Barcelona

Michael Eaude

Barcelona:
The City That
Re-invented Itself

Michael Eaude

Five Leaves Publications

www.fiveleaves.co.uk

Barcelona:
The City That Re-invented Itself
by Michael Eaude

Published in 2006 by Five Leaves Publications,
PO Box 8786, Nottingham NG1 9AW
info@fiveleaves.co.uk
www.fiveleaves.co.uk

ISBN: 190551204X

Five Leaves acknowledges financial support
from Arts Council England

Typeset and design by Four Sheets Design and Print
Printed in Great Britain by Russell Press

Contents

Part 2 — Decline and Renaissance

Part 3 — Re-inventing Modern Barcelona

For Marisa, with love

"From the very first, a city imparts a sense of poverty.
One sees, in the sea of roofs compressed into motion-
less waves, how it shrivels up and crushes
numberless lives."
VICTOR SERGE

"I love Barcelona very much because of what it has
done in the last 20 years. Barcelona is the ideal for
most planners and architects... It has achieved what
we are trying to achieve in other cities."
RICHARD ROGERS

Introduction

"Barcelona," Don Quixote exclaimed, is a "fountain of courtesy, shelter of strangers, hospice to the poor, land of the valiant, avenger of the offended, reciprocator of firm friendship, a city unique in its location and beauty."

Barcelonins, the people of Barcelona, purr with delight at Cervantes, Spain's greatest novelist, singing their virtues. There is a snag, though. Don Quixote is mad. The noble Knight does not easily distinguish reality from fantasy.

Cervantes' real opinion is as likely to be expressed in Don Quixote's experiences as in this exaggerated praise. While Sancho Panza wanders around on a sleepless night, he keeps bumping into feet that hang from trees. Terrified by this strange fruit, Don Quixote comforts his squire:

> *"— There is no need for you to be afraid, because these feet and legs that you touch but do not see undoubtedly belong to outlaws and bandits who have been hanged from these trees, for in this region the law usually hangs them when it catches them, in groups of twenty or thirty, which leads me to think I must be close to Barcelona."*

Today Don Quixote's first opinion prevails in the world's tourist brochures: *a city unique in its location and beauty*. This US travel ad sums up the message:

> *"Barcelona sweeps you up in a whirlwind of colorful historic sites, vibrant street life, and its creative approach to living life to its fullest. This Mediterranean seaport embraces the future as it honors the past."*

Since tourism began — in any mass sense, under 200 years ago — Florence and Venice have been *the* small cities of culture to visit. They are the prime examples of European museum-cities, whose attractions are the worn stones (or canals) of their mediaeval primes.

1

Barcelona also has majestic buildings from the Middle Ages, but these are only part of its beauty. The architect Richard Rogers caught a special quality of the city when he told me:

> *"The mediaeval town... plays off very wonderfully against the classical urban plan. The juxtaposition between nineteenth-century and mediaeval is quite breathtaking."*

Barcelona's old stones are overshadowed by its later buildings. Indeed, the main images that the name Barcelona evokes today date from the twentieth century: extravagant and/or elegant architecture, revolution, modern art, sordid bars, urban design, stylish living, attractive football, *chic* clubs and cafés... These contradictory images mixed into the Barcelona brand, sold in the world's tourism bazaars, are essentially modern.

As well as a beautiful tourist city of the twentieth century, Barcelona is seen by many as a model pointing the way to the future: a city that has overcome industrial decline and is becoming a sustainable city in the twenty-first century. Richard Rogers is an enthusiastic fan of the city:

> *"Five kilometres of derelict port cut off the sea from the rest of the city. This has been replaced, and the area now boasts a beautiful beach. The city is now a wonderful place to live and work in, with hundreds of new public spaces.*
>
> *Barcelona has become the most confident city in the western world in terms of urban regeneration. And the city is now at the top of all scales for livability and also for attracting tourists. It was ultimately successful because it used the games as a catalyst for improving the life of the city and of the nation."*

The extract is from an article published the day after London won the 2012 Olympic nomination. The games Rogers refers to were the 1992 Olympics. He believes Barcelona is the model that London should follow. This book argues that much of Barcelona's image of modernity and successful urban regeneration does not bear up under scrutiny. The Olympics took Barcelona down a tourism-oriented path in which the interests of construction companies were put above those of its inhabitants. Rogers is wrong: Barcelona is a less "liveable" city than it was 20 years ago.

Though Frank Gehry's giant golden fish on the sea-front glitters in the sun, the streets are not paved with gold or even with café tables. The city's residents are assailed by insecure employment, exhaust fumes and over-priced housing. These problems are common to most cities. Nevertheless, they undermine the high claims for sustainability made by many supporters of Barcelona.

One of the most striking aspects of the recent transfor-mation of Barcelona is that, despite its feeling and being a safe place today in comparison with London or Paris, its history has been extraordinarily violent, as Cervantes' hanged bandits signal. This is due to Catalonia's position as the easiest crossing-point over the Pyrenees, which means it has always been a cross-roads or thoroughfare, a *terra de pas* as Catalans put it. Hannibal and his elephants trudged through twenty-two centuries ago. "The Spanish March," it was squeezed between the Franks and the Arabs; then, in mediaeval times between the stronger French and Spanish states. In more recent centuries, its geographical position has underlain the conflict between Catalonia and the Spanish Empire, which conquered America and dominated Europe in the sixteenth century and reduced Catalonia to a subject province in the seven-teenth and eighteenth centuries. In the last 150 years, Catalonia's fight to regain its national rights has com-bined with Barcelona's intense class conflict. Those guns on the magnificent rock of Montjuïc, which now look out over the Mediterranean, within living memory pointed over the flat roofs of the city itself.

It is false to think there is one single true Barcelona to be revealed, as Manuel Vázquez Montalbán pointed to in the plural title of his book *Barcelonas*. There is though a shiny surface which is sold as true, yet is not the whole story. A shop-window, a simulacrum, a stage-set are words often used by recent observers grappling with the feeling that the beauty of the city has something artificial and posed about it.

This book looks at a number of the ingredients of the Barcelona tourism brand, and hopes to tease out both why they attract and how the brand has been put together. The first five chapters deal with some of the most common images British visitors have of Barcelona: the magic of the famous *Rambles*; the squalor of the red-light district, celebrated by Jean Genet; the 1936 Spanish Revolution of anarchism, recorded by Orwell; the *Art Nouveau* architecture of Antoni Gaudí and his contemporaries. At the same time, this first part moves geographically. From the Old City, the *ciutat vella*, walled in until 1859 and now the tourist heart of the city, it moves out and up to hills that look over the city, Carmel and Montjuïc.

The second part, Chapters 6-10, looks at some of the history that has moulded Barcelona: its mediaeval splendour, its great nineteenth-century Renaissance, and then the post-Civil War years of mass struggle against the Franco dictatorship and of mass migration from the rest of Spain. This is no simple historical account, but moves in each chapter through the Old City again, to bohemian Gràcia and to the *Eixample*, the nineteenth-century expansion adorned by *Art Nouveau* buildings. The last six chapters cover the modern transformation of Barcelona: the football club seen as a symbol of Catalan aspirations; Catalan *cuisine*, so internationally renowned today; sex and the family. It ends with a critical survey of the post-Franco councils, responsible for the city's model of reform and development, including the successful Olympics and the failed 2004 Forum of Cultures.

The city is usually celebrated for its art and architecture. This book does so too, but tips the balance towards literature: not just Genet, Malraux, Victor Serge, Orwell and other famous foreign writers drawn to the city, but some of Barcelona's own novelists: the Francoist Ignacio Agustí, who wrote brilliantly of the Industrial Revolution, the exiled Mercè Rodoreda, Juan Goytisolo (and his poet brother José Agustín Goytisolo), Manuel Vázquez Montalbán, Eduardo Mendoza or the recent Carlos Ruiz Zafón. Literature, I would venture, is more analytical, helps us see with fresh eyes the sights that dazzle on first view. It is great to be enchanted and carried away; and then good to reflect on that enchantment.

*****

The birth of modern Barcelona as a major tourist city can be dated (as precisely as a process can be dated) to the 1985-86 exhibition at London's Hayward Gallery, *Homage to Barcelona*. As recently as 1987 the *Guardian* could publish a travel piece on Barcelona with the sub-title: "Spain is the most heavily packaged holiday destination, but relatively few operators pitch on Catalonia." The Hayward exhibition was major and very official, organised jointly by the Arts Council of Great Britain, the Generalitat (Autonomous Government) of Catalonia and the Barcelona City Council. The 14-week exhibition and its large-format 325-page catalogue was sponsored by the car-firm Seat, Barcelona's largest industrial employer at the time.

The exhibition opened just after 1984, year when George Orwell's corpse was dragged back and forth between left and right in numerous exhibitions, articles, TV programmes and a feature film. The title of the Hayward exhibition was no accident: it deliberately evoked Orwell's *Homage to Catalonia*. And it didn't matter that Orwell's book was a homage to socialist revolution, which was hardly the goal of either Jordi Pujol or Pasqual Maragall, in 1985 President of Catalonia and Mayor of Barcelona, respectively. Orwell's book also ignored certain basic facts about Catalonia, such as that it is a nation within the Spanish state and that it has its own

5

language, which are of enormous importance to both Pujol and Maragall. The title was what mattered, not any irritating content. If Salvador Dalí, a mad-man of vociferous fascist opinions, could be turned in the 1980s into an icon of democratic Catalonia (a process that reached its apotheosis in 2004, the centenary of his birth), it wasn't difficult to render Orwell's views innocuous.

If the city's tourist boom started in 1985, its main transformation dates from the period between 1975, when Spain's dictator Francisco Franco died, and 1992, when Barcelona hosted the Olympic Games. The generation of upper-class youth known in the 1960s as the *Gauche Divine* — Divine Left rather than the 'Divine Right' which the monarchs, and dictator, of Spain claimed for themselves — took power in the city in 1979 through the PSC, the Catalan Socialist Party. It is they who have managed the transformation of Barcelona from the rather raffish run-down city it had been in the 1960s, the dirty port famous for absinthe, prostitutes and seedy bars, to the 1980s city of design and 1990s city of culture. From an interesting, untidy dump with a notorious red-light district to a more ordered and fashionable city. Barcelona has become a name synonymous with good urban living in beautiful surroundings. Examples abound: 1990s Glasgow advertised itself: "Glasgow: the latitude of Smolensk. The attitude of Barcelona." *Barcelona is hip*, the London publishers Serpent's Tail state simply in their publicity for Raúl Núñez's *The Lonely Hearts Club*.

A year after the Hayward exhibition, the International Olympic Committee awarded the 1992 Olympic Games to Barcelona. The Olympics became the event that justified the enormous cost of the reform of the city. Using a major event to attract business and regenerate sections of the city was not new, but a re-run on an even grander scale of Barcelona's Great Exhibitions of 1888 and 1929. 1888 had served to urbanise the Ciutadella Park; 1929, the Plaça de Espanya and the flanks of the Montjuïc hill.

The years before 1992 saw the most fevered construc-

tion since the 1880s. For the Olympic Village, old industrial and railway land in Poble Nou was converted to
housing, office and leisure facilities and the sea-front was
opened up. Ring-roads, high-class hotel space (since 1985
hotel space has multiplied four-fold) and a general housing
facelift accompanied the central Olympic developments.
The idea was: we will make Barcelona so socially and
financially attractive that tourists will pour into the city
and multinationals will relocate here.

It worked. Barcelona's success has aroused envy
throughout Europe, where other big-city mayors —
Rutelli in Rome or Livingstone in London — have seen
the Barcelona formula as a way out of urban decline.
Now London too has the Olympic hook on which to
hang its development package, though it does not have
the popular good will that Barcelona's rulers enjoyed in
the '80s, due to the city's emergence from 38 previous
years of dictatorship.

Barcelona's success was crowned by the 1999 RIBA
(Royal Institute of British Architects) annual Gold Medal.
The prize had never before been awarded to a city.
According to the citation:

> *"[Barcelona's] inspired city leadership, pursuing an ambi-*
> *tious yet pragmatic urban strategy and the highest design*
> *standards, has transformed the city's public realm,*
> *immensely expanded its amenities and regenerated its*
> *economy, providing pride for its inhabitants and delight in*
> *its visitors."*

Heady praise indeed. Such puffing is only matched by the
news that the architect Gaudí is being processed for saint-
hood.

The sub-title of the Hayward exhibition was *The city
and its art 1888-1936*. Art was to be the main attraction to
re-invent Barcelona: Picasso, Miró, Dalí and, most of all,
the politically reactionary yet artistically revolutionary
Antoni Gaudí and Catalan *modernisme* — Mediterranean
Art Nouveau.

Orwell and Revolution, Art and Architecture... in its title and sub-title, the Hayward exhibition looked back to the Civil War and the cusp of the nineteenth-to-twentieth centuries; but in its style and modernity, it looked forward to the Olympics. It set the tone for the message that Barcelona Council has been promoting ever since: here is an attractive city full of exciting history and art, where you will nevertheless have every modern comfort and be warmly welcomed.

Despite the hype, Barcelona is a genuinely exciting and comfortable place to visit. Becoming hooked on the city that Joan Maragall, one of its poets, called *la gran encisora*, the great enchantress, is only the first and easier step. This book is for those who do not want to take at face value initial impressions and one-track advertising. In short, for those who suffer the glorious ambition of distinguishing reality from fantasy. Like wise, mad Don Quixote.

****

Language

A word on terminology. I favour Catalan over Castilian Spanish almost throughout, even when it may look strange to an English eye: *Rambles*, for instance, rather than Ramblas (though the pronunciation of *Rambles* and Ramblas is the same) and *barri xinès* rather than barrio chino. There is a practical reason: in Barcelona all street-names are written in Catalan, so there is little use in indicating a name different from what you may see on the map or wall. There is, too, an ideological reason: Catalonia is a nation without a state, whose identity is linked strongly to its language. The cultural richness of Barcelona depends on that language's survival.

Exceptions occur in quotes from a writer or speaker in Castilian Spanish. There can be no full consistency possible in a place where two languages are spoken. For instance, I have stuck with the Castilian *tapas*, as it is almost an English word now, instead of the Catalan *tapes*. In avoiding anachronisms, it is easy to seem incoherent: for instance, the factory *La España industrial* is written in Castilian Spanish, for in the 1950s, the period referred to, Catalan was not used officially; yet *L'Espanya industrial* describes the park of the same name in the same place since the 1980s. Even people's names can vary. Books by Francesc Candel and Francisco Candel are listed in the bibliography. This is the same person but, as he changed his fore-name according to the language in which his books came out, the two fore-names have to stand.

****

Where a book or article is quoted in translation, it is from the published translation quoted in the Bibliography. If the book or article is quoted in Catalan or Castilian in the Bibliography, then the translation is by me.

Acknowledgements

I am especially grateful to Marisa Asensio, Mark Bardell, Andy Durgan, Anthony Eaude, Charlie Forman, David C. Hall and Stephen Hayward, who read parts of the text for me.

The following generously gave up their time to give interviews, offer opinions, provide material and/or give me specific information. Many thanks to: Brian Anglo, Quim Aranda, Daniel Asensio, Tricia Bickerton, Pere Comellas, Víctor Córdoba, Neus García, Germán Gutiérrez, Dan Lloyd, José Luis López Bulla, Margarita Martínez, Maria Molins, Ross Montgomery, John Payne, Carles Prieto, Albert Recio, Richard Rogers, Marçal Solé, Caragh Wells, Robin White, Simon Wynne-Hughes.

I would also like to acknowledge Gabriel Jackson, David Mackay, Tamzin Townsend, and the late Manuel Vázquez Montalbán (1939-2003) and Stafford Cottman (1918-1999), all of whom I interviewed for other purposes, but whose views have fertilised this book.

9

I want to record my debt to my aunt Mary
Eaude (1912-2000), whose legacy gave me
time to write this book.

The cover photo and maps are by Marisa
Asensio. Sadly, responsibility for mistakes
and stupid remarks is all mine.

Michael Eaude

Part One:

Images of Barcelona

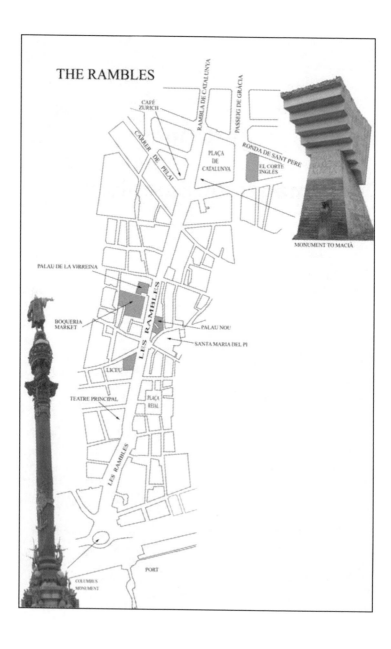

THE RAMBLES

CAFÉ
ZURICH

RAMBLA DE CATALUNYA

PASSEIG DE GRÀCIA

CARRER DE PELAI

RONDA DE SANT PERE

PLAÇA
DE
CATALUNYA

EL CORTE
INGLÉS

MONUMENT TO MACIÀ

PALAU DE LA VIRREINA

LES RAMBLES

BOQUERIA
MARKET

PALAU NOU

SANTA MARIA DEL PI

LICEU

TEATRE PRINCIPAL

PLAÇA
REIAL

LES RAMBLES

PORT

COLUMBUS
MONUMENT

Chapter 1
The Greatest Show

"The traveller who comes to Barcelona for the first time soon notices where the old city ends and the new begins. The streets become straight and wide instead of winding; the pavements, less crowded; tall plane-trees shade them pleasantly; the buildings are more distinguished. There is no shortage of people who are bewildered, thinking they have been carried magically to another city."
EDUARDO MENDOZA, THE CITY OF MARVELS.

Sitting

My father used to sing the first line of an old music-hall number that went "I'm one of the nuts from Barcelona," a reference, I learned later, not just to mental health but to the hazelnuts exported through the city. He loved the city. To be one of the nuts was a great compliment. It meant an alternative, more romantic life to going by train to the office each day and washing the car at week-ends. The Mediterranean represented the good life, leisure in perfect light by the gentle tideless sea. And it has represented this for generations of Northern Europeans since young middle-class men and women went South to evade the dread hand of Victorian society. To sit on a café terrace, in short sleeves, a drink on the table, time on your hands. Children shout and run round you: here they are to be seen, heard and cherished.

The Café Zurich is right in the middle of Barcelona. For many decades the Zurich has been Barcelona's main meeting-point for the native young and foreigners alike. Even today, in the age of mobile phones, when place and time are constantly re-negotiated on the way to the meeting, at seven in the evening round the metro entrance in

13

front of the Zurich, some twenty or thirty people are waiting.

Pleasure sitting at a Mediterranean café table is not just the warm air, clear light, the different drink. It is also the pleasure of the voyeur. It is legitimate to look. Spain is a place where one is licensed to stare. No-one jumps up as they might in an English pub: "And who do you think you're looking at?" From a café table you can stare at other customers, passers-by and those waiting. If you want, you tell yourself you're observing people, soaking up the local atmosphere or hoping to see someone you know. But no excuse is needed. The passers-by are part of the spectacle of city life. And you too, sitting at the table on the street, become part of this spectacle.

Founded in the 1920s, the Zurich closed in 1997 and re-opened in 2000. I was one of those who feared such a useful, popular, well-known place would not re-open. But there it is, a plausible imitation of its former self, now part of what is known as the *Triangle d'Or*, the Golden Triangle, the commercial block including the French leisure multi-national FNAC that gives onto the Plaça de Catalunya. The Zurich's rude middle-aged waiters in stained white jackets bang their drinks down onto the table and demand payment at the moment of service. This is quite unlike anywhere else in Barcelona or Spain, where the reverse is often true: on a busy day it may be hard to pay. Sometimes, after shouting for long periods, bank-note in raised hand, people are reduced to leaving without paying. Not at the Zurich. The one decisive alteration at the new Zurich: the toilets are no longer vile piss-stinking holes surrounded by a sodden saw-dust pile, a lack of authenticity only lamented by the followers of Jean Genet.

The Zurich's tables spread out over the pavements on the corner of Carrer Pelai and the Plaça de Catalunya. From the Zurich terrace you can dip into several Barcelonas. At the Zurich itself you are in the Eixample, the nineteenth-century grid expansion that turned Barcelona into a proper bourgeois city. Go on up the tree-

14

lined Rambla de Catalunya and you are on one of the city's classiest shopping streets. Leave the Plaça de Catalunya by the opposite corner and you are on the Passeig de Gràcia, once the path through fields from the Old City of Barcelona to the town of Gràcia. Its first blocks hold some fine examples of what one may call dictatorial architecture, the large square solid buildings built during the regimes of Primo de Rivera (dictator 1923-1930) or Franco (ditto 1939-1975). On the corner of the Gran Via is a magnificent example: fourteen stories of white stone blocks with stone statues of eternal truths ('Justice' or 'Beauty') clustered round the building's mighty doors. These dated monuments to eternity rapidly give way to today's famous Passeig de Gràcia, now packed with cafés, clothes shops, jewellers' and the densest cluster of *modernista* or *Art Nouveau* houses in the city (see Ch. 7).

Though at the Zurich you are sitting in the Eixample, on the other side of the bustling down-market Carrer Pelai, the *Ciutat vella*, the Old City starts. This roughly divides into three: the poor, packed Raval on the right of the Rambles (Ch. 2); the monumental political city, the Gothic city, one of Europe's best-preserved mediaeval areas, on the left (Ch. 6); and the Ribera district beyond the Via Laietana (Ch. 8). In Barcelona you find extensive mediaeval buildings and then dazzling architecture from the late nineteenth century on. Absent are the seventeenth-century architecture or grand eighteenth-century terraces and squares that grace Paris, Bath or London. A baroqueless city, for those centuries coincided with Catalonia's long slump.

From the Zurich you can go down too. A city of suburban and underground railways with its own shops and bars is buried beneath the square. Immediately below is an underground circle, known informally during the last years of Franco as the Plaça Lenin, for here short spontaneous rush-hour demonstrations could be held and the leaflet-scatterers themselves scatter through the numerous exits just ahead of the grey-uniformed police. *Els*

15

grisos, the greys, they were known as. From the Plaça de Catalunya the Ferrocarrils de la Generalitat, the Catalan Autonomous Government's local trains, run out to inland suburbs and on through the Collserola hills to the industrial cities of Sabadell and Terrassa, stopping at the leafy commuter villages on the way. Suburban RENFE lines running up or down the coast and two city Metro lines, the green and red, can be boarded here too.

The Plaça de Catalunya has been rebuilt several times, but has never quite worked. Even its underground section is confusing. Above ground, despite its many changes over the decades, the Plaça de Catalunya remains stubbornly unable to meet its function as a great city's central square. "An enormous mediocrity," wrote the novelist Manuel Vázquez Montalbán. The Plaça de Catalunya is geographically central because it is the hinge where the Old City opens into the Eixample; its irresolution represents the failure of these two parts of the city to really meet.

The Plaça has one great new monument, though, on the corner by the Zurich: a set of upside-down steps dedicated to Francesc Macià, the first President of the modern Generalitat of Catalonia in 1931. Its rough travertine stone expresses the solidity, the foundations of Catalonia; its upside-down steps, the stateless nation's unfinished construction. Or so I fancy. The monument is by Josep Subirachs, the sculptor hired to finish Gaudí's *Sagrada Família* cathedral. In front is a bust by Clarà of *l'Avi*, the Old Man, as Macià was known. On the travertine in small letters are carved the main events of Macià's life. Most people abhor this monument, but I like its open ending, its abstraction, the fact that Macià is remembered at the heart of Barcelona. Born in 1859, he retired as a career army officer in 1907 and entered politics as a radical Catalan nationalist. In 1926 he organised an army to invade Catalonia. One of his lieutenants Josep Rovira would later be George Orwell's commander on the Aragon front. The 130 separatists were detained at Prats de Molló, on the French side of the frontier, before a shot was fired. Macià turned farce into triumph at his trial in France, achieving worldwide publicity for the cause of Catalonia's independence. In the municipal elections that caused the fall of the monarchy on April 14 1931, Macià's newly formed party ERC, Republican Left of Catalonia, swept the board. From the balcony of the Generalitat on the Plaça Sant Jaume he declared Independence, though backtracked a few days later in return for an extensive Statute of Autonomy, similar to the one re-introduced in 1979. He died suddenly on Christmas Day 1933. There is a good anecdote about Macià, famed for his combination of military firmness and gentle calm. After April 14 he called in the President of the Regional Council who blustered: "I refuse to hand over power. My loyalty is to the King. I will only be forcibly removed." Macià leaned over and pushed him lightly on the arm. "Will that do?" Honour was saved.

For the rest, the Plaça stubbornly resists modernisation. Young couples canoodle, office workers eat their packed lunches, back-packers make *xoriço* sandwiches and tramps doze on benches, as they might have thirty years ago. Many-coloured helium balloons hover on ribbons above the vendors' heads. Ice-cream stands. And pigeons. The square has as many pigeons as London's Trafalgar Square used to have, constantly fed by the mad and lonely and by children.

The lamentable pigeons of Barcelona reflect no credit on the city fathers and mothers. Many stagger across the square, on their last legs, deformed, poisoned, feathers falling out. Many have just one foot: have they been run over by Barcelona's thrusting young executives in four-wheel drives and dark glasses? Others' feet lack claws: the birds limp like foreign drunks (rarely do you see a staggering Spanish drunk). Flying seems beyond them. In recent years the City Council has put out contraceptive food for them (a pity the Spanish Church has not been so generous). More recently, kestrels were released into the city sky to control their numbers, though these appear to have disappeared as mysteriously as the Slovenian bears let loose a few years ago to repopulate the Pyrenees. To complete pigeons' misery, Barcelona has a steadily increasing number of handsome green and red parrots. Originally escaped from private hands in the '80s, the parrots have successfully survived cold winters and colonised the city. Their flashes of colour in the tree-tops, their raucous shouts above the traffic like the mockery of the free, represent their success over the poor docile pigeons, lowing below like foolish cows. Once I saw a group of pigeons and a parrot all eating bread. The parrot had the evolutionary advantage for it clutched the bread in one claw, hopped onto a branch and tore the bread with its beak, all the while staring at me with a bulging brown eye. The poor pigeons are reduced to pecking around on the ground, their heads continually bobbing into the dust. Their misery is completed by the increasing number of sea-gulls, big noisy greedy birds, invading the city as the Mediterranean rots. It is not uncommon to see a sea-gull tormenting then eating an ailing city pigeon.

The other new note in the Plaça de Catalunya is struck by black faces, groups of young men from Africa. They may well not know it, but they are only the latest in successive waves of migration to Barcelona. They look too, though are careful not to catch your eye. In Summer 2001, several dozen, homeless and jobless, slept out under the trees, but now the City authorities, who as we will see are very careful not to damage their tourists' sensibilities, make sure they sleep out of sight. The irredeemably ugly *Corte inglés* occupies one whole side of the square, opposite the Zurich. The *Corte inglés*, the English Cut, Spain's première department store that has gobbled up all its rivals, is a nine-storey concrete ocean liner, with slim lines of port-holes lit up after dark on the upper storeys. In the doorways of the undistinguished banks and office-buildings round the rest of the square sleep the white homeless on opened cardboard boxes. They are not cared for either, but at least are not moved on.

At the Zurich, you will be struck by the large numbers of people passing. And not just because this is the city centre. Barcelona is very densely populated: the surface area of the city is no greater than that of Bristol, yet it has four times more inhabitants. People live on top of each other in flats. The number of people you see in the streets 365 days a year is like London during a tube strike. Spanish cities are all like this: there are huge open spaces of bare uninhabited land all over the country and everyone lives huddled up in enormous cities.

Population density makes it a rowdy drink on the Zurich terrace. Traffic hurtles down Pelai, motor-bikes with enlarged exhausts rev at the traffic-lights, buses hiss and trucks grunt, and the crowds on foot shout at each other. John Langdon-Davies, pioneer British interpreter of Catalonia, wrote in the 1950s:

> *"(The Barcelonan) seems impervious to noise of any sort. When a Catalan and especially a Catalan woman greets our infant son it is almost certain that stolid individual will burst into tears. This is because they put their heads within a foot of his and scream their affection."*

If you know some Spanish, you will realise too that the machine-gun chatter of Castilian Spanish is more common here in the city centre than the explosive consonants and slushing watery sounds of Catalan, what the novelist Matthew Tree calls "a mixture of after-dinner belches and little waves breaking." This tends to confirm to a Catalan nationalist that his/her language is in severe danger of being lost. It is also a surprise to visitors from other parts of Spain, who have been led to believe by a mainly anti-Catalan press that Catalans will spit at you in their own language, specially designed to be awkward, if you dare to speak in Castilian to them. Nevertheless you will hear some Catalan too, though a first-time visitor is unlikely to distinguish between it and Castilian Spanish. Foreign languages may well predominate round the Zurich. A sea of tourists wears away the stones of central Barcelona, talking not just in English, French, German and Japanese, those familiar languages of tourism, but Romanian, Lithuanian, Arabic, Czech...

The tourist is not exempt from Barcelona's linguistic contradictions. All the guidebooks now give phrases in Catalan. However, no waiter, shop assistant or passer-by being asked directions would imagine a foreigner was going to speak to him or her in Catalan. If at the Zurich you ask in Catalan for a *tallat*, a small strong coffee cut with a dash of milk, you are less likely to be understood than if you mouth the expected Castilian *cortado*. But persist, for this is Catalonia, and to defend the existence of Catalan, the weaker stateless language, special effort is needed.

Walking

When the time on the Zurich terrace bought by your *tallat* has expired, set off down the Rambles. Your company includes the laughing ghost of Lorca, poet from the deep South for whom the flower-sellers and bird-stalls made the Rambles "the prettiest street in the world". That was before the Civil War, when the painter Ramon Casas married his model, a flower-seller, and groups of intellectuals used to discuss the world by the flower-stalls. 1936 changed all that. Discussion was not possible under Franco. And when the dictatorship ended, football had established itself as the theme of the men who gather by the Fountain of Canaletes.

The Catalan word *ramblejar* comes from Rambla and means just to wander up and down, to saunter aimlessly, to stroll about. The Rambles developed as the outlaw edge of the city outside the mediaeval city walls, a stream of sewage washed clean by the Spring and Autumn rains. Still today, through all its changes, the Rambles is a mix of the sordid and elegant. On the right lies the Raval, subject of the next chapter. On the left lies the old walled city, exalted by the *Ajuntament*, or City Council, as the 'best-preserved mediaeval city in Europe.' Bologna or Venice might dispute the title, one of the many examples of the City Council's *autobombo* or self-puffing. Self-promotion that is particularly effective because there is little cynicism involved: the Council usually believes its propaganda.

The Rambles is a pretty tacky street. The Argentinean Raúl Núñez, in his bitter-sweet master-piece *The Lonely Hearts Club*, catches its 1980s seediness:

> *"He checked out the rent boys at the Liceo subway station. He watched the girls, curly-headed and showing white knickers through thin dresses. He watched plainclothes policemen — all casual jackets, dark glasses and unconvincing moustaches... He watched henpecked husbands drinking iced lemonade on café terraces next to fat, sleepy wives. He watched obstreperous, red-eyed drunks as they cursed the full moon."*

The news kiosks where you can buy the foreign press and over-priced post-cards are splashed with gaudy pornography. Unemployed men hang about and stare. Drop-outs sprawl on the ground. Beggars exhibit stumps or deformed limbs — a throw-back to the post-war period when Spain was full of the mutilated. More enterprising and fitter unemployed cover themselves with silver make-up and clothes and powdered wigs, and perform for hours on end as human statues: mediaeval soldiers, Greek athletes, cowboys, Columbus, a Cleopatra painted in gold... Most of them have a gimmick when you put money in the tin: pointing suddenly, smiling manically or raising a hat. Competition is fierce. The best this year is a man in white powdered jacket, wig and face, his trousers round his ankles, sitting on a toilet. His bare legs are also painted and powdered white. He sits quite still, reading a book. Every now and again he grimaces and twists in the ecstasy of relieving himself. The crowds adore it, making an effort with him, leaning sideways, clenching their fists. Children peer round behind him to see if the toilet is connected to the drains. He has found a successful theme, for Catalan society is particularly fascinated by shitting – or perhaps just open about it. Nativity cribs include the *caganer,* a model of a man squatting, and the steaming coils of excrement he has just dropped. Blasphemy to Protestant minds.

Everyone will form their own view of this boulevard, whose distinguishing charm is its number and variety of people. A dizzying parade of people moving up and down, across, in and out of side streets, or just hanging out, whether at the hyper-expensive tourist cafés or leaning against a tree. The Rambles is a spectacle, a show. As such it feeds itself: it attracts performers and it attracts those with little else to do but watch a show.

In the nineteenth century, all social classes would walk here. In the twentieth the upper class withdrew to the upper, more salubrious part of the city; the working-class had its own great avenue, the Paral·lel. By the twenty-first, the Rambles is dominated by tourists and the businesses that line it are currency exchange booths, hotels, cafés, fast-food rooms, souvenir shops, and a 24-hour Internet café with 140 computers. At one point there are four souvenir shops in a row, all identical and run by Asians. They sell post-cards, guide-books, Barça football shirts, porcelain or plastic dolls dressed in flamenco dress, and wide-brimmed straw hats, of the type James Coburn wore when asleep under a tree in *The Magnificent Seven*. This is one of the unsolved mysteries of modern Catalonia. You see families stagger with their bags off the midnight planes at Manchester or Stansted carrying enormous Mexican straw hats. They have come very likely from Reus, Girona or Barcelona, the three Catalan commercial air-ports. Yet in Catalonia, no-one wears these hats. They are invented souvenirs, souvenirs of something that has never existed, souvenirs of an idea of Spain that only exists in British tourists' minds. "Oh no, they are Spanish," an Indian shop-keeper insists. And so they are. The label he shows me states "Made in Alicante."

Despite the tourism show, the Rambles is still used just as it has been for centuries. People come in from other parts of the city to buy seeds on the Rambla de les flors (of flowers), to buy a pet from one of the animal stalls or, like Vázquez Montalbán's fictional detective Pepe Carvalho, to hunt for delicacies in the Boqueria market. Girls bunking off classes still stride arm-in-arm down the Rambles. Office-workers digest long lunches by strolling on the Rambles.

Monuments or great buildings are not profuse. Three emblematic buildings, from each of the last three centuries, are worth looking at. One is the Virreina Palace, built in the 1770s by Manuel Amat, the only Catalan to become a Viceroy in the Americas. Forerunner of the ostentatious industrial magnates who paid for Barcelona's *Art nouveau*-style buildings a century later (see Ch. 7), Amat wanted to use the untold riches he had robbed from Peru to build the biggest house on the Avenue. Known for his many mistresses, Amat became the subject of a romantic novelette by Prosper Mérimée and an 1868 operetta by Offenbach, *La Perichôle*. These French writers plundered Spain for romantic stories just as Amat had pillaged America. This was not just literary looting, for in the 1840s Mérimée succeeded in inventing a view of Spain with his Carmen, the fiery, dark-haired Andalusian woman, stamping and snorting fire. These French Romantics saw Barcelona as a typical Spanish city. More business-like than Sevilla, yes; less flamenco, too; indeed, more frenchified, but otherwise just like Sevilla, where Théophile Gautier drooled over the scantily-clad Carmens working in the cigar factory. Like many foreign visitors, they had no understanding that Barcelona was in Catalonia, a nation within the Spanish state.

For moralists, Amat's story of womanising and ostentation has a happy ending. His premature death meant that his palace became his spurned wife's and to this day is known as the Palau de la Virreina, the Palace of the Vicereine. The Palace is now used for art exhibitions, so is easy to walk into. It is not a beautiful building, but it's still the biggest house on the street.

The Rambles' most spectacular twentieth-century addition is half-way down on the left. It is the shining white 1990s *Palau nou*, New Palace, designed by the famous MBM partnership (an architectural practice not a Hollywood producer). When I asked David Mackay, one of the Ms of MBM, which of all the buildings they had designed was his favourite, he gave the standard answer: "the one we're designing at the moment." And then added:

> "As a building we're very pleased with the Palau Nou. We persuaded the Japanese client to put a gap in it and juggled with all the volumes, so that from the Rambla you can see the tower of Santa Maria del Pi. That we're terribly pleased about."

The *Palau Nou*, equally praised and scorned like most surprises, is an example of the MBM practice's cut-and-paste approach to urban design. It sums up their ideology: integrating their new buildings into the space available and the environment given, not imposing them on their surrounds. MBM have been the most influential Barcelona architects of the last 40 years and played a key part in the post-Franco redevelopment of the city: more on them in Chapter 15.

Singing

The Rambles' middle section is dominated by the third building, one of the great opera houses of Europe, the Liceu. At 10am on the sunny morning of Friday 31 January 1994, black smoke began to pour through its roof. Fire caused by an electrical fault gutted the interior in three hours, though the facade remained intact. Not just an opera house burned down that day: the fire ended a century and a half of swank and luxury. The Liceu had opened in 1847, supplanting the Teatre Principal (still there, now used as rehearsal premises for the Liceu) of which the irascible Tory Richard Ford had asserted in his 1845 *Handbook for Spain*:

"...the lighting is bad and the odour worse, for the atmosphere is impregnated with the filthy fumes of a garlic-fed audience; the edifice was built on a suppressed convent; now the farce and fandango have supplanted the monastic melodrama."

Josep Pla, one of Catalonia's best-known prose writers, an astute conservative peasant with a prose style as smooth and flowing as honey, wrote of the Liceu at its apogee nearly a century ago:

"Except for the music-lovers up in the gods and a few others scattered about, everything in the Liceu of those years was exhibitionism... It was such a fabulous show-case that the anecdote was told of a Barcelona magnate with a girlfriend he liked to show off. He took her to the Liceu — he himself did not stay — covered with the most brilliant and costly jewels. At the end of the function he picked her up in his car and immediately took off all her jewels, made a thorough inventory and returned them to his strong-box."

That was how the rich stayed rich. Anecdotes and scandals of the Liceu abound. Precisely because it was a place where the *nouveaux riches* flaunted their wealth, it was on October 7 1893 the target of Barcelona's most notorious anarchist bomb outrage. During the opening night of the season, in the intermission after the first act of Rossini's *William Tell*, Santiago Salvador threw two Orsini bombs from the fifth floor into the stalls. The first killed twenty people in rows thirteen and fourteen; the second fell on a dead body, failed to go off and can now be seen in the Museu d'Història de la Ciutat. A spiky metallic ball, looking like every cartoonist's drawing of an anarchist bomb. Unrepentant, singing a song of freedom, lamenting only the failure of his second bomb, Salvador was executed by public garrotting at the nearby prison of Cordellers in the Raval, subject of a famous and terrifying painting by Ramon Casas *El garrote vil*. Inadvertently, Salvador founded the legend of Barcelona being packed with fanatical bomb-wielding anarchists. Barcelona's anarchists were the Al Qaeda of the 1890s, demonised as ubiquitous, lethal and heartless. And hounds of repression were unleashed on the anarchist movement after the Liceu bombing, which led to a cycle of further bomb attacks and more repression.

Ignacio Agustí integrates the Liceu bombing into his fine novel of the Barcelona upper-class, *Mariona Rebull*. His heiress heroine is caught in her lover's box by the bomb. Agustí evokes the bourgeois dream of the Liceu before that bomb that ended an era:

> *"The theatre filled again. Just as men feel during the course of a drinking session that the world's getting steadily better, that they are taller and freer, that life lies before them with a thousand attractions, so in the middle of the theatre everyone imagined himself a hero in a wonderful world; that the arm of the woman beside him, lying on the same velvet arm-rest, belonged to the realm of dreams, of sensual and poetic intoxication. The magical dimming of the lights wiped away any possible error of God's..., transforming human beings into pure perfection, in an unearthly magic land."*

Opera was, of course, the nineteenth-century *bourgeois* art form *par excellence*, so it is entirely appropriate that Barcelona, the Manchester of Spain, should have had a luxurious, internationally renowned opera house, second in size only to La Scala, Milan; whereas Madrid, with no real middle class in the nineteenth century except state bureaucrats, could never sustain one. As well as being a symbol of Catalan wealth, inevitably the Liceu was an object of envy from the state capital. Nothing pleased the Catalan industrialists more as they discussed business over their lobsters and *cava* in the sumptuous private rooms of the Liceu. For it was not just a theatre, it was a private club for conducting business with pleasure.

Until the January 1994 fire, the opera house was owned by the members of the *Cercle del Liceu* (Liceu Circle). Much the same families had owned the boxes and stall seats since its opening in 1847. Women were excluded from the club rooms, something which infuriated even such a conservative figure as the soprano Montserrat Caballé. The Liceu took five years to rebuild after the fire. Huge sums of public money (some 100 million euros) were spent on restoring the Liceu to its former glory. Neighbouring houses were compulsorily purchased. To justify such expense and palliate protests, changes had to be introduced: the *Cercle* transferred its private ownership of the Liceu to a public consortium, consisting of the Barcelona Council, the Spanish State and the Generalitat. The consortium invested public money and raised some from multinationals. Effectively, the opera was nationalised. In a time of privatisation of most public companies in Spain as elsewhere, creating vast fortunes for a few, this was a case of private property going broke and being taken into public ownership.

The Catalan upper class retains numerous privileges in the Liceu, but it no longer owns its own flagship. The 1994 fire revealed a decline in the wealth and influence of the great families dating back to at least the Spanish industrial boom of the 1950s and '60s, when the family companies that characterised Catalan industry began to open to Madrid and international capital (Chs. 7 & 13). Yet if you sit up on the fifth floor, peering straight down over the low rail as Santiago Salvador once did, below it still seems as plush as ever. The bejewelled women and plump-fingered men who fill the stalls and boxes dress and look much the same as 100 years ago. The difference is that many of them today may be Nestlé executives or Nissan management rather than textile magnates.

Fire has played a significant part in the Liceu's history. The monastery-burnings of 1835 cleared a great deal of space throughout the still-walled city. The new industrialists took advantage of most of these newly vacant lots to build their *vapors*, their steam-powered factories, but the Liceu too owes its existence to the destruction of a convent on its site. The new opera house burnt down by accident in 1861, but was rebuilt within the year: the *Cercle* had more cash then than in 1994.

Salvador's Orsini bomb was also conceived in terms of fire: as a purification of sinful humanity by flame. It ushered in a period of violent class struggle that lasted until Franco decisively settled the matter in 1939, and that gave to Barcelona the nickname of the *Rosa del Foc*, the Rose of Fire. Bosses hired assassins, most famously killing in 1923 Salvador Seguí, *El noi del sucre* Sugar Boy, the leader of the anarchist union, the CNT. Workers responded by arming themselves.

A rather milder version of these conflicts was played out ritually in front of the Liceu in the late 1970s. On gala nights, when the wealthy were tipped out of their taxis and chauffeured limos, hundreds of demonstrators on the Rambles would spatter them with rotten vegetables and abuse. The bins in the square behind the nearby Boqueria market provided a ready supply of old vegetables. This changed nothing; it was merely a nostalgic echo of that powerful anarchist movement of the early twentieth century. José Luis López Bulla, opera lover and General Secretary of the left-wing trade union federation *Comissions obreres*, was infuriated by these demonstrations:

> *"So the opera is a bourgeois affair, is it? Meaning Count Godó can chat away with Donizetti and we're left with Baa-Baa black sheep."*

High culture is not to be disdained by the working-class, but appropriated. López Bulla's argument was not likely to convince the tomato-hurling followers of Buenaventura Durruti, who in proud defiance had thundered in 1936:

> *"We are not afraid of ruins, we are going to inherit the earth. The bourgeoisie may blast and ruin their world before they leave the stage of history, but we carry a new world in our hearts."*

28

Barcelona's reputation as a music-loving city cannot be reduced to opera for ostentation. Agustí describes the fifth floor of the Liceu, the *galliner*, hen-house, or "the gods" as it is more nobly known in English:

> *"...full of Wagner fanatics who listened score in hand and hissed at the first beats to impose silence... artisans who spent their savings rather than miss the function, workers who had walked from Horta or Sarrià, who waited three hours in the box-office queue just to see and hear, without showing off and unseen, anonymously, dramatically."*

In the Rambles and Old City, there is a high proportion of classical buskers. I remember an afternoon twenty years ago in a *pensió* in the Old City, with the sound of a street-singer performing opera arias lulling me into a sweet-sounding siesta. Two decades later, Víctor, who plays the violin in the Rambla dels Caputxins (one of the five sections into which the Rambles is divided) opposite the Liceu, told me: "I play here to pay my violin teacher who costs me fifty euros a class. And as I practise six hours a day anyway, I might as well do some of it here." As he plays for the money he needs in order to learn to play better, he is unknowingly fulfilling tourists' preconceptions of beauty in the city of art.

Sailing

The Rambles ends at the monument to Columbus: an ambivalent figure in Catalonia. No evidence at all backs occasional nationalist claims he was Catalan, though it is not impossible. Usually thought to be Genoese, and maybe a *converso*, a Jew forced to convert to Christianity, Columbus returned from his first trip to the New World in April 1493 to be received by Ferdinand and Isabel in Barcelona, but that is because they were there at the time and not because Columbus was a native. His pigeon-dropping covered head, resembling Dr. Johnson's in his dusty white wig, looks out towards the open sea, and his raised arm points languidly towards Libya, not America.

The monument dates back to the Catalan nationalist fervour of the 1888 Universal Exhibition, one of those cyclically recurring times when everything seems possible, the city is torn up for building works, and overnight fortunes are made by the ruthless. Yet Columbus' trips hastened the decline of Barcelona as a port and city, for the trade with the Americas that his voyages opened up brought riches to Seville but was forbidden to Barcelona for nearly three centuries (from 1518 to 1778).

A replica of Columbus' Santa María galleon — the original foundered due to the crew's drunkenness in Hispaniola — used to be moored in the harbour in front of the statue, but it was burnt mysteriously in 1991. The fire saved Catalans the embarrassment of participating in the highly Spanish-nationalist celebrations of the 1992 fifth centenary of Columbus sailing the ocean blue. For the low-life writer Mandiargues, in the 1960s, the Columbus monument was the great phallus that presided over the *barri xinès*, the erect beacon of sex above the dark streets.

In modern times it is often said that Barcelona turned its back on the sea until the Olympic development opened access again. It is more accurate to say that the sea was prohibited to Barcelona. In the fourteenth century imperial Catalonia had ruled Sicily, Naples, Genoa and parts of Greece. Even today Catalan is still spoken in L'Alguer on Sardinia. Buildings along the water-front bear witness to this maritime glory: the Customs House and the *Drassanes* ship-yards. The *Consolat de Mar*, Sea Consulate, was the Catalan arbiter of maritime law that was accepted for several centuries as standard throughout the Mediterranean. The Catholic monarchs of Spain feared the more democratic constitution and maritime power of mediaeval Catalonia, its greater wealth, its desire for independence. The city was penned in its walls, denied the sea.

Eduardo Mendoza flatly rejected, in *The City of Marvels*, the idea that Barcelona lived apart from the sea:

"That Barcelona went about its business 'turning its back on the sea' was already a well-worn phrase by the end of the nineteenth century, though in fact daily life in the city gave the lie to that cliché. Barcelona... lived off and for the sea; it was nourished by the sea...; the streets of Barcelona guided the wanderer's steps down to the sea, and that sea linked the city with the outside world... The streets and squares of Barcelona were blinding sea-white in fair weather and dull sea-grey on stormy days."

The nineteenth-century official buildings around the Columbus monument have a French air[1]. More than one tourist has sought a bed in the Port Authority, which looks like a hotel on the French Riviera. These were buildings put up after the city walls came down in 1859. Before, Henri Beyle *Stendhal*, most clear-headed son of the French Revolution and ironist on the sort of Romantic fantasies that dizzied Mérimée and Offenbach, walked down the Rambles in 1837:

"Barcelona is, so they say, the prettiest city in Spain, after Cadiz. It looks like Milan, but instead of standing in the middle of a perfectly flat plain, it gives onto Montjuich. From Barcelona the sea cannot be seen; this sea which so ennobles everything is hidden by the fortifications which stand at the bottom of the Rambla."

I like the 'so they say'. For sure many *barcelonins* will have boasted to Stendhal how pretty their city was. Like Cervantes, he does not leave you quite sure what his real view was — but the fact was clear enough: the sea was not seen because of fortifications. And Barcelona's fortifications have been as much to confine as to defend it.

---

[1]*Trotsky thought so too. Escorted under arrest through the port in December 1916, he jotted in his diary: "Big Spanish-French kind of city. Like Nice in a hell of factories. Smoke and puffs of flame, then lots of flowers and fruit." (21/12/1916)*

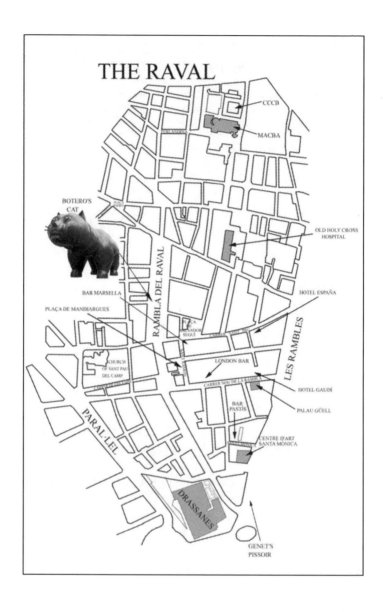

THE RAVAL

CCCB

MACBA

BOTERO'S CAT

OLD HOLY CROSS HOSPITAL

BAR MARSELLA

RAMBLA DEL RAVAL

PLAÇA DE MANDIARGUES

PLAÇA DEL SALVADOR SEGUÍ

HOTEL ESPAÑA

LES RAMBLES

CHURCH OF SANT PAU DEL CAMP

LONDON BAR

CARRER NOU DE LA RAMBLA

HOTEL GAUDÍ

BAR PASTÍS

PALAU GÜELL

CENTRE D'ART SANTA MÒNICA

PARAL·LEL

DRASSANES

GENET'S PISSOIR

Chapter 2
Mouldering Alleys

"Foreigners in this country, wearing fine gabardines, rich, they recognized their inherent right to find these archipelagoes of poverty picturesque, and this visit was perhaps the secret, though unavowed, purpose of their cruise."
JEAN GENET, *THE THIEF'S JOURNAL*.

Orgy of Humiliation

The Raval, meaning merely 'suburb' in Catalan, spread over the centuries from the Rambles and the city wall towards the Montjuïc mountain. The name of the Romanesque church hidden today among its bustling streets indicates the area's origins: *Sant Pau del Camp*, St. Paul's in the Fields, like London's St. Martin's.

In mediaeval times, undesirables were excluded from the walled city, with its monumental Government and Church buildings and twisting, narrow streets. Those forced to live outside included vagrants, prostitutes and butchers, whose dead animals smelt bad and attracted vermin. The destitute were brought to die in the Hospital, not then a place you entered for a cure, a careful few hundred yards beyond the city wall.

Somewhat luridly, with fascinated disgust, the early twentieth century Catalan poet Joan Maragall wrote of the Raval as if the soil were diseased:

> You have this Rambla which is so beautiful.
> And there, right beside it, much broader
> And more feverish, the Rambla of the poor
> Trembles in the dark of its infernal lights.

Today the name Raval describes the upside-down triangle between the Paral·lel, the Rambles and, inland, the

Rondes de Sant Antoni, Sant Pau and Universitat, following the line of the city walls and dividing the area from the Eixample. The Raval's status continues to be, in part, what it was 500 years ago: for much of it is the *barri xinès*, the rough brothel and bar quarter that most port cities have. 'Xinès' (or 'chino' in Castilian) not because of any Chinese connection, but because in the 1920s or perhaps earlier it was dubbed *Chinatown* in imitation of red-light districts in San Francisco or New York.

Jean Genet (1910-1986) has left the most famous account of Barcelona's *barri xinès* in its squalid heyday in *The Thief's Journal*. Genet was, of course, no ordinary tourist, and his journal no common travelogue. On his arrival in Barcelona in late 1933, he was, in Edmund White's words, "destitute, homeless, orphaned, friendless." White, his recent biographer, believes Genet stayed in Barcelona for less than three months, although in *The Thief's Journal* Genet exaggerated his stay to six months to play up "the most miserable period of my life." Genet lived in the *barri xinès* in winter: "My clothes were dirty and shabby. I was hungry and cold," he wrote. It even snows, a rare event in Barcelona. "We dared not wash it was so cold." The beggars he talks of as vermin, himself as a louse.

Genet sleeps for a while under a wall, then in cheap rooms: sometimes six to a bed without sheets, he says. He lives with gentle Salvador, then with Stilitano, a one-handed Serb. He survives by theft, begging and prostitution. He witnesses a murder during a card-game.

The Thief's Journal is a celebration of Genet's life as a down-and-out. Genet not only inverts the moral order, but undermines everything that he himself asserts. Thriving on contradiction, he insists he robbed because of poverty, then, as if casually, affirms he was "*hot* for crime." He describes his time in Barcelona as a series of humiliations. He is searched during a police raid and the cops mock his used tube of Vaseline. He dresses as a woman to go to the transvestite cabaret the *Criolla* (once in Carrer Tàpies), but he feels humiliated by a middle-class woman asking him when he started liking men (the prickly Genet was as quick to take offence as he liked to give it). At Carnival, he steals clothes from a hotel, dresses as a woman again — with the greater licence of Carnival misrule — and gets into a row in a bar. "Furious and humiliated, I left under the laughter of the men and the Carolinas [Genet's name for transvestites]."

In yet another orgy of self-abasement, Genet describes at some length how French tourists off a cruise ship take photos of the picturesque beggars and toss them coins. The tourists line up on a parapet to stare at the beggars below. This parapet, incidentally, is probably the remnant of city wall, with a garden now laid out on top of it, just behind the *Drassanes* — the mediaeval shipyards. Then as now, this wall divides the tourist waterfront from the *barri xinès*.

The scene of watchers and watched is reminiscent of a theatre, the sort of theatre of cruelty revealing the relationships of power that Genet was to write in the 1950s. Below, some beggars pose or perform, making themselves appear more wretched than they really are, whilst others look on with Olympian disdain. Both are ways to escape pity and conserve dignity. The tourists above compare the beggars with Goya or Doré compositions, or remark that they are less noble than their counterparts in Casablanca. Intolerably, all these comments are broadcast loudly in Genet's native tongue.

This would merely be another station in Genet's Calvary of humiliation, were it not that he dares to speculate that looking at beggars is the *real purpose* of these tourists' cruise. Genet's lurid description of Barcelona's red-light district drew foreigners to the city from the 1960s on. The motive of many of these later tourists is foreshadowed in this remarkable scene of tourists and down-and-outs. The unconfessed purpose of the cruise-ship passengers, formally in Casablanca or Barcelona to tour the sights, was to see the sights of poverty and so feel their own position up on the parapet — or the *balcony*, to echo the title of one of Genet's plays — reinforced.

If the above is the most resonant image of *The Thief's Journal*, the best-known describes the march after "one of the dirtiest, but most beloved pissoirs" was torn down by rioters, though not apparently for any homophobic reasons but as a protest against the right winning the November 1933 elections. About 30 *Carolinas* paraded in formal silk dresses, jackets and *mantillas* down the Rambles at 8 o'clock in the morning, mid-winter dawn, and laid red roses on the scrap-iron remains of the urinal.

For Genet, the city is merely a stage-set for his obsessions. Nevertheless, he names a number of the streets where he begged, stole, prostituted himself or hung out with his companions: Hospital, Carmen, Mediodía... These are streets you can enter by turning off the Rambles into the Raval. Within a block or two, you find yourself in narrow alleys reeking of urine, cats, reheated cooking oil and rubbish. The sun never reaches the pavement or even the washing pegged over the street below the windows of the tiny flats. Genet's territory was this entire *barri xinès*, which ran from Carrer Hospital down to the harbour and spilled across the Rambles into Escudellers and the surrounding streets (*barris* are no respecters of municipal boundaries).

> *"The barrio chino was, at the time, a kind of haunt thronged less with Spaniards than with foreigners, all of them down-and-out bums. We were sometimes dressed in almond-green or jonquil-yellow silk shirts and shabby sneakers, and our hair was so plastered down that it looked as if it would crack."*

Like Orwell, Malraux and Mandiargues, Genet now has a square named after him — surprisingly, if you supposed that the modernity-obsessed City Council might not be too fond of Genet's sordid Barcelona. But this would be to misunderstand the tourist industry's ability to assimilate the past and transform it for its needs. Like George Orwell,

Genet, once dead, safely dead, becomes a brand emptied of content and context. His name is used to sell ersatz decadence as a commodity. The *frisson* of sin and danger for the modern tourist.

It is not just a case of the Council re-moulding images of the past to its purpose. A city needs fine writers to bring it to life in the imagination. Thus, London is defined by Dickens or Glasgow becomes the 'Lanark' of Alasdair Gray. The Barcelona City Council has grasped that Genet's is one of the several Barcelonas (the "sinful, grim, port city," in Montalbán's words) lurking in Europe's collective imagination.

Genet, of course, really was a "down-and-out bum," not a middle-class tourist slumming. The authenticity of his experience as an outcast was key to his influence on French and European youth in the cultural rebellion of the 1960s, many of whom are today's well-heeled middle-aged tourists. His books became available to a mass audience at just the right time: in Britain the paperback *The Thief's Journal* came out in 1967.

Drunk, Ill or Dreaming

Other French lovers of *la boue* also used Barcelona as a landscape for their novels, most notably André Pieyre de Mandiargues in *La marge* (The Margin) and Georges Bataille in *Le bleu du ciel* (The Blue of Noon). Mandiargues (1909-1991) took the portrayal of the *barri xinès* into the Franco era: *La marge* is set in the 1960s. It was widely read, because it won the 1967 Prix Goncourt, France's main literary prize, and the author was openly anti-Franco. Translated into Catalan and Castilian, it was banned in Spain, which helped popularise it there, too.

La Marge's main character Segismond wanders the *barri xinès*'s labyrinth of streets. He is seeking vainly to ward off impending disaster. The book describes in detail heightened by Segismond's fevered mind the bars and streets Mandiargues trod in his months in the *barri xinès*. As if in homage, the prostitute- and acacia-filled square named after the author seems determined to remain stuck in the squalid '60s.

Surrealist librarian Georges Bataille (1897-1962) was in Barcelona in 1934, the same year as Genet, and wrote *Le bleu du ciel* immediately afterwards, though it was not published until 1957. His first-person narrator Troppmann is fleeing blindly into the future. He leaves his respectable wife and children in Brighton; he runs from his mad upper-class lover Dirty, who drinks, vomits and shits herself in the servant-pampered luxury of London's Savoy Hotel. He flees Paris, too, and the puritanical Communist Lazare, "a girl of twenty-five, ugly and conspicuously filthy". Troppmann himself is, in Will Self's introduction to the recent paperback edition, "throughout the action of the novel either drunk, ill or dreaming."

Le bleu du ciel, like *The Thief's Journal*, has 50 pages set in Barcelona — what better stage for demon-driven Troppmann? Like Genet, Bataille describes the transvestite bar *La Criolla*:

> *"A boy in girl's clothing was performing a number on the dance floor. The dress he was wearing left his back bare to the buttocks. The heel-drum of Spanish dancing resounded on the boards..."*

While Lazare is plotting armed actions with anarchists, Troppmann wastes time in a squalid cabaret:

> *"As I entered, a woman on the verge of deformity — a blonde woman with a face like a bulldog's — was performing on a small stage. She was practically nude; the coloured handkerchief round her loins failed to conceal the deep black of her pubis..."*

And so on...

Just as, in the nineteenth century, the French were the main creators of Spain's romantic image as a country full of scantily clad Carmens, so in the twentieth century, Genet, Bataille and Mandiargues created the legend of the *barri xinès.* Geographical proximity, the perception of Spain as a more thrilling and wilder country, and sexual voyeurism are all factors underlying these French *débauchés'* fascination with the *barri xinès.* A more immediate reason was absinthe, banned in France during the First World War, but available in nearby Barcelona.

Absinthe hastened Baudelaire, Toulouse-Lautrec, Van Gogh, Alfred Jarry and Oscar Wilde, along with many thousands of less celebrated drinkers, to their early deaths. It was the subject of Zola's *L'assommoir* and Degas' *The absinthe drinker.* If you ask in France for Ricard or Pernod, modern *pastis*, you will catch something of the taste of absinthe and have the pleasure of watching its magic transformation into cloud as water is added. The real absinthe is different: distilled from wormwood, its taste is bitter and its effects not just alcoholic, but hallucinogenic too. Oscar Wilde, broken by prison and ending his days in Paris, wrote:

> *"After the first glass, you see things as you wish they were. After the second glass, you see things as they are not. Finally you see things as they really are, and that is the most horrible thing in the world."*

The absinthe (*absenta*) sold now in Spain is no longer the genuine article, either. Today's *Bar Marsella* (the French connection again), where Mandiargues used to hang out, is tamer too. A visitor wrote:

> *"In 1978 I spent a lot of time in the Bar Marsella, where I imagine that now there are more customers with Lonely Planet guides in their pockets than barcelonins. Back then, it was the seediest bar I'd ever visited — I remember a thin, pallid man with stolen watches extending from wrist to elbow, just like a character in a Graham Greene novel... That the Bar Marsella sold absinthe was, of course, part of its magic."*

Its new proprietors have conserved the fading wallpaper, the browning mirrors for people who have given up looking at themselves, the posters advertising long-unavailable drinks, and the dim yellow lighting. If grey is the colour of the *barri xinès*'s streets, surely speckled yellow — dead flies on dim light-bulbs — is the colour of its interiors.

Other drugs have since made the *barri xinès* a more dangerous place. Or is that just nostalgia for supposedly kindlier ways of killing yourself? As Doña Concha, the *pensión*-keeper in Vázquez Montalbán's *Off Side*, mutters: "These days there's no control on anything. You get these dirty little junkies out on the street, and they end up giving you some lethal disease."

In the mid-80s there was a surge of heroin use, heroin-linked robberies and heroin deaths in the Old City. AIDS too killed more than in many other European countries: through lack of government education and of practical condom or needle programmes. Like other social problems, heroin has not gone away, but police pressure has pushed it off the streets of the Old City. It just won't do for tourists to stumble over people shooting up in hotel doorways. Heroin has been removed to outlying estates, or just along the waterfront to Can Tunis, under the Montjuïc mountain and beside the cemetery. Here the junkies can remain in their ghetto, or even kill themselves darting across the coastal ring-road.

The *Marsella* is not the only bar to survive as an echo of how the *barri xinès* once was. Wandering, you stumble on a number of nameless or ordinarily named bars, usually full of old men. One is called with majestic simplicity the *Bar Barato,* the Cheap Bar. The Raval is a plebeian quarter — in these bars you find retired waiters, retired sailors, retired pimps, retired prostitutes, the retired unemployed. People who have worked casually. Morning or afternoon, these relics of the past gaze out of the doors of bars and doze in the new squares. Plebeian like Naples rather than proletarian like Coventry: it is no accident that in Vázquez Montalbán's detective novels, Pepe Carvalho's extended *barri xinès* family consists of a call-girl, a boot-black and a failed car-thief.

Just behind the super-modern Santa Mònica Art Centre at the bottom of the Rambles, the *Pastís* has an honoured part in the history of the *barri xinès*. It's odds on that this tiny bar, stuffed with Left Bank memorabilia, will be playing Edith Piaf or Juliette Greco when you get there. If the *Pastís* represents the left-over French perfume of the intellectuals' *barri xinès* of several decades ago, then the Santa Mònica Art Centre (just opposite the site of Genet's *pissoir*) is very much part of the Olympic regeneration of the city. The Pompeu Fabra University also located its library and some faculties at the bottom of the Rambles in 1996. Just fifteen years ago, aged prostitutes lined up as if they were in a bus queue along this dingy section of the Rambles, but the memory of them is now drowned under the chatter and bustle of students and art tourists. Yet still, just along from the Santa Mònica Art Centre on the Rambles itself, a peep-show is gaudily advertised. And behind the Centre, on the corner opposite the *Pastís*, a transvestite bar is packed at nine in the evening. For a few years yet, left-overs of the old *barri xinès* will still float, like memories adrift, alongside the city of culture.

This multi-layered reality can be savoured on a 500-yard walk down Nou de la Rambla, which cuts straight through the *barri xinès* from Rambla to Paral·lel. At the Rambla end stands a tourist Mecca, the Palau Güell, the house that Gaudí designed for his patron. An *Art Nouveau* masterpiece, with a link to the Civil War: in 1936 its private chapel was destroyed by anarchists, and in 1938 a *cheka*, a Communist Party-controlled prison, was located in the basement. Opposite the Palau Güell is the Hotel Gaudí (Barcelona's famed creativity hasn't extended to the naming of hotels). The hotel used to be the Eden Concert, a casino and brothel for the upper-class. A trace of its past is recalled by the neon sign of the Parking Eden, underground garage beside the hotel. Right by the Palau Güell, two new clubs have opened. The daily *El Periódico* wrote: "The Old City is washing the face of its night life... it's acquiring brush-strokes of sophistication and design.

Where before the filth of years ruled, now a newly created modernity is beginning to flourish."

Move on down the street, you will see an old fountain on the left, from the days before running water, and on the right the London Bar, founded in 1909 and relative of the *Pastís*. It too boasts a bohemian tradition, conserved in its *Art Nouveau* décor, long-haired clientèle and late-night jazz. At the Paral·lel end of the street, the Bagdad club, notorious for live sex acts on stage ("the most daring cabaret in Europe"), stands near the police station built after clashes between Gypsies and Africans in the late '80s[1]. All along Nou de la Rambla, refurbished buildings mingle with crumbling tenements. *Art Nouveau* monument and Civil War jail, tourist hotel and '20s casino, workers' tenements and gentrified apartments, bohemian bar, sex club... it's all there, both co-existing and layered in time.

Only in passing do Genet's, Mandiargues' and Bataille's books describe the place itself. And then it is merely the backdrop for their own performances: Genet's remark of how there were more foreigners than Spaniards in the area betrays the narrowness of the circle in which he spun. Though their Barcelona is more phantasmagoric than real, it is their Raval that has lingered seductively in the minds of travel and guide-book writers.

Good and Bad Girls

There was one famous foreign writer who offered a brief but demystifying view of the *barri xinès* in a little-known 1950s book, the energetic and intelligent *Pagan Spain*. This was the Paris-based American Richard Wright, who is taken by two young men to a bar in the *barri xinès*, to meet 'bad women'.

> "...we entered an oblong dive whose background was lost in smoke. An unshaven, greekish face, with an unlighted cigarette stub in its partly-open lips, eyed us coldly from behind a cash-register... Strips of bamboo covered the

walls; I suppose that that tropical ornamentation was to make sailors feel they were in an emotionally abandoned atmosphere. Some thirty women of all ages and descriptions and sizes sat at tables and at the long bar, their shiny black purses — the international trademark of their profession — blatantly in evidence."

Wright's few pages make most of the romancing about the *barri xinès* seem self-indulgent, morbid curiosity. There is no disgust or self-disgust in Wright, as there is in Bataille; nor erotic role-playing, as in Genet. There is smoke, decor to entice sailors, a cash-register and women, whom Wright does not describe for atmosphere or titillation. "A tall, angular, not pretty, not ugly girl" is the nearest he gets to a physical description. Wright interrogates the prostitutes who approach his table about religion:

"...in one half hour I had plunged my hands into Spanish life and had brought up poverty, fear, prostitution, illiteracy — and all of this was but half a mile from... the white marble basin [in the cathedral] in which Columbus's Indians had been baptized."

As he returns to his *pensió*, Richard Wright sums up:

"Poor, 'bad', illiterate girls... The tall, dark middle-class apartment buildings... were filled with respectable Catholic families in which all the women were 'good'. The sailors, soldiers, the men who were married to 'good' women and the young sons in 'good' families became the clientele of 'bad' girls..."

The poverty, women's oppression and hypocrisy of Franco's Spain were felt in their bones by most of the writers who grew up then. Manuel Vázquez Montalbán was born in 1939, the year of Franco's victory, in the upper, more respectable part of the Raval. Many of his novels are set in or around the *barri xinès*: notably *The Pianist* and the Pepe Carvalho novels – his detective Carvalho has a gloomy office somewhere on the middle of the Rambles.

Round the Plaça del Padró, near the Sant Antoni market, where Montalbán was brought up, there was extreme poverty after the war, though not destitution in his family's case. He describes how people from his father's native Galicia were always turning up to stay and look for work, part of the long process of emigration off the land; how even at the door of a poor flat like his mother's (his father, like many, was away: in jail), women with children would knock asking for scraps of food. The residents of the *barri* felt defeated politically, economically and linguistically. One of Montalbán's characters in his greatest novel *The Pianist* explains:

> *"I know the neighbours, almost all of them have lost the war and they carry the post-war round on their backs like a dead body."*

Defeat was the reality underlying the mass prostitution that went on a few streets down towards the harbour from Montalbán's childhood flat, in Robadors, Tàpies or Sant Pau streets. As José María Carandell points out in his *Secret Guide to Barcelona*, many prostitutes had children. Given the death, imprisonment or exile of so many men during and after the Civil War, and the lack of any state assistance for the poor, numerous women with young children in 1940s Barcelona sold sexual services in order to survive.

A large industry grew up around these thousands of prostitutes — of women to look after children while their mothers worked, of venereal disease doctors and quacks, abortionists, condom shop owners (you still see some of these old shops with tiny frosted windows and the single word GOMAS —- rubbers — above the door), pimps, taxi-drivers, and barmen, washers-up and cleaners in bars and brothels. Some of these were as wretched as the prostitutes. Others made fortunes: Carandell tells of a man who paid, in 1972, the huge sum of 2,850,000 pesetas (some half a million euros in today's money) to buy just the lease of a twelve-room *meublé*, or brothel, on the slummiest street of the *Ciutat vella*, Robadors. A year later he had made enough to buy outright a bar in the same street.

For sure, not all the bars of the *barri xinès* were *bares de camareras*, sex bars. The Paral·lel, the great avenue of theatres and cafés along one side of the *barri xinès*, was before the Civil War the city's centre of working-class politics and entertainment; and after the defeat, the street of popular music-hall that ran the gamut from *risqué* to respectable. The entertainment on and off-Paral·lel in many theatres or cafés shaded into the sex industry. For every idolised Raquel Meller or Bella Dorita (the 1920s *vedette* who died in 2001, 100 years old), there were a thousand girls who never made it off the casting couch.

What of the clients, the men? The poverty-stricken Barcelona of the post-war coincided with the imposition of a rigid morality by Church and State. There was no shortage of clients, often married to women with Church-inculcated ignorance and fear of sex. Carandell's flat reporting style catches the rites of sex in grim Robadors in the 1960s:

> *"In just a few metres, there are almost thirty bars and a dozen* meublés, *where the prostitutes trade with the motley crowd of customers. These come, in steadily growing numbers, from the start of the afternoon until the small hours. They walk slowly but nervously, they enter one of the bars, they study the women with more or less intensity and pleasure, some stay, most go out to the street again to enter in the next bar, and so on, in a kind of labyrinthine route, repeated a number of times... The women's art is to wait with infinite patience."*

In 1973 the government closed down these bars in the name of 'public hygiene.' In *Tatuaje*, Vázquez Montalbán comments on the effect of these raids:

> *"As if by magic the red and green bulbs had disappeared, and new 100-watt lamps threw shop-window brightness over everything. Everything looked unfamiliar in the crude white light."*

45

Residents remember seeing the strips of sticky paper, duly dated and signed by the pertinent authority, sealing the doors. Poet and publisher Carles Barral liked to tell how, looking for a writer at a Raval address, he enquired "Ferlandina street?" and was told bluntly "It's closed." An entire street closed? Locals could not imagine that an outsider would actually be looking for a street, rather than the *meublé* bearing its name.

Sex for sale, of course, cannot be banned, only driven underground. It cannot be suppressed without the structures of society being profoundly changed. The anarchist movement tried to do just that in the revolutionary upsurge of 1936, when it campaigned among men against prostitution and offered practical alternatives to women. Many visitors to Barcelona in those heady days were impressed by the posters against prostitution[2], but after the withdrawal of the women's militias from the front line in early 1937, coinciding with the political defeat of the anarchists, the campaign died. Women returned to war-support industries, one of which was prostitution. The public campaigns against prostitution were replaced by notices *inside* brothels urging men to respect the women. The experience underlines how deep a social revolution is required to uproot prostitution. Under Franco and the rule of the Church, it reached its apotheosis.

Tourist-led Gentrification

The Raval is more than just the *barri xinès* and its legend. Though it cannot match the mediaeval monuments of the Gothic Quarter across the Rambles, it has its share: the fifteenth-century Holy Cross Hospital, now the National Library of Catalonia, as well as buildings already mentioned such as the Palau Güell and the restored Romanesque Sant Pau del Camp church. If you want an unrestored Romanesque church, you can still find one on the Plaça del Padró, its stones propped up in practical fashion by red brick. The Raval also contains the four-teenth-century ship-yard, the *Drassanes*. Restored as the

Maritime Museum, one of Barcelona's finest, it is a rare mediaeval industrial building (churches, of course, abound).

The Hotel and Restaurant España deserves mention, too. On the Carrer Sant Pau, just beyond the side-door of the rebuilt Liceu opera-house as you come from the Rambles and behind an unimposing facade, the dining- and ball-room of this hotel, designed by Domènech and painted by Ramon Casas a hundred years ago, are *Art Nouveau* masterpieces. You can still walk off the street (book on Sundays) dressed any old how and for the price of a couple of pints in a West End pub eat a good mid-day set menu. The restaurant's high ceiling is crossed by wooden beams with hundreds of tiny tiles dotting the spaces in between. Dark, almost black, wood, with carved fishes twisting out into coat-pegs, covers the entire room to shoulder height. Deep-blue tiles with a fish design run round above the panelling. The bar is framed in a wood-sculpted cornucopia of vines. Most amazingly, the room is full of respectable families eating lunch at the week-end or of local office-workers during the week. In London or Paris, such beautiful surroundings would be priced for high society.

Spain's first modern industrial workshops were founded in the 1830s on the still-remaining fields of the Raval, or on the smouldering sites of the monasteries burnt in the riots of 1835 – a sudden Spanish way of disestablishing the Church. The destruction of feudal property allowed the up-and-coming bourgeoisie to re-fashion the city: theatres and factories replaced the convents and monasteries. The very first *vapor*, or steam-driven factory, in Spain was located in the Raval, just off the Ronda de Sant Antoni. The Raval became a densely populated proletarian quarter, as well as the red-light district.

The industrial workshops have long gone, though some buildings remain, such as the Can Ricart textile factory on Sant Pau. And, as part of the modernisation of the city, both the street-sex industry and squalid bohemia

47

have been squeezed. Emblem of today's new city is the Rambla del Raval, a wide pedestrian boulevard hacked out of the centre of the *barri xinès* by demolition of five city blocks and 62 slum tenement buildings. Inspired somewhat pretentiously in Rome's Piazza Navona, it aims to be "one of the most beautiful squares in Europe" (Council leaflet!). Botero's enormous, smiling cat sculpture is a start. Young Pakistanis playing cricket add as exotic a touch as if bulls were being fought in the Birmingham Bull-Ring.

Wide new roads such as the Rambla del Raval which open up 'dangerous' neighbourhoods are a tried and tested device of social control. Shaftesbury Avenue, driven through London's Soho in the nineteenth century, is one example; and it was one of the functions of Barcelona's own Via Laietana, built like a lance straight through the *Ciutat vella* in 1910 after the 1909 revolutionary uprising against conscription for the colonial war in Morocco, known as the *Setmana tràgica*. The police can charge freely along open avenues, and anarchists less easily glide away up back alleys.

The current flagship project of Council reform of the Raval is the Robadors block. Rat-ridden vertical slums between the Rambla del Raval and the infamous Robadors street of brothels have been demolished. They are being replaced with a ten-storey glass-fronted elliptical hotel, housing, offices and green space. The Council is proud of this project, designed to 'dynamise' the centre of the Raval. The project epitomises many of the contradictions of the Council business-led reform programme. First, though slums, the demolished buildings housed people and had shops at street level. Now hotel and offices, with their underground parking places attracting cars into the historic centre, have replaced housing. Second, the project is the responsibility of a joint public-private company, the main tool of development the council has used since the 1980s. In a recent publication on the *Ciutat vella*, the Council argues:

> *"This body [the joint public-private company] was the first experience of the Council in incorporating civil society in redefining the city. Citizens and shop-keepers of* Ciutat vella *gave the most significant reply, organising themselves and pooling their efforts to take out shares in the new company."*

There is a certain slippage here, for shop-keepers are not the same as 'civil society'. Nearly all the many Residents' Associations of the area denounce speculative investment, lack of consultation and a model of development based on tourism- and business-oriented projects rather than reconstruction of houses. A hotel replacing housing is a case in point. Green space is welcome, but much or all of it may end up being private[3].

If you stroll down the brave new Rambla del Raval, you will notice the number of blocks being overhauled and the 'lofts' — the English word used, in fashionable imitation of New York — and flats for sale. You will also see, in the evening, a large number of Arabs and Asians chatting in the streets and immigrants' restaurants and shops.

Groceries, small supermarkets, fax and telecom shops, Pakistani, Filipino and Senegalese hair-dresser's, *halal* butcher's. Young Asians, often sharply dressed in Western clothes, contrast with the young Spanish *colgados,* dropouts, smoking dope or drinking. It is the usual mix of inner-city areas throughout Europe, but in Barcelona this mass presence of black immigrants is a new phenomenon. About 5% of all Catalans today are of African or Asian origin: ten years ago, it was under 1%. The figure is over 15% for the *Ciutat vella*. These emigrants have revitalised the Raval in a way that the conservative nationalists fear, for these often non-Catholic darker people are ungrateful, do not want to 'integrate' and wish to build outlandish mosques (more on this in Chapter 10). Ironically, it is these new Catalans, more than the empty boasting of Socialist or *Convergència* politicians, who are converting Barcelona from a provincial capital to an open cosmopolitan city.

Just as the Rambla del Raval is a gouge out of the middle of the Raval, so Richard Meier's 1995 Museum of Contemporary Art (MACBA) is a wedge shoved into the area. It stands beside the spectacular reformed *Casa de la Caritat*. Deyan Sudjic wrote rudely in *The Guardian*:

> *"...[Meier's] work is always instantly recognisable, an attribute that clearly appeals to those who are unsure of their own taste... Meier is always designing essentially the same building, using the same geometries, the same nautical imagery, and above all the same white stove-enamel cladding."*

White concrete and glass. Safe, international glamour architecture. The real-estate logic of this museum is that its prestige re-values the area: property prices rise, a different class of people move in, galleries and hotels open, fancy boutiques and bars replace traditional shops. This is "benign metastasis," a term coined in Council circles; or "Culture fertilises real estate," in Mike Davis' more waspish phrase[4]. Round behind the MACBA, by Carrer Ferlandina (yes, the same, once closed), houses are left deliberately by landlords to fall apart, with a view to redevelopment. The landlords can afford to wait as the roofs sag, walls crumble, their tenants age and property prices rise (see Chapter 8).

The Raval is being rapidly gentrified, with building work everywhere. Without proper municipal control of property, prices soar and the former residents are excluded. Whether the Council and the building speculators ("the public and private sectors working hand-in-hand") can carry it off is not clear. Such reforms to transform an entire neighbourhood are always a challenge, their effectiveness an open question. Like the East End of London, the Raval has seen successive waves of immigration: first the Catalans coming out of the hills to work in nineteenth-century factories, then from other parts of Spain, then this new wave from Latin America, Africa and Asia. Most of the new African and Asian emigrants are poor, fleeing the effects of war, famine, IMF cutbacks and "debt" repayments in their countries of origin, and living several families to a flat in crumbling buildings with shared toilets, like the Galicians who stayed in Vázquez Montalbán's childhood home in the 1940s. Even worse, as the buildings are now sixty years older. Their presence appears to contradict gentrification, but in reality may not do so. Emigrants by definition are dynamic, and odds are that some of the moneyed Catalan young will be excited by the new cosmopolitanism of the multiracial Raval.

Vázquez Montalbán summed up the process of change in the *barri* of his childhood with his customary succinct irony:

> *"I'm not at all sad to see the disappearance of these streets where it's impossible to live. But it concerns me that behind the clean-up of the Raval and old Barcelona, there is a speculative operation designed to expel the Indians to a new reservation on the outskirts... The city's shit is being swept under the carpet. There are no solutions offered to the people living in this shit so that they can get out of it definitively. They are just being exported to the outskirts so that the city centre can be converted into an inhabitable territory for new social layers and an agreeable area where tourists can snap photographs and see how Barcelona has changed and what a pretty city we have."*

The poor of the Raval will not be buying lofts on the new Rambla. Many of the people of the area are rehoused in the Old City, but others end up in the balconyless tower-blocks you see on the outlying hills of Santa Coloma and Montcada i Reixach when you drive out of the city on the motorway towards France. Barcelona's conversion from industrial to service city demands that the city centre be made safe and attractive for the visitors who are bringing the revenue to restaurateurs and hoteliers. But if it's so safe, will people still want to come? Genet could be right about the secret, though *unavowed* thrill of danger and poverty that tourists savoured from the parapet above the beggars' vacant lot. Could too sanitised a city lose its edge, even become too boring to visit?

---

[1] *There are two small areas in Barcelona where Gypsies have been settled for several generations. One is the area round the Plaça de Raspall in Gràcia and the other is on Nou de la Rambla. The origin of the clashes referred to is unclear, though it was believed that two Gypsies who died from overdoses had been sold bad heroin by a black dealer.*

[2] *"In the streets were coloured posters appealing to prostitutes to stop being prostitutes," Orwell,* Homage to Catalonia, *Chapter One.*

[3] *Chapters 8, 15 and 16 develop this discussion of Barcelona's model of development.*

[4] *In* City of Quartz *(1990), Davis' sustained polemic against the Los Angeles model of urban development. Barcelona is very different, because of its compactness and long history. Yet, as I discuss in Chapter 16, Barcelona is not wholly untouched by the L.A. model.*

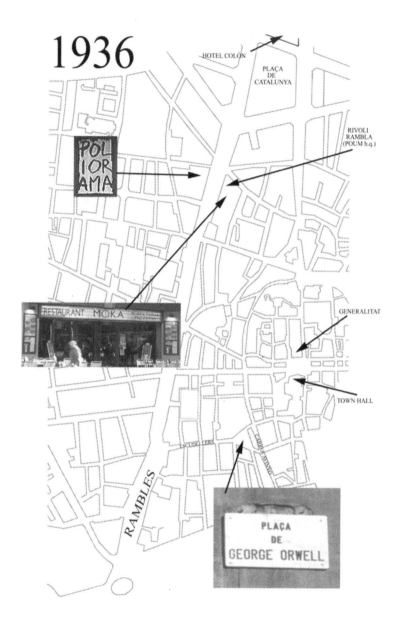

1936

HOTEL COLÓN

PLAÇA
DE
CATALUNYA

RIVOLI
RAMBLA
(POUM h.q.)

POL
IOR
AMA

RESTAURANT MOKA

GENERALITAT

TOWN HALL

L'ESCUDELLERS

RAMBLES

PLAÇA
DE
GEORGE ORWELL

Chapter Three
Strange and Valuable

"I had dropped... into the only community of any size in Western Europe where political consciousness and disbelief in capitalism were more normal than their opposites... One had been in contact with something strange and valuable."
GEORGE ORWELL, *HOMAGE TO CATALONIA.*

Plaça Orwell

At the end of the century, we Orwell fans were excited to see that a new Barcelona square was to be named after him. From New York, Christopher Hitchens hailed this lyrically:

> *"In Catalonia three years ago, the history of the defeated was finally celebrated as a victory. A square near the Barcelona waterfront was named Plaça George Orwell..."*

The Plaça Orwell is a small triangular space opening off the Carrer dels Escudellers (Street of potters). Though hardly a stone's throw from the City Hall and Catalan Government buildings on the Plaça Sant Jaume, Escudellers is one of the most irreducibly rough streets of the *Ciutat vella*. Novelist Stephen Burgen called it "a gloomy piss-drenched street cheered only by the aroma of chickens spit-roasting on a wood fire outside Los Caracoles restaurant" — and he wasn't writing of Genet's day, but in 2002.

The creation of the Plaça Orwell is part of the City Council's strategy of knocking down slum buildings in the *Ciutat vella* to create small open spaces. This policy, known as *esponjament* — i.e. inserting little holes, as in a sponge — both reduces the area's extremely high population and leads towards gentrification and making the area more tourist-friendly. The square's troubled short history reveals some of the contradictions. After it was sponged out in 1997, the Plaça Orwell rapidly became a hang-out for late-night drinkers and drug users. Conflict between youth using the square and the police erupted into skirmishes several times in 1999 and 2000.

As a result, in Summer 2001 the Plaça Orwell was selected for a pioneering social experiment. Street cameras connected directly to the police station were installed. Drug dealers would be deterred and unsuspecting tourists straying down from Carrer Avinyó would be properly protected. Manu Chao, son of Spanish exiles, brought up in Paris and now master of the *mestissage* of styles that has become the main style of today's anti-capitalist movement, lives on Carrer Avinyó, where 100 years ago Picasso had a studio[1]. This uncompromising radical poet did not miss the irony: "It's symbolically just incredible that the square named after George Orwell is among the first in the city to be under video surveillance."

However, resistance to 1984 lives: the camera cables have been frequently cut. Even uncut, their effectiveness is slight: there is less bag-snatching or drug-dealing in the Plaça Orwell, but these activities have just moved further along Escudellers.

In the Plaça Orwell I met a man with definite ideas about tourism. Drawn by our camera tripod (the photo on the cover of this book), in dark glasses and with hunched shoulders and long white hair, he stomped across the square towards us. "So what do you see in these old houses?" he asked.

"They're pretty, don't you think?" I said.

The old man placed both his hands on my defensively folded arms.

He took off his dark glasses to reveal he had just one functioning eye with which he stared at me for several seconds.

"You know what's in these houses?"

"Yes," I said provocatively, but he was going to tell me anyway.

"Behind these pretty facades are *mierda y ratas*, shit and rats. Decent people are forced to live here. And if you're making money out of taking photos, you're *hijos de puta*, sons of bitches."

One could speculate he is hired by the tourist board to perform as a resentful old anarchist in the Plaça Orwell, but he is just one of many old people left high and dry in the changing Old City. I have a friend who lives on Escudellers whose whole building is falling to pieces. Pipes growl like bears; the spring and autumn rains pour through the cracked roof; the communal stairs are uneven, the banisters and windows removed. Nearly all the mostly elderly residents of the twenty flats, four per storey and five storeys, live on minimum pensions — some 300 euros per month. No-one has the money so that they can collectively do up the building and Council cash is spent elsewhere. Orwell Square (or triangle), crumbling and under surveillance, is not quite where, in Hitchens' words, *the history of the defeated was finally celebrated as a victory*. It reminds me rather of the enduring consequences of the Civil War defeat (see Chs. 5 & 9).

Many, particularly the British, know something of Barcelona through George Orwell's classic account of revolution, *Homage to Catalonia*, nowadays widely seen as his best book, though a failure when it first came out. It is a vivid, sincere and strangely poignant book: written by a man in his prime before illness and disillusion cut him down. Alongside *The Thief's Journal*, it has been one of the main factors drawing British people to Barcelona. This is especially so for the generation which lived young through the cultural and political upheavals of the 1960s and '70s and was fascinated by the Spanish Civil War and the international solidarity it inspired. The City Council knows this. It knows visitors like to stumble across the Plaça Orwell, even if they do not believe that the revolutionary change Orwell fought for is possible.

Days of Hope

Twenty pages near the start of André Malraux's *Days of Hope* describe in his urgent prose the fighting in Barcelona on Sunday July 19 1936 in response to the Generals' uprising the day before.

> *"... the Colon Hotel with its pineapple tower and nests of machine-guns loomed above the square. Troops from the Pedralbes Barracks in separate detachments occupied the three main buildings on the Square...*
>
> *"Some thirty workers made a rush across the central portion of the square, which stands above the level of the roadway, taking what cover they could behind the trees that border it. The machine-gun chattered, and they fell in bunches. Shadows of the pigeons wheeling above at no great height glided across the fallen bodies, over a man who still was staggering, waving his gun at arm's length above his head."*

The central portion of the square referred to, the Plaça de Catalunya described in the first chapter, still stands above the level of the roadway and is still bordered by trees. The Hotel Colón stood on the mountain side of the square, just along from the exit into the Passeig de Gràcia. Thousands of workers, mainly from the CNT (National Federation of Labour), the anarchist-led trade union, gathered that Sunday in the side streets, aware that if they took this central square, the city could be theirs. Thousands more assembled near the *Drassanes*, then used as a barracks. Telephoned information reported more soldiers marching down the straight roads of the Eixample from the outlying Pedralbes barracks. Many of the workers could recall that the Catalan uprising in support of the Asturian revolt of October 1934 was crushed. In both 1934 and 1936, the Generalitat refused to arm the workers. In 1936, though, the CNT, which had not taken part in 1934, was prepared. Arms had been stock-piled. The night before, they raided an arms depot in the port for more. Some 2,000 anarchists in 200 self-defence groups knew this Sunday morning that victory or defeat depended on themselves.

As their victory is now history, it can easily seem no other outcome was possible. But it was touch and go. In many other towns of Spain the workers lost; in Barcelona it was only after intense fighting and sections of the police being won over to opposing the military revolt that the Army was defeated by the end of that long Sunday. Dozens of people died in the Plaça de Catalunya. On the Monday, in the final attack on the *Drassanes*, the anarchist leader Francisco Ascaso was shot in the forehead.

After July 19 a full-scale social revolution erupted in Barcelona. The CNT pushed forward the collectivisation of society they had dreamed of. Workers took over production, transport, everything but the state. As the anarchists did not believe in states, they ignored the state apparatus. On Tuesday July 21, they met with Lluís Companys, the President of the Generalitat. Anarchist leader Diego Abad de Santillán described this famous meeting of the Government and the people who did not believe in Government.

> *"We went to the seat of the Catalan government, clutching our weapons, not having slept for several days, unshaven, confirming by our appearance the legend that had formed about us. Some members of the Generalitat were trembling, white-faced, at this interview from which Ascaso was missing."*

The canny Companys, a labour lawyer who knew well how the anarchists would respond to noble sentiments, told them:

> *"—You are masters of the city, because you defeated the Fascist soldiers on your own... You have won and everything is in your power. If you do not need me, if you do not want me as President, say so now and I shall become just another soldier in the anti-fascist struggle."*

The anarchists told him to stay on. "We did not believe in dictatorship when it was being exercised against us and we did not want it when we could exercise it ourselves only at the expense of others," wrote Santillán. Thus the state apparatus, which at that moment could have been destroyed by Santillán giving Companys a light tap on the arm just like Macià's push only five years before, survived to re-group and return nine months later to break anarchist power.

Barcelona 1936 is one of the very few social revolutions in history, comparable to the Paris Commune of 1870 and the Russian Revolution. This is often obscured, for it is linked by almost the entire political spectrum, from Franco to the Communist Party, with anarchist disorder and uncontrolled killings. For the first two months of the Revolution, bodies would be found at dawn on the Carretera de la Rabassada, the winding path up through the woods to the Tibidabo hill overlooking the city.

Eduard Pons Prades, a young anarchist, told a devastating story that explains the context. The owner of a small wood workshop had stayed after July 19: known as a good employer, he had nothing to fear. However, when he disappeared a few days later, his family came to the CNT to inquire for him. The CNT investigation found he had been killed by three men. Hernández the CNT woodworkers' leader lambasted one of the assassins:

> "— How many times had you seen this man? Only once! You mean, you dared to kill a man you had seen only once. Like a dog! He was one of our best employers. Everyone knew he was a good man."

The young man struggled for words:

> "— He couldn't have been good. He looked like the land-owner in our village in Córdoba, the scoundrel who ruined my father's health, led him to his grave, forced us to emigrate to Catalonia."

Pons Prades comments:

> "The world suddenly shattered for me. What could have happened in that Cordoban village? He was only twenty,

had been living in Barcelona ten years. What could have happened that, from the age of ten, he had kept alive such hatred, such rancour for a man, that he could kill, kill another merely for looking like him?"

The revolutionary order that leaders such as Abad de Santillán argued for was well-nigh impossible in these early days, given this depth of hatred for the Church, the bosses, their gunmen and the State.

Anarchism was widely associated with Barcelona from the time of Santiago Salvador's bombing of the Liceu. Later, two Spanish Prime Ministers were assassinated by Catalan anarchists. The bomb attack on the King's wedding procession in 1906 killed six guards and several horses and spattered with blood the bridal dress of Victoria Eugenia, Queen Victoria's grand-daughter newly arrived from England. The CNT, however, was not a bomb-throwing organisation, but a trade union that sought to use the mass strike as a revolutionary weapon. Its membership fluctuated enormously, but from its foundation in 1910 through to 1937 it was the main organisation of the Catalan working-class. The Iberian Anarchist Federation (the FAI) worked within the CNT to give it its anarchist orientation. The CNT still exists, but only as a small grouping with little influence. A 1980s split-off, the less uncompromising CGT, has succeeded in providing a militant though minority alternative to the two main unions, the UGT and *Comissions Obreres* (see Ch. 9).

It is not surprising that Bakunin's ideas, reaching Spain around 1870, fell on fertile ground. Here "peasant riots, short, violent revolts, and banditry by outlaws were the time-honoured form taken by popular explosions of anger and revenge" (historians Broué and Témime). In Spain the ground was less ripe for gradualism, the ideas of slow reform that dominated the mass social-democratic parties of France, Germany and Britain. Anarchism was an ideology that suited Spain's particularly violent history and raw class struggle.

In February 1902 a General Strike was drowned in blood. 1909 saw the *Setmana tràgica*. On these and countless other occasions, the bosses and state reacted with violence, barricades went up and churches were burned.

The class struggle reached its highest point before 1936 in the years 1917-1919, culminating in the Canadiense electricity company strike, which plunged the city into winter darkness. In the following years the CNT had to wage a defensive battle against the bullets of the bosses' union the *Sindicats lliures* (the misnamed 'Free Unions') and of the police of Martínez Anido, the Governor appointed by Madrid to root out anarchism.

Victor Serge, who reached Barcelona in 1917 with nothing and worked in a print-shop, catches the atmosphere of these early years of the CNT in *Birth of our Power*:

> *"They don't have much reason to ponder over the value of their lives, these people. Never will they escape from these shacks (which stink from cooking oil and bedbugs), from the factories (where their bodies and brains are drained each day), from the stifling slums, from the swarms of kids with their dirty, matted, lice-infested hair... Only by force will they break out of the closed circle of their fate. And tough luck for those who fall by the wayside (losing nothing of importance anyway). The others, the victors, would open the way of the future. What kind of future?... Any future would be better than the present."*

This was the background to those workers who went up against machine-guns with bare hands in July 1936.

In the Saddle

When George Orwell arrived in Barcelona on Boxing Day, 1936, he was enthused by the still-glowing embers of that Revolution unleashed five months before. At the start of *Homage to Catalonia* he comments on the atmosphere: "It was the first time I had ever been in a town where the working-class was in the saddle." This quaint phrase introduces Orwell's famous page-long paean to revolutionary Barcelona:

"...every building... draped with red flags or with the red and black flag of the Anarchists; Churches... being systematically demolished by gangs of workmen... Waiters and shop-walkers looked you in the eye and treated you as an equal..."

No tipping, no *Senyor* or *Don*, no private cars, no 'well-dressed' people at all. No evidence of this remains today, of course, except in one thing: the ugly newness of many churches. If you wander through the workers' suburb of Poble Nou, now up-and-coming, or through the Eixample, you do not see many pretty old churches. You see 1940s-style utilitarian brick churches, for Franco had the sacked, burnt and systematically demolished churches of this godless city rebuilt. On occasion, with Republican prisoners' forced labour.

It is often remarked that *Homage to Catalonia* is a misnomer. Orwell spent little time in Catalonia and showed no appreciation of how Catalonia differed from the rest of Spain. This is so, but misses the point. Catalonia, for Orwell, was where the Spanish Revolution enthused him and then where the events of May 1937 crushed that Revolution. Catalonia was the place where Orwell lived the most intense political experiences of his life. It gave him the raw material not just for *Homage to Catalonia*, but for *Animal Farm* and *1984*.

Volunteering to fight with the POUM, the small revolutionary party to the left of the Communist Party, Orwell trained for two weeks at its Lenin barracks on the Carrer Tarragona. In January he was sent to the Aragon front, at first overlooking Saragossa, and was soon transferred to besiege Huesca when the contingent of the Independent Labour Party (ILP), which was linked to the POUM, arrived. This tiny group of thirty people made not the slightest military difference to the war, but their presence boosted the morale of the besiegers of Huesca and galvanised solidarity movements in Britain.

Orwell and the ILP group were based at *La Granja* (The Farm), a complex of white-washed farm-buildings still standing near Monflorite, at a cross-roads just four kilometres South of Huesca. Living here in primitive conditions aroused his admiration for the militia:

> *"Many of the normal motives of civilized life — snobbishness, money-grubbing, fear of the boss, etc. — had simply ceased to exist."*

The Big Lie

To those familiar with the Communist Parties' onslaughts on Orwell, it may come as a surprise that Orwell at first disagreed with the anarchist and POUM view that the revolution and war should go hand in hand. In the endless debates on the relatively inactive Aragon front Orwell argued the Communist Party line, which was that a social revolution should be postponed while a centralised army was built to win the war. Defeating fascism had to be the main priority. When the ILP contingent left the trenches on leave for Barcelona on April 25, 1937, Orwell and several others hoped to transfer to the International Brigades in order to see more action on the Madrid fronts.

During their stay in Barcelona, the decisive events that completely changed Orwell's view took place. On May 3 1937 the Generalitat and the Communist Party moved against anarchist power in Barcelona, occupying the telephone exchange (still there, though now reduced to a cell-phone shop) on the Plaça de Catalunya, which the anarchists had taken from the Army on July 19. Several hundred people were killed in the four days of street fighting that followed. Like other ILP volunteers, Orwell defended the POUM, which supported the anarchists. He was sent to the roof of the Poliorama Cinema (now a theatre) near the top of the Rambles. Here they had a stock of the infamous "indifferent grenades", indifferent as to whether they killed the thrower or the enemy.

Luckily they didn't have to throw any. Orwell read detective novels for three days.

Orwell's job was to watch out for attacks on the POUM Executive Committee Headquarters on the opposite side of the Rambles, where the 4-star £150 a night Rivoli Rambla Hotel at No. 128 is now located. The Café Moka (still there), beside the POUM offices, was occupied by Assault Guards loyal to the Government.

The only sign today of the Rivoli Rambla's revolutionary past as the POUM headquarters is a somewhat weather-beaten plaque on the wall, recalling the detention of POUM leader Andreu Nin there on June 16 1937. Originally put up in 1983 with Socialist Party support, the plaque declared Nin a "victim of incomprehension." Blandness which falsifies the record. In 1987, pressure from the Andreu Nin Foundation corrected this to "victim of Stalinism."

The 1992 film *Operació Nikolai*, made by Dolors Genovés and Llibert Ferri for the Catalan station TV3, used material found in the Moscow archives to show that Nin was abducted by Comintern agents, tortured, killed and buried in an unmarked grave near Alcalá de Henares, in the province of Madrid. In 1987 I had interviewed Stafford Cottman, only eighteen in 1936 and the youngest of Orwell's colleagues in the ILP contingent ("I was known as 'the kid'"). Stafford recalled emotionally:

"The death of Nin was a terrible shock to us. I remember him very well. The first day we were at the POUM HQ, we were sitting around, as you do in these situations, waiting for someone to take us somewhere and we heard these roars of laughter from one of the committee rooms. It was Nin, they told us. Later he greeted us very warmly. The murder of Nin has always made me very angry, even to this day. He was Spain's most erudite Marxist, you know, but I always remember those peals of laughter. The point is, he was a very serious man, but absolutely able to enjoy life. And you know, the fact he never 'confessed' under torture as the defendants in the show trials in the Soviet Union did was heroic and saved countless lives. It meant

Nin has been treated in modern Catalonia in a similar way
to Orwell: his revolutionary politics have been emptied of
content. Nin has become a "universal Catalan," internationally famous and therefore *good*. He has no square in
Barcelona, but he has a street in *Nou barris*, ironically
where a new *Corte inglés* and the new giant Heron City
leisure development, one of Saramago's 'cathedrals' of
modern capitalism, with its shops, movie screens, walk-
ways, sports facilities, discos, cafeterias and fast food
outlets, are located. When Andreu Nin is remembered, as
often as not it is for his translations of Dostoievsky into
Catalan rather than his politics.

I have run ahead of the story. After the May events, the
Communist Parties' propaganda drive went into top gear.
The POUM were denounced as fascists. A widely circu-
lated cartoon showed the POUM drawing aside its mask of
hammer and sickle to reveal a swastika beneath. Orwell
saw this slander stencilled on the walls of Barcelona.

An empiricist who believed in facts, Orwell *knew* the
POUM were not fascists. He had lived with them at *La
Granja*, he had fought with them against the fascists. To
the argument that the rank-and-file were dupes, but its
leaders were fascists, he could contrast his experience of
knowing the leaders, too. Like Cottman, he had met Nin
and other leaders. This *big lie*, the mask in the cartoon
apparently being stripped away when in fact the truth was
being masked, sowed the seed of *Animal Farm* and *1984*.
This was not a question of differing interpretations of
complex events, but a deliberate inversion of the truth.

Orwell believed that most of the Communist Party
ranks consisted of honest revolutionaries, but he became
convinced that they were being systematically used by a
leadership that acted in the interest of Stalin's geo-polit-
ical strategy. Despite paying lip-service to international
revolution, Stalin prioritised the national interests of the

Soviet Union over revolutionary movements such as the one in Spain. Thus, Communists gave their lives in Spain for a policy of diplomatic manoeuvres with the Great Powers, which was subsequently to lead to the 1939 Hitler-Stalin pact. This was the harsh story Orwell was to tell in *Animal Farm*. He learnt it in those few days in May.

He and the other ILPers told Wally Tapsell, the International Brigade representative, there was no way they could now transfer to the Communist-controlled International Brigades. The ILP contingent returned to the Huesca front, where at dawn on May 20 Orwell was shot by a sniper. It is curious how little echo in Orwell's later writing this serious wound left. The bullet passed right through his neck, amazingly missing nerves and arteries, only affecting his vocal chords. Orwell had finally got rid of the Eton accent he disliked, for afterwards he spoke in a monotone.

His writing, though, became more distinguished. John Lehmann called the style Orwell developed in *Homage to Catalonia* a 'close-to-conversation' style. This is so, though notably there is hardly any actual dialogue. Orwell establishes a warm colloquial voice, far from the pompous pseudo-proletarian tones characteristic of too many Civil War memoirs. Orwell's book has the feel of someone writing a chatty letter: "I remember..." "I wish I could convey..." "I do not know if I can bring home to you...". He tells you quirky, interesting details: in the Spring, "you met peasants wearing wild roses over their ears."

The subject-matter of this style was decidedly anti-heroic. The cold and mud, the insolent rats "as big as cats" that nibbled your boots at night, the lice on your testicles, the clothes and rifles falling apart. Orwell did not believe a just cause makes war any more bearable. The night attack is masterly: he filters it through his own reactions, fears and feelings, but without playing up his leading role. In fact, we only know he played a leading role from other sources. Such plain writing is, of course, not artless. It has the effect of pulling in the reader to share more vividly the experiences — and views — of the writer.

Awkward Message

Homage to Catalonia has always been a particularly difficult book for the Communist Parties, precisely because Orwell started off supporting their line of "defeat fascism first; leave revolution till later." It was the common-sense line. But 'common sense' is not always good politics. ("Common sense is the sum of the prejudices we have accrued by the age of sixteen," said Lukács). Orwell's opinion changed because of his experience in May 1937. In Aragon, before the May days, he accepted that the revolution had to be postponed. He was then outraged when he saw that the Communists did not want to postpone it, but were engaged in reversing and crushing the revolutionary gains already made.

Thus, actual experience changed his pro-Communist preconceptions, which was particularly uncomfortable for the Communist argument. As a result, Communists have tended towards *ad hominem* attacks, of which "upper-class," "not a Marxist," "petit-bourgeois" are the politer ones acceptable today. At the time Orwell and his comrades were described in the Communist press as "Trotsky-fascist traitors" and "spies for Franco," words which could have led to his death and did lead to the death of some of his comrades in the POUM militia. Cottman told me:

> *"When I got back to Bristol, I found out that the Young Communist League of which I had been a member had expelled me and had been marching up and down in front of my mother's house in Shirehampton every Saturday morning with placards saying* Cottman accepts Franco's gold. *My mum was disappointed, I can tell you, to find I'd come back without a penny."*

In his 1995 film, *Land and Freedom*, Ken Loach used the power of Orwell's central argument and took it a twist further. Dave the protagonist does not just sympathise, as Orwell did, with the Communist line, but is a Party member, making his change of position because of the May Days even sharper.

Land and Freedom, its Barcelona sequences shot in unchanged alleys in the Born area in 1994, is not a film of *Homage to Catalonia*, but in its characters and story it draws on the composite experience of the ILP contingent. The film, a Loach project from at least the mid-80s, was often discussed with Stafford Cottman, a neighbour of Loach's in Bath.

In Spain, *Land and Freedom* was a surprise 1995 hit, with a release in 41 cinemas. It remained in the box office Top Ten for three months and was one of the year's most popular films. Historian Andy Durgan, an adviser on Loach's film, told me:

> *"You could feel the interest created by the film was something special because of the numerous well-attended meetings and film presentations I spoke at and the applause at the end of the film when it was shown in Barcelona. Again and again young people commented to me that they were unaware there had been a revolution in 1936 and that this had been crushed by the supposedly 'revolutionary' Communist Party. They had never learnt this at school."*

The young people Andy Durgan refers to were of course a post-Franco generation, yet the Civil War has remained little discussed till recently in the new Spanish democracy (see Chapter 9).

The POUM/ anarchist version of the war, that Orwell basically expressed, has been heard still less. Even today, the overall consensus of the huge swathe of democratic opinion that did not support Franco has been that the Communist Parties were right, but just went a bit too far. The eminent historian Raymond Carr argues:

> *"It was not that Communist overall strategies were mistaken; their plea for strong government, the maintenance*

of a popular front that included the bourgeois Republicans and concentration on the war effort was, in their own jargon, 'objectively correct'. The policies of the POUM, the consequences of a naive Marxist-Leninist dogmatism, would have been a disaster... It was Communist methods which stank: the night-time rap at the door by the secret police, the mysterious disappearance of once-valued comrades..."

The awkward message in Loach's film and Orwell's book is that you cannot separate policy and methods. The *methods* Raymond Carr dislikes were an integral part of the policy he likes. The repressive, murderous methods were necessary precisely to crush the popular revolution witnessed by Orwell, so that the Popular Front could govern.

The militia besieging Huesca used to encourage each other with the catch-phrase: "Tomorrow we'll drink coffee in Huesca." They never did. Bob Edwards, the leader of the ILP contingent, went back in 1959 when Labour M.P. for Bilston to attend a trial of anti-Francoists as an international observer. While there he made a special trip to Huesca. He wrote of his bitter pleasure in toasting the POUM militia with a bitter Spanish expresso drunk in Huesca's main square. Later on that trip, to his credit, Edwards was expelled from Spain.

Orwell did not live to go back. He died of tuberculosis in January 1950. After the suppression of the POUM and abduction of Nin on June 16 1937, Orwell, still recovering from his neck wound, had to go underground and flee the country. Barcelona had changed in the six months since his arrival. The ILPers had to tear up their militia cards and retrieve their passports. Some volunteers spat on the hated passport signature of Foreign Secretary Anthony Eden, so sick were they at British non-intervention, which meant denying arms sales to the Republic whilst doing nothing about Hitler's and Mussolini's support for Franco. In contrast with the tie-less egalitarian city of December 1936, the fugitives got out by posing as tourists. They dressed in their best clothes and sat in the dining-car of the train for France. The train stood for many long minutes in frontier town Portbou's Euston-like railway station, with its huge curved cast-iron roof. The four tourists, Eileen and Eric Blair (Orwell), John Mcnair and Stafford Cottman, nervously sipped their cups of coffee in the dining-car whilst wondering whether they would soon be safe, or hauled off the train to prison and possible death as Francoist spies. The fate they must have already divined for Nin.

---

[1] Les demoiselles d'Avignon, *his ground-breaking 1907 picture, refers to women on this street, not the old papal city of Provence.*

WALK ALONG THE HILLS

CAMP DE LES CANONS

ANTI-AIR BATTERIES

VISTA

MÜHLBERG

CARMEL RESIDENTS ASSOCIATION

GUINARDÓ PARK

BAR DELICIAS

PATH

PARC DEL CARMEL

CASA-MUSEU GAUDÍ

COTTOLENGO HOME

LA SALUT TENNIS CLUB

PARK GÜELL

ENTRANCE TO PARK

SANT JOSEP CHURCH

KASAL DE LA MUNTANYA SQUAT

PLAÇA DE LESSEPS

TRAVESSERA DE DALT

METRO

Chapter 4
Architecture and Housing

"Mount Carmel is a bare and arid hill on the North-east side of the city... [It] rises beside the Park Güell, whose green leafiness and fairy-tale architectural fantasies it looks at sceptically over its shoulder."
JUAN MARSÉ, *ÚLTIMAS TARDES CON TERESA*.

Sugar Plum Dwellings

Many a visitor to Barcelona only leaves the bars and monuments of the *Ciutat vella*, Barcelona's historic heart and terrain of the first three chapters, for a quick raid on the Sagrada Família. This chapter goes out, and up from the top of the old village of Gràcia to one of Gaudí's greatest creations, the Park Güell. And then up again, beyond the Park and Gaudí, to the very roof of the city. Then it drops down the hidden side of Mount Carmel, to a working-class Barcelona that has not benefited from the investment that has made tourist Barcelona a famous city of art and culture.

From the Plaça Lesseps metro station on the green line, follow the signs for the Park Güell and the poor and more independent tourists heading that way. The wealthier are taxied; the organised are coached or ride the tourist bus. Once across the disastrous jumble of the square, cross the *Ronda*, the inner ring-road known here as the Travessera de Dalt, follow it along and take the steep road up to the left called Avinguda del Santuari de Sant Josep de la Muntanya, passing the modern sanctuary of this name, designed by Berenguer, disciple of Gaudí. Throughout the *Ciutat vella*, the Eixample and Gràcia, Barcelona slopes very gently back from the sea, but at this point it begins to climb more steeply the line of low hills within the city boundaries.

The street continues up some steps, at the top of which you reach the long-running (since 1989) squat in a house with battlements, the Kasal de la Muntanya. The tower of the Kasal proclaims its ideology to the city below: "No boss, No king, No god". It is a great site for a political squat: the building used to be a police station and was specially constructed to provide protection to the Park Güell. In front of the door a mural welcomes the visitor, a huge painting of a middle-aged man in coloured shorts and glasses, with a plump red face and a camera. The caption reads alarmingly in English: "TOURIST YOU ARE THE TERRORIST".

This is one of many squats dotted round the city. Housing is disproportionately expensive. Shortage of building land is fuelled by speculation. The ageing young are forced to live with their parents, share slum flats if they can find one, or occupy some of the 15% of property that is estimated to lie empty in the city. Many squats have considerable local support. Some have become organising centres for the anti-globalisation movement, influenced by a residual tradition of anarchism and something of '60s situationism. This latter is reflected by the other squatters' command that greets the visitor approaching the Park Güell: "Eat the rich."

Look across the valley and you will see the brown walls of the Cottolengo, home for mentally handicapped children, and below it the sixteen courts of the La Salut tennis club. A hundred years ago, these slopes were one of the areas where the new middle-class built holiday chalets with gardens. This was the longed-for *una casa i un hortet*, a house and a vegetable plot, which Francesc Macià desired for all Catalans. The air was fresher and there was no cholera, endemic in the Old City till the twentieth century. The rather exclusive tennis club claims to be the only club in Europe with two Masters champions as members: Manuel Orantes, son of an immigrant family from Carmel, who in classic fashion started as a ball-boy, and Alex Corretja, who won the title in 1998.

Climbing further, you reach the Park Güell, the place in Barcelona where tourists and residents most contentedly mingle. Japanese fans of Gaudí wander through the park's many areas and levels, while staid residents take their exercise strolling back and forth along the esplanade, and the younger roll on the grass and seek to go as far as they can without actual copulation. Sheer numbers sometimes affect the contented mingling. At times in 2002, Gaudí Year, the lower part of the Park was completely over-run by school students hurtling round to fill in their project sheets mixed with hordes of polite tourists trying not to photograph each other.

The Park wasn't meant to be a park at all, but an exclusive wooded residential suburb for the rich, inspired by the English garden-city idea. That is why Park is written *Park* on the front wall and not the Catalan *Parc*. In fact it was a distortion of the original non-exclusive idea of the garden city, associated in the late nineteenth-century with Fabians, Quakers and socialists such as William Morris. An ideal not unlike Macià's. Gaudí and his sponsor Güell took some of the arts and crafts passion associated with the Garden City movement, but had a completely different concept of their park, as architect Juan José Lahuerta has explained:

> *"The city was a place of sin and class struggle. The Park Güell was conceived as an island apart, outside the city."*

A refuge for the rich, not a place to enrich the lives of the poor.

However, only two of Count Güell's plots were sold. This was perhaps, Robert Hughes ventures in his *Barcelona*, because buyers were frightened off by Gaudí's eccentric designs. This may have been so, but more scaring was that the development came at a time when Barcelona was shaken by class conflict, culminating in the 1909 *Setmana tràgica*. Churches were burnt (Gaudí himself fell into a depression), hundreds died and the libertarian teacher

74

Francesc Ferrer who had nothing to do with the uprising was executed. The rich preferred to stay in their flats in the Eixample than risk being eaten up on the hill. The idea of an enclave for the wealthy behind high walls, commonplace today, was still ahead of its time.

This failed real-estate development has been cited as a justification of capitalism: investment in private development of the land 'trickles down' into later use for public benefit. The theory, however, omits the important detail that Güell's heirs sold the Park to the City Council in 1922. Property does not trickle anywhere, but is bought and sold. Indeed, in the 1960s the Park came under threat from speculators, who proposed a fourteen-storey hotel with the Park as its private garden. Prominent in this project was the hotelier Joan Gaspart, whose father founded the family fortune at the time of the 1929 Exhibition. The latest Gaspart, also Joan, is President of the family hotel chain, of the City's Tourism Board and, recently and disastrously, of Barcelona Football Club (see Chapter 11). Father to son to grandson: this is 'trickle-down'. The 1960s Gaspart was a relative of the man responsible for Public Works in Porcioles' notorious Barcelona City Council (see Chapter 9). Popular pressure, led by a generation of progressive architects, who were later to lead the '80s transformation of the city, defeated the hotel project in October 1971.

The Park Güell is Gaudí's happiest creation, with what Rose Macaulay called, in *Fabled Shore*, the "sugar plum dwellings of elves" poking up between the trees. Gaudí and his partner Jujol enjoyed themselves smashing coloured tiles and sticking them onto cement to form the great lizard, or dragon, on the stair-way and the abstract pattern round the long snaking bench-parapet of the enormous plaza raised on 86 pillars. This collage mosaic style, known as *trencadís*, was a forerunner of later styles, such as cut-up and colours in abstract art.

It has often been argued that Gaudí left no school, was a one-off. This has some truth, though one can trace influence in Santiago Calatrava's bridges (such as the *Bac de Roda* bridge in Barcelona) or in the eggs and curves of Dalí, a great fan. More than specific influence, though, Gaudí was a general liberator because he smashed the limitations on what an architect was permitted to do. One specific influence of *trencadís* was, curiously, on the Argentinean writer Julio Cortázar, who lived in Barcelona in 1917 when he was three years old. Cortázar's earliest memories were of shadowy, multi-coloured forms, which his mother later confirmed were those of the Park Güell where he had been taken to play. For Cortázar, whose most famous book *Rayuela* (Hopscotch) was a literary fragmented multi-coloured pot stuck together again, the ideas that came to him for a story were always "pieces of mosaic."

In the Park Güell, Gaudí intertwines nature and architecture. Gardeners often struggle to conquer nature. By eliminating slugs and weeds and growing lettuces and dahlias, they impose order. Gardeners fence a patch of the world to stave off chaos. Science tells us, though, that the natural world is chaotic, ruled by chance. Our lives are disordered, the fight to impose garden fences lost from the start. Gaudí is different. Despite his religious beliefs, hierarchical from God to King to Boss, as the anarchist squatters have just reminded us, Gaudí is no ordinary gardener. In this giant garden he seeks to imitate, not to conquer, nature. Look beneath the bowl of water right at the bottom of the cascade by the main gate, and you will see two stone supports carved to look like roots. The famous long colonnade of sloping pillars along the palm walk imitates tree trunks. So real that, though you know they are stone, you run your hand over them to feel their texture, just in case they are wood. The tops of the walls bulge as if they were the tops of rounded Mediterranean pines. The stone used is untreated, unsmoothed, looks just the same as the rock in the ground. Imitate, be part of nature; not dominate it.

In recent years, as artistic-technical analysis has examined the architect's life and views in greater and greater detail, several monographs explain the Catalan nationalist and theocratic symbolism Gaudí embedded in the park. In Robert Hughes' *Barcelona* (pages 504-512) there is a summary of these. Yet this contradiction is tenable: Gaudí can be theocratic and ultra-nationalist, driven by these beliefs to build his park on symbolic lines. At the same time he can express the way things actually are, the way he sees, rather than the way he wanted them to be. If Antoni Gaudí was only that reactionary nationalist who, had he lived, would surely have been, like Foix and Dalí (see next chapter), closer to God and Franco than to anarchy and Durruti, his art would not be so exciting. He expressed the chaos of nature despite his views. He was a revolutionary artist *and* an ultra-conservative traditionalist. For him there was no contradiction. To have dominated nature would have been a blasphemy. God disposed Nature. Gaudí wrote: "Those who search in the laws of nature to create new works collaborate with the Creator."

The Unmodern Revolutionary

The history of taste in Gaudí is an outstanding illustration of how Barcelona has re-invented itself in the light of overseas perceptions. Gaudí's rise to world-wide renown is a story of how, first, international taste rescued him from obscurity, and then this international regard was picked up vigorously in Barcelona and exploited for profit. From the 1930s to 1950s he was considered an eccentric dead-end in architecture — non-functional, over-loaded baroque. This was Orwell's philistine view. He lamented in 1937 the anarchists' failure to demolish the Sagrada Família and dismissed Gaudí as a religious fanatic. Picasso, painting prostitutes on the Carrer Avinyó at the same time as Gaudí was overhauling the Casa Batlló on the Passeig de Gràcia (Ch. 8), was part of a bohemian, radical Barcelona. The ideas of Gaudí, Catalanist and

Catholic, were the antithesis of the outlook of Picasso, who from Paris sent a famous postcard to a friend in Barcelona:

> *"If you see Opisso [an associate of Gaudí's] tell him to come here, as it is good for saving the soul. Tell him to send Gaudí and the Sagrada Familia to hell."*

Orwell and Picasso disliked Gaudí for political reasons. Politics that one can only assume blinded Picasso to Gaudí's artistic radicalism. Gaudí was also isolated in his lifetime for artistic reasons. The philosopher Unamuno, a contemporary of Gaudí, thought him guilty of "drunken architecture". The *noucentistes* — the artistic movement of the new twentieth century — rejected Gaudí's religiosity and extravagance in the name of reason and straight lines. One of their most admired pieces of architecture is pure anti-Gaudí: Mies van der Rohe's minimalist German Pavilion in the International Modern style, built for the 1929 Exhibition on Montjuïc. Orwell's prejudice merely reflected the popular dictum that you could always recognise a *noucentista* because he/she looked the other way when passing the Sagrada Família.

Oriol Bohigas, Barcelona's most famous living architect, explained Gaudí's neglect in a similar way, though less polemically:

> *"Gaudí didn't have too much confidence in the benefits of the new systems of construction, of new technology, but stubbornly continued building in stone, something hardly anyone else was still doing... In his day he seemed too traditional and unmodern. This out-datedness was one of the reasons that isolated him from international movements and deprived him of the recognition he deserved. While everyone else was employing iron and new technology, he was still reforming and improving stone structures based on Gothic architecture."*

The English novelist and travel-writer Rose Macaulay criticised Gaudí in 1948 in strictly artistic terms. She found him a *reductio ad absurdum* of Spanish (not even Catalan) bad ecclesiastical taste:

> *"There is a naïve endearing quality in these magnificent extravaganzas of bad taste, as in the tawdry décor, the simpering painted plaster figures of saints and choir boys with alms-plates who posture like pious puppets within the sombre magnificence of Spanish churches."*

The doyen of British architecture criticism, Nikolaus Pevsner, hedged his bets. Writing in 1936, at the nadir of Gaudí's reputation, he couldn't quite make up his mind:

> *"Gaudí's details of the lodges [of the Park Güell] with their minaret and their wildly heightened Orientalism everywhere, of the parapets snaking up and down, the covered promenades of stone-work as rough as in eighteenth-century sham ruins and of the Doric columns placed out of true like wooden posts shoring up a wall, all this goes in many ways beyond Western Art Nouveau, and yet can only be understood within the terms of that short-lived style. Here is the frantic desire for the unprecedented..."*

And so for decades Gaudí's reputation rested, wonderful perhaps but, as Pevsner says elsewhere, *outré*.

It was the generation that began to visit Barcelona in the 1960s that uncovered a different Gaudí and started the heady climb in his reputation. It is a pleasant twist of history that Gaudí, so pious he took communion daily and was once rebuked by the Bishop of Vic for following his Lenten devotions too strictly, was re-discovered by internationalist hippies. Robert Hughes describes how a good week-end in '60s Barcelona took in an afternoon in the Park Güell smoking a joint: helped along by the Alice-like toadstool on top of the lodge at the main gate, inspired apparently by Hansel and Gretel, that would have made a good Jefferson Airplane LP cover.

After 1979 Gaudí's reputation was fostered by a Socialist City Council which recognised how his genius generated tourism. For the Christian Democrat nationalists who from

1980 ran the Generalitat, Gaudí was a politically congenial figure: Catholic and Catalanist. There is even talk today of his beatification, fed by stories that he gave away his clothes to beggars. The opposite is also told: that he tried to give his coat to a beggar, but the beggar refused because Gaudí's coat was too ragged.

This architect, who, unusually for an architect, had no interest in money, did not even build a house for himself and dressed so shabbily that when he was knocked down in the street in 1926 he was taken to the poor-house to die, has generated endless millions for the hoteliers, restaurateurs and ice-cream manufacturers of Barcelona. Gaudí Year in 2002, commemorating 150 years from his birth, rounded off his fame. Gaudí Year saw numerous exhibitions, restorations of many of his buildings, books, videos, school projects, a new bus itinerary, greater access to several of his buildings and a glut of what in Mackintosh's Glasgow is called *Mockintosh*: Gaudí pencils, pens, erasers, chocolate bars, lamp-shades, stools, greetings-cards, post-cards and note-pads. Gaudí Year showed Barcelona's genius for self-publicity: despite the fall-off in American tourism after the terrorist attacks of September 11 2001, and despite the 5% drop in visitors to the Spanish Costas in Summer 2002, Gaudí Year was instrumental in Barcelona itself receiving more visitors in 2002 than ever before.

The place to think these thoughts is sitting in the shade on the *Passeig de les Palmeres*, Avenue of Palms, where the bourgeoisie's carriages used to parade up and down. Those big stones like cannon-balls are to stop the horses trotting onto the down slope. You're unlikely to be pestered here by the city's mainly African *venta ambulante* — street hawkers — because they are firmly excluded from the park, at the risk of confiscation of goods and a 120-euro fine. Don't forget, foreigners are welcome at the temples of art, but you have to dress better than Gaudí and have money. You can even be African, but make sure you're not poor. Head towards the Casa-Museu, contrary to general belief not built by Gaudí but where he lived for the last twenty years of his life, when he wasn't sleeping on a cot in the Sagrada Família workshop.

On Top of the City

Instead of going on round the park, back to the main front gate and back towards the city centre, follow on upwards from the Casa-Museu, past the Park's other completed house, ever upwards. Here the Park begins to be wilder. Unpruned bushes, broken branches, piles of leaves and litter, brambles and nettles. Gullies filled with undergrowth run off down the back. As you step out of the top of the park onto the path along the hills, fancy that you are stepping out of beautiful Gaudian Barcelona, with its *trencadís* dragon in the grottoes of the wooded park and magic houses overlooking the sea, through the looking-glass into another world. Step onto a breathtaking walk along the hills through what were post-war slums.

From the top of the Park Güell, this path runs along the hills in the middle of the city towards the River Besós. As Barcelona is not on a North-South axis (the coast runs roughly North-east to South-west), directions are often given with reference to the mountains and sea and the two rivers that enclose the city: the Besós on the French side and the Llobregat on the Tarragona side. "I'll meet you on the corner of Roger de Llúria and Mallorca, side Besós and side sea," your friend may say, and you would know on exactly which side of that street junction to wait.

Up here on a working day, the companions on the path are old men, propping up walls or clacking down dominoes on the stone tables. They sit on opened cardboard boxes, to soften the benches. Some carry their canaries, budgies or goldfinches with them, in little cages covered with a cloth, hoping to meet another bird-owner. At times a group forms and the cloths come off like hoods from race-horses as the stalls open. Released to the light, the small yellow or green birds burst into song. The owner-breeders tell each other bird stories.

"He sold me a little brown one. I exchanged it for one I myself had bred plus 20,000 pesetas. But he died a month later, *me cago en...* I shit on," familiar Spanish exclamation tailing off. *Dios...* God, the oft omitted last word. Often *Diez*, Ten, is used as a euphemism.

"What was his name?"

"Sweet baby."

"No, you fool, the man who sold it you."

"Juanito."

"Juanito! What do you expect? I wouldn't pass the time of day with that two-timer."

Caged birds are common among the older immigrants from other parts of Spain. In a small flat, a bird's song lightens the gloom of poverty. You see them on sale on the Rambles. If you criticise the keeping of wild animals in cages, the reply is two-fold: they are bred in captivity, and it is better to cage animals than children. If not logical, the latter response is unanswerable. Here children run free and shout, are welcomed in restaurants. Extra beds are available in hotels. Gruff old men grin at the sight of them. Animals are inferior in the order of things, but children are the kings and queens of society. The English are regarded with suspicion: as torturers of children.

The retired and unemployed often sit among the scrub stretching up to the bare hill top — this is known as the *Muntanya pelada*, the peeled mountain — or walk their dogs along the path. Urine and faeces of dogs and humans mingle with the smells of vegetation. It was not always the *Muntanya pelada*, for during the Civil War the low round-topped pines were chopped down for firewood — unlike the Guinardó Park further along or the very last hill on this inner ring, the Turó de la Peira in *Nou barris*, blessed with a 1950s vertical slum on one side (Ch. 15) and a wood of beautiful leaning pines on the other.

Follow this path and you reach a road crossing the hills. It is the road that winds up the mountain from the Plaça Sanllehy to Carmel. Down to the right is a line of tower-blocks along the curving road. Down to the left, the main part of the *barri* of Carmel, dropping away behind the mountain, a hidden world of improvised buildings packing the steep slopes. In front, the Bar Delicias, frequented by Juan Marsé's fictional *charnego* or *xarnego (Cast : Cat)*, Manolo the *Pijoaparte*. *Xarnego* is the word, racist or proud according to who says it and how, used to describe a migrant into Catalonia from another part of Spain. The *Pijoaparte* would sit on rainy afternoons playing cards with the old men in the Delicias, while his girl-friend, a maid who had walked up the steep hill from the Plaça Sanllehy on her half-day off, waited meekly by the door. The Delicias is now a gaudy bar, cheaply done up, with fruit machines, T.V. and a large number of different brandies behind the bar. It smells strongly of pork products — sausage, hams, *xoriços* — and cheese. Big round oily cheeses piled on the bar.

Juan Marsé's series of novels of the Civil War defeated in the 1940s and 1950s are set in this area. Marsé's portrayal of Carmel-Guinardó is a Spanish equivalent of Faulkner's depiction of the defeated South in his fictional-real Yoknapatawpha county. Born in 1933, Marsé came to fame in 1966 with *Últimas tardes con Teresa*, *Last afternoons with Teresa*, the bitter story of Teresa, an upper middle-class university student, and Manolo the *Pijoaparte*, an invented nick-name meaning something like Toff-apart. The *Pijoaparte* is a petty crook with ambitions living in Carmel. As you follow this path out the back of the Park Güell along to the Bar Delicias, it is to the *barri* of Carmel that you have come:

> "In the grey post-war years, when empty stomachs and green lice demanded daily some dream to make reality more bearable, Mount Carmel was the favourite and fabulous field of adventures of the ragged children of the quarters of Casa Baró, Guinardó and La Salud... The hill rises beside the Park Güell, whose green leafiness and fairy-tale architectural fantasies it looks at sceptically over its shoulder."

This is how Marsé introduces the area in his direct, realistic and then lyrical style, unexpectedly lyrical because you do not at first realise that this most apparently realist writer is writing about the dreams of the dispossessed, the dreams and desires of someone living on a bare hill in a shack and looking over his shoulder at the bright-tiled chimneys of the gingerbread houses poking up through the forest of the Park Güell.

Before the Civil War this series of low hills was sprinkled with retirement or holiday chalets for the middle-class dreaming of Macià's little house and garden, like those round Alex Corretja's tennis club a little further across, direction Llobregat. With the arrival of mass immigration from Andalusia, Extremadura and the other poorer parts of Spain in the 1940s, shanty-towns sprouted, 'like wild mushrooms' as they say in Spanish, across the mountain-sides. Streets of dust or mud. Home-made houses without water, electricity, sewage or transport.

From the Delicias, carry on up the Carrer Mühlberg; to the left, bare rock with houses perched on top; to the right, flats hanging like sea-gulls' nests off the edge of the hill. Following along, across the newish wooden bridge over a quarry, you reach the edge of the Guinardó Park. Here you can find among the yellow broom and morning glory — a luxuriant weed in the Mediterranean — the remains of the last shanties on Carmel, cleared by the City Council just before the Olympics. Peach, fig, olive and plum trees still grow among the scrub-covered foundations of the demolished shanties. Ironically, these squatters had achieved their little house and garden.

Veer left up the slope, up one of several flights of stairs and you come out on the road right along the crest of the highest hill. A few big old houses in their gardens show what an attractive place this hill-top is. Most of the houses, though, are self-built. Today, it has become an area ripe for luxury re-development: the wind that blows across the hills is refreshing, the views are unbeatable.

The Council is planning to develop this marginal area. This is progress. Welcome, if it means proper paving, proper street-lighting, rubbish-collection and bus services. Welcome, if the wildest park within the city limits, now gouged by deep erosion gullies and spattered with rubbish, becomes better cared for. The pattern of municipal development has always been a game of musical chairs in which the same people are left sitting on the floor. Most residents have signs out "Park yes! Eviction no!" They are fighting against being chucked out to make way for new wealthier residents.

On this route you will probably have stopped more than once to admire the view of the city spread out below, but you should really wait until you're at the ruins of the old anti-air raid batteries built to defend the city during the Civil War. Here, the view is almost like the aerial photos taken by the Italian pilots as they bombed the city in 1938. The city's divisions stand out clearly: the polygonal *Ciutat vella* with its jumble of twisted lanes, the rectangular blocks of the Eixample and the wiggly streets of the old villages of the plain. Its landmarks are clear too: the twin sky-scrapers of the Olympic Village on the water-front, the adorned towers of the Sagrada Família, the three towers of the power-station at Sant Adrià del Besòs, the new 'gherkin' near the Forum site, the Montjuïc Hill to the right with the domes of the National Palace on its flank. If you're lucky, you can make out the line of the Maresme coast to the left along to Mataró. If, like 60% of the days, it's hazy, you will be driven to clean the dandruff off your glasses on your shirt-tail. If you don't wear glasses, you will wonder whether you need them. Barcelona smog blurs every line. The carbon dioxide filtering the sun brings on a heavy head and lethargy. At times it is not possible to see the sea.

From here above the city, on a day after rain has washed the smog from the sky, you see the light as Gaudí perceived it a century ago. A fellow-architect, César Martinell, recorded him saying:

"Don't go to the North to search out art and beauty. These are found on the Mediterranean, from whose shores — Egypt, Assyria, Greece, Rome, Spain, North Africa — all art has emerged. In the North and in the Tropics, they do not receive light at 45 degrees, which is how things can most clearly be seen. If there is scarcity of light or it is too much overhead, things appear deformed in their inadequate illumination. More than the thing, they see the ghost of the thing. Their heads fill up with ghosts and fantasy predominates... In the Mediterranean our eyes are not accustomed to ghosts, but to images. We are more imaginative than fantastical, and thus more skilled in the plastic arts."

You can appreciate the character of this light from up here, looking down on the city. Not so different from what Picasso found at Horta de Sant Joan near Tarragona, Matisse at Collioure ("There is no sky in France bluer"), or Dalí at Cape Creus. The object, the thing itself, is seen hard and clear.

From the air-raid batteries, make your way down the back of the hill. Here on the side away from the sea is working-class Barcelona, from the home-made houses interspersed with jerry-built blocks along Carrer Gran Vista to the tower-blocks of Canyelles climbing the Collserola hills on the other side of the valley which contains the old village of Horta. These outer immigrant suburbs make up the fourth Barcelona — the Old City, the Eixample, the old villages like Gràcia or Sarrià are the first three.

Here is Marsé's *Pijoaparte*, after parking a stolen motor-bike on Gran Vista, running down the hill-side to the house of the fence, 'the Cardinal':

"He dropped down the hill-side populated with white-washed little houses, almost hanging in the air, whose particular positions on the uneven slope formed an intricate network of alleys with steps, sharp bends and short ramps."

The *Pijoaparte* reaches the Cardinal's house:

"At the bottom of the slope, he moved round the wall of a neglected garden and stopped before the small wooden door that had captivated him one day. It was different from other doors because it was old, carved with some complicated drawings that the rain had almost worn away, and more than anything because of its implausible knocker, a tiny, delicate, moulded hand — a woman's hand, he always thought — clutching a ball. There wasn't another door in the barrio *like it. It belonged to a small, ruinous two-storey house. In front of it lay the empty lot with the screeching of crickets."*

Marsé is describing Gran Vista as it was 50 years ago and much has changed. But you still get a sense of the jumbled housing, still see ramshackle houses with yards full of scrap like the Cardinal's, and imagine the *Pijoaparte*, the delinquent who had arrived in Barcelona with just a cardboard suitcase a few years before, now full of the joy of youth jumping and twisting down the slope. Up here in Carmel, among the elderly — that '50s population of young immigrant workers has aged — you can still see young *Pijoapartes* in garish clothes, nowadays with tattoos and two-style hair-cuts.

Marsé's *Pijoaparte* grew up in Murcia with dreams of a different life, based on a brief few weeks' contact with a French couple on caravanning holiday. Like most immigrants, he arrives in Barcelona with no prospects, but an address: in his case, a relative in Carmel where he can sleep for a few days. In his mind, he can be and do anything. In the opening scenes of the novel, he steals a motor-bike on *Sant Joan*, Mid-Summer Night's Eve, when Catalonia devotes itself to *verbenas*, all-night firework and *cava* parties. He gate-crashes a *verbena* in classy Sant Gervasi: big cars outside, a garden, swimming-pool and coloured lanterns.

The Struggle for Carmel
Follow Gran Vista and you return to the pass across the mountain at the Bar Delicias. If you go a few yards down

the back of the hill, a bus down Calderón de la Barca runs to the route's end-point, the metro station of Horta. This is the steepest bus-ride you will have ever been on, unless you live in La Paz, Bolivia. People standing are held up by their neighbours, as the bus turns and twists slowly down the narrow streets. Women with swollen legs trudge back from the market with plastic bags of shopping, and the numerous small bars, *chiringuitos* or holes in the wall, are full of men drinking and looking. Displacement of immigration, small dark flats, tough lives, all lead to a tendency to congregate in and outside bars — for company, to get out of the house, to drink.

Just about everything that has happened to improve Carmel, a quarter of some 40,000 residents, is down to the activity of the Residents' Association. Their office is a dark hall up a flight of steps on the Carrer Feijoo. The people staffing it during the afternoon are four retired men. "You'll find us here most days. Keeps us out of the bars," said Adrián, grinning. They are as friendly a group as you could find, but their discourse is melancholy. "You can't get the young involved," Adrián went on. "You know, 25 years ago, the PSUC [the Catalan Communist Party] won more votes than the Socialists here. The Residents' Association had hundreds of active members. Now we're just a handful." He grins again.

Whenever I've been there, a steady stream of people comes in: to ask about the water campaign, to inquire how to get a cracked kerb-stone fixed, to complain about rubbish not being removed. In these years, the Residents' Association, despite having fewer and fewer active members, has won campaigns to get escalators installed in the steepest parts and bus services. It has run a mass water bill boycott against abusive charges, and got a Health Centre, a nursery and a library (named after Marsé).

Its most famous campaign, though, was for an extension of the metro to Carmel. After twenty years' agitation, work started on this in 2004. In January 2005, disaster struck: a service tunnel collapsed. It had been drilled through a gully filled in with rubbish and rubble. The technicians hadn't bothered to ask the residents what was there. A block of flats on top fell down and more than a thousand people in neighbouring blocks had to be evacuated. Amazingly, no-one was killed. The political furore became the biggest to hit the Socialist Council and the new three-party Government of the Generalitat. A series of demonstrations called for compensation for affected residents, which they won. It emerged that proper geological surveys had not been conducted; that out-of-date tunnel technology was used; and that the resistance of the concrete was inadequate.

By collective effort, the people of Carmel have taken their hill that no-one wanted because it was too steep from a light-less, road-less, sewer-less, running water-less shanty town to an area more integrated into the city, with services. When you look at the *favelas* on the hills of Rio de Janeiro or the slums on the collapsing slopes circling Caracas, you can picture what Carmel was like fifty years ago. Agustí, a retired factory worker, told me:

> *"None of the changes that have occurred in Carmel have been given us by the Council. The Council talks a lot about* Barça és bona[1], *but every improvement in Carmel has come about through the Residents' Association organising and fighting for change. And don't think it was easy."*

Carmel's grave problems of services and investment date from the time of the dictatorship. If the Council cannot treat Carmel, and many other such *barris*, with special priority, if they place tourist facilities and jamborees with a speculative undertow like the Forum (see Chapter 16) before basic services for poor residents, what are we to say of them? This is a theme that runs through this book: Barcelona is beautiful, but it is ugly too. It is resumed in the contrasting quotes from Richard Rogers and Victor Serge at the front of the book.

The leaders of the Federation of Residents' Associations are scathing. They wrote in their paper, *La veu del Carrer* (The Voice of the Street)[2] about the tunnel collapse:

"This crisis has brought into question the serious deficiencies of the Barcelona model *– a city of show, design, tourism and services that foments speculation and forgets old and new residents and popular barris."*

Six years earlier, in 1999, the RIBA (Royal Institute of British Architects) citation talked of "inspired city leadership" when awarding their famous Gold Medal to Barcelona – the first time, remember, this was ever given to a city rather than to an individual architect. Jonathan Glancey reported in *The Guardian*:

"...the ambitious, intelligent and co-ordinated democratic local government... the men and women who have raised Barcelona to new international heights over the past 24 years see their city as an organism to be nurtured and treated as a whole."

I put this to the activists of the Carmel Residents' Association. Adrián answered, serious:

"Perhaps it sounds good in England. But all the money they've spent on the Olympics, on the Liceu, on the museums, on the ring-roads, or the millions for the Forum hasn't benefited areas like Carmel. So you can't say they treat all Barcelona as a whole, can you?"

---

[1] *One of the Council's more inane and best-known slogans: "Barcelona is good."*

[2] *Marc Andreu and Andrés Naya,* La veu del Carrer, *March-April 2005.*

Chapter 5
The Defeated

"A craggy mass of sheer rock — shattering the most beautiful of horizons — towers over this city... We would have loved this rock... had it not been for those hidden ramparts, those old cannons with their carriages trained low on the city, that mast with its mocking flag, those silent sentries with their olive-drab masks posted at every corner. The mountain was a prison — subjugating, intimidating the city, blocking off its horizon with its dark mass under the most beautiful of suns."
VICTOR SERGE, *BIRTH OF OUR POWER.*

"What shit Marxism is!"

The scents of two 1930s Barcelonas, the revolutionary city of the Civil War and Genet's City of Vice, still linger as tourist attractions in the post-Olympic city of design and culture.

Another less celebrated Barcelona, neither '30s revolution nor '90s glitter, was the hungry, defeated city after the Civil War, when the Franco dictatorship set out to extirpate systematically the three sins of Catalonia: Anarchism, Republicanism and Separatism. Mussolini's son-in-law and Foreign Minister, Count Ciano, wrote in his diary on the fall of Barcelona to Franco's troops in January 1939:

> *"The Duce was imperturbably calm. But he has good reasons to be really pleased, because the victory in Spain bears only one name, that of Mussolini, who conducted the campaign with bravery and firmness."*

Ciano is presumably not referring to the Battle of Guadalajara in March 1937, when Mussolini's troops were

routed by the Garibaldi Battalion of Italian internationalists, among others, but to the Italian airforce's
bombardment of Barcelona during 1938 from its bases on
Mallorca. Barcelona's civilian population was the first in
Europe to be subjected to mass bombardment from the air,
harbinger of what followed in the Second World War.
Curiously Churchill, no great friend of red Barcelona but
an early user of its image, recalled during the Blitz: "I
trust that our citizens will be able to resist just as the
valiant people of Barcelona did." By 1939, some 1750
apartment buildings had been destroyed, mainly in the
working-class areas of the city. Few planes were brought
down by the air-raid batteries on the hill above Carmel.

Hundreds of thousands of *barcelonins* were delighted to
see the return of the established order, the end of the war,
potentially the end of hunger and of restrictions on com-
merce. On the day Yagüe's troops occupied the city,
marching down the Diagonal on the freezing January 26
1939, its residents stayed prudently indoors, watching
from behind the slanted slats of the city's green wooden
shutters. Tens of thousands had already fled, in a pitiful
exodus through the snow to the French border. The
French could not understand why so many wounded had
left their hospital beds to cross the frontier. The reason
was simple: in several cities that fell to Franco's advancing
armies the mere fact of being wounded was taken as proof
you were a red and many had been slaughtered in their
hospital beds. Fascism had decisively changed the rules of
war.

Yagüe's nick-name was the Butcher of Badajoz. He liked
to boast of his slaughter of two thousand people machine-
gunned on his orders in that city's bull-ring on August 14
1936 — the worst single atrocity of the Civil War. An
exhausted, frightened Barcelona fell to the Butcher without a shot being fired.

In the following days, the city's residents poured into
the streets, many of them giving the fascist salute at
Franco's victory parade, blessed by Cardinals, as an oppor-

tunist act of survival, others in an outburst of relief that they had survived the bloody red revolution.

The Catalan bourgeoisie, expropriated in 1936, followed Yagüe's army into the city. They came to re-possess their properties. After the conservative nationalist party, *Convergència*, won power in Catalonia in 1980, this history was re-written, as if the whole of Catalonia had always been anti-Franco. It is not unlike France in 1945 when everyone was miraculously transformed into a *résistant* and there were no collaborators or Petainists to be found. In truth, most wealthy Catalan families supported Franco for sound economic reasons. The most prominent was the financier and leader of the right-wing *Lliga Catalana*, Francesc Cambó, who did considerable business financing Franco's armies. His enormous statue near his former mansion on the Via Laietana (by the Urquinaona metro station) is periodically spattered with red paint as a reminder.

The most famous Catalan supporter of Franco was the painter Salvador Dalí. In 1933 he had professed his support for the Workers' and Peasants' Bloc, one of the two revolutionary parties that later fused to form the POUM. He had even spoken on their platform in Barcelona. By 1939, now making his name in New York as a show-man, Dalí wrote "What shit Marxism is" in the letter that signified the end of his friendship with the film-maker Luis Buñuel. During the Civil War Dalí often praised the Spanish Falange and in 1939 was expelled from the Surrealist Movement for his white-supremacist views. André Breton nick-named him with the anagram Avida Dollars. Quite a few circles had to be squared, quite some pages of history quietly torn out, in order to turn Dalí into a "universal Catalan" in the 1980s. Nowadays Dalí's museum in Figueres is the most visited museum in Catalonia, bringing millions of euros every year to the town's *Convergència*-voting burghers.

In Sarrià, formerly an outlying village nestling under the Collserola hills, swallowed up by Barcelona as it expanded across the plain in the nineteenth century and since then one of its wealthiest suburbs, a major poet whose face for three years had been covered with flour, and his body with a linen apron, emerged like a ghost from his family bakery. This was J.V. Foix (pronounced *Fosh*). Foix was associated with the Surrealists, had been a friend (if anyone could really be a friend) of Dalí, and was an ardent supporter of Catalan independence. So nationalist was he and so hostile to outside elements that his views bordered on fascism. Throughout the war, in fear for his life, Foix baked cakes and bread, ruminating under his white mask that when the anarchists and Republicans were defeated he would emerge and with his reputation and Falangist friends become one of Catalonia's leading cultural figures.

This indeed was the view of certain Falangist intellectuals such as Dionisio Ridruejo, who thought Catalonia could not be run unless the Catalan language was permitted and Catalan 'difference' respected. Foix never recovered from his shock when Franco immediately banned the use of Catalan. "Talk in Christian, not like a barking dog," became the humiliating insult of supporters of the regime to anyone talking Catalan. After hiding from the anarchists in his bakery, Foix now had to hide his native language from the fascists. By his death at the age of ninety in 1980, he had become an emblem of the rebirth of Catalan culture *against* the dictatorship.

Vengeance was fierce after the war. Despite the mass exodus to France, which left some 60,000 Catalans in long-term exile, about 3,000 people who had stayed behind were executed in the months following the occupation of the city. Historian Albert Balcells explained:

> "Most of them were little-known, minor officials of parties and unions who, not considering their lives to be in danger, had not gone into exile... More people from rural areas were executed than from industrial and urban areas. Those who denounced them or who acquired goods confiscated from those sentenced to death or in exile made up a

group of unconditional Catalan collaborators with the Franco regime."

Some 25,000 Generalitat civil servants were sacked. These included school-teachers, imbued with the revival in progressive education under the Republic and with the belief that education in Catalan and concerning Catalonia were essential components of a longed-for independent country. Franco agreed: 700 replacement teachers were drafted in from other parts of Spain to ensure that Catalan could not be used, and an infamous system of appointing teachers not because of their qualifications, but because of their political affiliations, was adopted.

Vázquez Montalbán sums up the immediate post-war period:

> *"While half of Barcelona tried to find guarantors or sponsors to petition for the release of relatives from prison or permission for their return from exile, and Republican soldiers were forced into national service for the conquering army, post-war deprivation fell upon the city. Cripples, beggars, stub-end tobacco sellers, charlatans, street singers, organ grinders, rag-and-bone men, uniformed Falangists marching to their epic songs..., Fascist commandos who shaved their heads to the scalp and forced people to drink castor oil...* estraperlo *[black-market] white bread and Virginia-tobacco sellers..."*

In his 1966 novel *Els plàtans de Barcelona,* The plane-trees of Barcelona, Víctor Mora, inventor in the 1950s of the famous Captain Thunder comic-strip, documents the stifling day-to-day atmosphere: the ubiquitous official notices in the streets, "Avoid blasphemy and foul language" or "Spain, united, great and free"; the bizarre graffiti scrawled on walls, "Death to the Jew Churchill"; the grandiloquent radio programmes, "On the genius sent by Providence, Adolf Hitler, falls the great honour of leading the Crusade...". In one scene, Mora describes how a petty official travelling as a passenger stops a packed city bus and drags off a man who had used Catalan during an exchange occasioned by an umbrella poking him accidentally. A litany of insults from the bullying official like a string of sausages as the argument increases in tone: "Talk in Christian.... In Spain the language of the Empire is spoken... *catalán de mierda*... and now you will come with me, dog." Marching him off down the street. The bus drives on. Its humiliated passengers are silent.

Montjuïc

The Montjuïc mountain, close to the industrial areas of Sants, Poble Sec and the Raval, was where thousands of working-class families escaped from the slums 100 years ago for a Sunday picnic. Covered with springs, pitted with quarries from which the stone was extracted to build the city and harbour walls, Montjuïc remained semi-wild until the 1920s, when it was urbanised on the city side with the Olympic stadium and, lower down, the buildings for the 1929 International Exhibition. These included the grandiloquent Royal Palace, never occupied by the monarchs who fled into exile in April 1931. It is used today to house the magnificent paintings from the Romanesque churches of the Pyrenees; the Pueblo Español, a village showing all the architectural styles of Spain, now for tourists buying craft goods by day and for clubbers by night; the famous Mies van der Rohe pavilion (what you see today is a 1986 replica); and the exhibition halls, used for Barcelona's trade fairs. Even in the 1980s, you could still find hidden corners and overgrown gullies on Montjuïc, before the 1992 Olympics finally tamed the whole hill.

Low on the city side, just above the exhibition halls, is the *Teatre Grec*, the Greek-style amphitheatre. Every July sees the Grec theatre festival. Attending a performance in the open-air Grec is not unlike watching Shakespeare in Regent's Park or in a garden of an Oxford College, but has the added beauty of the adapted quarry on the mountain's flank, with its sheer rock face behind the stage, cypresses, stone seating and candle-lit gardens you pass through between the entrance and your seat and where you sniff jasmine with your interval glass of *cava*. Social realities do impinge on this summer dream of the good life. Once a performance of *Othello*, in Sagarra's Catalan translation, coincided with one of Spain's World Cup football matches. As Othello, a huge white man whose black paint was dribbling in the heat of his performance and the night, tightened his scarf round his wife's neck, cries of "Goooo-o-o-o-l" flew from a Poble Sec bar across the theatre. "Who's scored?" my neighbour muttered, for in Catalonia there is no automatic support for the Spanish side.

Since its construction in the eighteenth century, the heavy, squat fortress on top of Montjuïc has been both symbol and reality of Spain's military occupation of Catalonia. Richard Ford, doyen of English travellers in Spain, wrote succinctly in 1845: "The panorama, with the prostrate city at its feet and mercy, is magnificent."

Up until the mid-1990s the flowers in the moat in front of the fortress were laid out in the form of the Roman fasces, the symbol of fascism adopted first by Mussolini and then by the Spanish Falange. For a foreign visitor, it was a shock, as if you found a giant swastika flying over Berlin's Charlottenberg Castle. The Army has finally adapted to democratic forms: the flowers in its beds now form a less explicit pattern. It has even hitched its tanks to the tourist industry, opening a cafeteria inside the Military Museum which the castle has become. The café terrace overlooking the city has been closed. To get a drink on top of Montjuïc now, you have to pay a euro to enter the castle[1].

Victor Serge in 1917 found the same combination of magnificent view and sinister fortress as Ford had:

> *"It is from the height that one discovers the splendours of the earth. The view plunges down to the left into the harbour, the gulf lined with beaches, the port, the city... But our eyes, scanning the faraway snowcap at leisure, or following a sail on the surface of the sea, would always light on the muzzle of a cannon, across the thicketed*

> *embankment. Our voices would suddenly drop off, when,*
> *at a bend in the path, the stark, grass-covered corner of the*
> *citadel's ramparts loomed up before us. The name of a*
> *man who had been shot was on all our lips."*

The man whose name was on their lips was Francesc Ferrer, executed in 1909 despite a storm of protest throughout Europe for his supposed part in the *Setmana tràgica*. The legal murder of the libertarian teacher Ferrer was an act of brutality aimed to cow Barcelona's anarchists. Its effect was the opposite: more than any other single event, it pushed large numbers of workers into explicitly revolutionary thinking.

In more recent times, Juan Goytisolo, scourge of Catholic Spain, brought his novel *Marks of Identity* to an intense climax on Montjuïc. He juxtaposed the "flocks of tourists" (already there in the early '60s), the view and beauty of the site, and its use as a place of execution:

> *"foreigners and natives were walking slowly along the*
> *paths.*
> *they would stop to admire the begonia pots take pictures of*
> *the walls that had been the scenes of the vengeful execu-*
> *tions...*
> *brigades of workers had carefully erased the bullet marks*
> *and opened to the indiscreet looks of the curious the place*
> *seemed to proclaim to the four winds its innocence"*

These foreigners were the tourists whose presence in 1964, without historical memory or curiosity, was helping Franco deny the murders of the past and keep his regime afloat by transforming Spain's economy[2]. There is something still strange about the visit to the top of Montjuïc. Tourists take photos of each other against the battlements, while locals pick out the sights of the city below and their kids clamber over the gun emplacements. The drawbridge over the grassed-in moat with its pretty flower-beds and the cobbled steep slope up inside the castle make it seem a fairy-tale castle, like the Tower of

London. You know atrocities happened here, but it was so long ago. Just part of our heritage now, detail lost.

The strangeness of Montjuïc is because the atrocities *were* so recent. Things happened here that are still felt by the living. That decommissioned artillery pointing out harmlessly over the Mallorca ferry gliding into the harbour was used to shell the city several times in the nineteenth century. Whereas for Genet the *secret though unavowed* intent of the cruise-ship tourists was to confirm their own well-being by observing the *archipelagoes of poverty* suffered by others, for Juan Goytisolo the function of tourists was to whitewash the past and present of a disreputable regime. Montjuïc in 1964 was once again a pretty look-out point and place to catch a breeze on clammy July or August evenings, not a grim hill where thousands were shot.

1964 was the year of celebrations throughout Spain for "twenty-five years of peace." The black humour of those living under a dictatorship is reflected in the widespread joke about a tourist reacting to the ubiquitous posters proclaiming the event:

"— '25 years of peace'. Is that a film showing in Barcelona?
— No, it's a long-running farce in Madrid."

Of the many monuments to Franco that existed forty years ago, a giant slab behind the Montjuïc fortress is one of the few to remain. Today it is often splattered with ritual red paint and just as ritually scrubbed, to leave a stain like the memory of blood. Till recently, though, there was no memorial to Lluís Companys, whose death Goytisolo evokes, joining again, like Serge and Ford, the horror of the place to its natural beauty:

"Although there was no plaque that said so the President of the abrogated Generalitat de Catalunya had lived in Montjuich during the last moments of his life
turned over by the Nazis after the fall of France the politician feted one day by the crowds in Barcelona went down

into the moat of the castle escorted by the soldiers' bayonets
he thought with pain and nostalgia about his beloved city
he breathed in the pure wild air of the mountain
he looked at the clear blue sky for the last time"

It was in this fortress, on October 15 1940, that Lluís Companys the elected President of Catalonia was executed by firing-squad after a summary trial. Companys faced his death with great dignity, telling his daughter in a letter written on his last morning not to live her life in bitterness and shouting "For Catalonia" as the order to fire was given. His extraordinary composure helped many Catalans in the dark decades following to find their better selves and resist.

His death certificate expressed the cynicism of the Franco regime: "...died in Montjuïc castle of a traumatic internal haemorrhage." His corpse was thrown into the common grave filled with quicklime, in the quarry furthest away from the city and on the opposite side of the Montjuïc mountain from the Greek theatre.

The Fossar de la Pedrera

I visited this common grave on a sunny late-October day with a friend from London, Stephen Hayward, author of a book on the pilgrims' route to Santiago. Stephen was here on a pilgrimage of another kind. He had come to lay flowers on behalf of the daughter, born posthumously in French exile, of one of the many thousands executed by Franco in the weeks and months after the fall of Barcelona. The quarry is quiet except for birds, a surprise after the constant noise of the city. Its bare walls climb steeply and jaggedly on three sides and shut out the hum of traffic from the *Ronda Litoral*, Coastal ring-road, close by. No steadily-rising cambered wall of seats as in the Grec. This quarry was tucked out of sight behind the mountain, a place for action, not for spectacle. The quarry floor has been levelled and laid out as a lawn, dotted with little white crosses and, in the autumn, hundreds of small wild mushrooms. At the end, against the back wall, is the common grave. On the left are rocks placed more recently and inscribed with the names of the Nazi concentration camps where Catalans were interned and died. Along the right-hand side runs a long pond and the memorial to Companys and to all those who died for the freedom of Catalonia. It is covered with wreaths: we are here only a few days after the anniversary of his death, when numerous Catalan organisations and political parties render homage to this unlikely hero of Catalan nationalism.

Unlikely, for Companys was a left-wing Republican labour lawyer with separatist tendencies, whose views are certainly not shared by his successor as elected President, Jordi Pujol, or Pujol's party *Convergència*, nor by the modern Esquerra Republicana, which is merely a shadow of the party Macià and Companys founded. Companys inherited the Presidency of the Generalitat on the sudden death at Christmas 1933 of Francesc Macià. Companys' photos show a wiry, lean-faced, middle-aged man with a mop of unruly hair. A dapper dresser, with a hankie in his breast pocket and lively eyes. One can imagine his energy: quick-moving, talking fast, enjoying life.

You enter the quarry through a forest of pillars that record the name of each person known to have been dumped in the pit. Stephen finds the name of his friend's father and places red carnations at the foot of the white pillar. It is a suddenly solemn moment that brings us close to tears. "It's strange," he says. "This must be one of only very few memorials to the victims of Franco's terror, and certainly the biggest one, whereas all over Spain you still find monuments to Franco's dead." We look round this tranquil and moving quarry. His sadness turns to anger. "It's a disgrace that all the tourists are bussed up to the Olympic stadium and the fortress, but none are told about this place."

A look through the Barcelona guide-books in my possession confirms that this is so: there is not a single reference to the *Fossar de la Pedrera*, Quarry Graveyard, con-

101

structed in the 1980s as a memorial to the Republican and Catalan Civil War dead. I go to the Palau Robert at the junction of the Passeig de Gràcia and the Diagonal, the Generalitat's main tourist office in Barcelona. They have no leaflet on the Quarry Graveyard and suggest I go instead to the monument by the Santa Maria del Mar church called the *Fossar de les Moreres*, the Mulberry Graveyard, where the heroes of the 1714 siege of Barcelona are buried (see Ch. 8).

Death needs to be more distant to become a tourist attraction. Sight-seeing is meant to make us feel good. Only perverts, of a political sort, will want to go poking round the sites of major atrocities. "The Civil War, it's long ago now," sighs the kind woman in the Palau Robert. Yet the effects of this defeat, even nearly seventy years on, are still with us. Go to the Montjuïc military fortress, then visit the quarry. Take a taxi. And if the taxi-driver has not heard of it, say it is beside the Montjuïc cemetery.

City of the Dead

The city's biggest cemetery covers the wind-swept Southern side of the Montjuïc hill. Here you find beside each other, overlooking the harbour, three slabs: the grave of Francesc Ferrer and memorial slabs to the anarchist leaders Francisco Ascaso, who died in the assault on the Drassanes barracks on July 20, 1936 mentioned earlier, and Buenaventura Durruti, killed on the Madrid front in November, 1936. On Durruti's great block of stone are carved his famous words "We carry a new world in our hearts." Poignant words of hope for a dead man's memorial.

In Spain, the dead are not usually buried in the ground but immured in niches, just as city-dwellers live not in houses side by side, but on top of each other in flats. In Montjuïc the rows of niches are several stories high. From a distance they look like cheap housing projects, brown block above brown block running up the hill-side, like the tower-blocks of Canyelles climbing the flank of Collserola that you can see across the valley from the fortifications above Carmel.

Before many niches a glass window protects a curled brown photo of the deceased, severely dressed, looking out through plastic forget-me-nots. If you pay, the niche is yours for ever. If you don't, the bones are evicted after five years to the ossuary of bleached bones at the top of the hill, where rustling cypresses guard the upper border of the cemetery. The paupers' graves bear no photo: just crumbling cement, a hand-cut name and cross.

Relatives look after the niches. They clean the glass, light a candle, place fresh flowers or adjust the photo. To reach high niches, these often elderly people climb ladders to tall platforms, similar to those used in grand old-fashioned libraries to search the top shelves. If you go on November 1, the Day of the Dead and a bank holiday in Spain, you will see the cemetery as packed as the Carrer Pelai on a working day by the bereaved with window-cleaning fluid, dusters and flowers.

In a high immurement, the coffin is wound up on a creaking platform, while priest and congregation stand below, then pushed into the niche. Workmen close the niche with brick, cement and plaster. In England grave-diggers are country-men with spades; here they are brick layers with trowels and buckets. So large is the city of the dead that police on motor-bikes protect its numbered streets against vandals.

There is room for everyone on Montjuïc, the ancient burial place of the Jews (hence the mountain's name): victims of execution in their quick-limed pit, non-Catholics (Protestants and Jews) in the heretics' section, the workers in their rented niches, the destitute in their unmarked niches and the rich in their *Art Nouveau* family pantheons adorned with seraphs and surrounded by plants. The current cemetery was opened in 1883 when the old one on the waterfront at Poble Nou was full. This was just when the new Catalan bourgeoisie's confidence and wealth were reaching their peak. Their tombs were designed in the

103

same styles as their houses. Many of these architectural wonders are bigger than workers' family homes. If you can't take it with you, you can remind the future generations what you had. Yet it is in this section that the most spectacular decay is seen. Cracks in the walls, lids of coffins forced off by roots, years of leaves piled up, all making the mausoleums of the rich look like a set for a Hammer horror film. Property, of course, needs to be kept up; and few families maintain expensive small villas housing the remains of the long-dead. Tidier to rent your niches on a five-year renewable plan.

Hell

José Agustín Goytisolo was a month short of his tenth birthday when his mother died suddenly. He explained in a 1980s interview how it happened:

> *"My mother died on March 17 1938 in the Paseo de Gracia, in a bombardment by Italian planes, I think... They came in over Tibidabo to avoid the Republican artillery and plunged down low. All the North-South streets were machine-gunned or bombed by the fascist planes. My mother was killed by a bomb. Apparently due to the shock-wave and not the shrapnel... She had gone down to Barcelona to buy some things for me and my father, because March 19 was our Saint's day."*

Elder brother of the more internationally renowned Juan, José Agustín was one of his generation's finest poets. Juan Goytisolo got out of Spain as soon as he could, in the mid-50s, and has remained consistently unseduced by the charms of modern Barcelona. He opens *Count Julian* with the rejection of Spain spat out with pain: "Harsh homeland, the falsest, most miserable imaginable. I shall never return to you..."

José Agustín stayed in Barcelona. From a Spanish-speaking Catalan upper-class family, he became one of the 1950s generation of anti-Franco, anti-academic poets. He played an important bridging role with Catalan by his '60s translations and anthologies of modern Catalan poetry. Many of his own lyrical, gentle but fierce, poems return to the death of his mother, Julia Gay. He was tossed out of paradise by her death:

"You explained to me a world
without fear without ghosts without punishment...
a boy like me
who did not know
that a hell existed on the other side."

In his direct, emotional poetry he avoids all self-pity. "Someone is not a poet because he feels or is moved... the poet makes others feel, causes emotion in others, by using words," he affirmed in a lucid rejection of the cult of poets' sensibilities. And in his life he was a celebrant: conversationalist, *bon vivant*, friend, lover. One of those courageous Spaniards who, in finding the strength to grow up against a dictatorship, lived their lives to the full.

He and his wife named their daughter Julia after his mother, and one of his most famous poems, *Palabras para Julia*, Words for Julia, when set to music and sung by the Basque troubadour Paco Ibáñez made him known to a post-Franco generation:

"My daughter it is better to live with the happiness of men
than weep before the blind wall...
Life is beautiful
you will see how despite grief
you will have love
you will have friends."

Like Companys, he wanted his daughter to live without bitterness. José Agustín Goytisolo killed himself on March 19, 1999, throwing himself from the balcony of his second-floor flat. Unkempt in hair and clothing, Paco Ibáñez sang in his beautiful hoarse voice memorial concerts to José Agustín, tears coursing down his face.

Numerous depressions assailed José Agustín Goytisolo's

last years. The long shadow of the Civil War stretches right down to today. Even those who faced explicitly the trauma of violent death in war, as José Agustín did, had no guarantee of coming through. It is understandable that so many millions in Spain, Barcelona no exception, chose not to talk of the war. Such pain, though, was only increased by government institutions also remaining silent. Nor were reparations made or memorials erected, with the honourable exception of the *Fossar de la Pedrera*.

---

[1] *In 2005 negotiations were under way to transfer the castle from the Army to the City Council.*

[2] *These tourists were, by definition, not left-wing. Throughout Europe, the left boycotted Spain during the Franco regime.*

Part 2

Decline and Renaissance

Chapter 6
Freed from the Dragon of Anger and Hate

"Julieta said, dance, dance... The kids set off rockets and bangers at the corners. On the ground there were water-melon pips and in the corners, water-melon rinds and empty beer bottles and from the roofs they were also setting off rockets. And from the balconies. I saw faces glistening with sweat and boys wiping their handkerchiefs over their faces. The musicians happy and let's play. Everything like a decoration. And double speed. I found myself going up and down and as if it came from a long way away, it was so close, I heard the voice of that boy who said, well, look, you do know how to dance! I smelt strong sweat and stale cologne."
MERCÈ RODOREDA, *THE PIGEON GIRL.*

The Secret Core

The *Call*, the former Jewish quarter between the Cathedral and the Rambles, is the part of the *Ciutat vella* with the narrowest, most twisting streets and the oldest houses. The Jews were expelled from Spain in 1492. But they didn't just pack their bags and go. There were few left in Barcelona by that year. Before 1492, they had been confined in the *Call* for two centuries and were periodic targets of murder and expropriation. In Barcelona in 1391, dismal year of a wave of assaults on Jews throughout Spain, Christian fundamentalist agitators piled rubbish against the gate of the ghetto on the Plaça Sant Jaume, rats proliferated, and the Jews were accused of being pestilent. Despite being formally defended by the authorities, the *Call* was over-run on 5 August 1391,

109

unknown numbers of Jews slaughtered and their houses burnt.

It is only very recently that the Jewish history of Barcelona has been partially recovered, due mainly to the tenacity of Miguel Iaffa. He is the son of a Catalan woman and an Argentinean Jewish volunteer with the International Brigades in the Civil War. Born in Barcelona in 1939, he left at once and only came back after Franco's death. Passionate about Jewish history, Iaffa searched the *Call* for the site of the synagogue and found it. With much of his own money, but some support from the City Council, the synagogue was restored. Further excavations have suggested that it dates from the third century: if so, this would make it one of the very earliest Jewish remains in Europe[1].

In the atmospheric opening of *The South*, his first novel, Colm Tóibín describes Katherine's 1950s discovery of the *Call* and the area nearby:

> *"I walked down a narrow passage which I had thought was a cul-de-sac. The air was still warm and when I touched the stone I was shocked at how cold it was. I remember I stood there and I shivered. I was going to turn back but around the corner I could see an archway leading into a square so I kept on.*
>
> *...The square was irregular and dimly lit; there seemed to be another narrow passageway at the other side... I... sat on a ledge. I had been in Barcelona for about a week and suddenly I felt as though I had found the place I had been looking for: the sacred core of the world, a deserted square reached by two narrow alleyways, dimly lit, with a fountain, two trees, a church and some church buildings."*

Katharine's epiphany takes place in the Plaça de Sant Felip Neri, the most secret Venetian square in the Old City. It is a place easy to feel is the sacred core, hard to find and often stumbled on only by chance. The allure of these thickly-walled, softly-lit alleys that muffle noise ("even the electric light from the walls resembled light from a torch," Tóibín) is the absence of anything modern. It seems magical that there can be empty corners and such quiet so close to the Cathedral Square, in this packed Old City.

Mr Hyde Without Dr Jekyll

The Plaça de Sant Felip Neri is not so secret now, for it is one of the main scenes of Carlos Ruiz Zafón's best-selling literary thriller, *The Shadow of the Wind*. After publication in 2001, *The Shadow of the Wind* was on both Castilian (its original language) and Catalan best-seller lists for four years, and in 2005 reached Number Two in the UK sales list, an extraordinary success for any literary novel, and even more so for one in translation. So successful has it been that an enterprising British company is already organising *Shadow of the Wind* tours of Barcelona. I wonder what they will find, for, strangely, the book has very little to do with Barcelona.

The strength of the 500-page novel is its complex story with several narrators that grips readers to the end. The plot is original, bold and well worked out. At times, too, the writing is fine, with powerful phrases and imagery. Some of its characters are memorable: the blind and cruel Clara, Daniel's long-suffering father and several minor cameos. The protagonist Daniel is taken by his father, a widowed book-seller, to the secret Cemetery of Forgotten Books. There he selects a book to guard. By chance or fate, his strange choice attracts the interest of several people. As Daniel grows up, he begins to investigate the mystery of the book and its vanished author, Julian Carax.

The story of Daniel's quest is set almost entirely in Barcelona, but it is an unreal city of drizzle and fog swirling through cold streets, of a haunted mansion on the Avenida de Tibidabo and a mysterious man in a mask who looms out of the rain and dark. Sometimes in Barcelona winters you can look up at cloud scudding over turreted mansions on Collserola or can feel winter chill in the crumbling mediaeval alleys of the old city, but Ruiz Zafón's city is unrecognisable. He has converted Barcelona into a nineteenth-century Northern city of phantoms and

111

mist, a Gothic, literary Barcelona more like Dickens' London or Robert Louis Stevenson's Edinburgh than a Mediterranean port.

Not content with the geographical removal of Barcelona a thousand miles North, Ruiz Zafón ignores history as well. And this too is odd, given that the novel is full of precise dates, from the action opening in 1917 up to 1955. It is not, though, a book that explains anything at all about Barcelona in those forty years: the action could just as well be occurring in the nineteenth century. For example, it is nothing like Eduardo Mendoza's *The City of Marvels*, which narrates the history of the city through the rise and rise of an unscrupulous gangster-capitalist.

In *The Shadow of the Wind*, historical events only impinge when they can help the plot along. For instance, the Civil War allows Carax's death not to be properly recorded or the Franco regime enables murderous policemen to thrive (surprise!). Ruiz Zafón deliberately makes his book timeless, with the evocative invention of the Cemetery of Forgotten Books and with the repetitive patterns of behaviour in different generations, which he suggests by making Daniel and Bea's love story the mirror-image of Julian and Penelope's thirty years before. For a Gothic terror story transferred from the nineteenth to the twentieth century, a real city in real time would only be a nuisance.

Ruiz Zafón names lots of real Barcelona places: the *Quatre gats* café, the Ronda de Sant Antoni, Carrer Balmes, Sarrià... The list is long, but they are places named, not described. There are two exceptions, the haunted mansion at Avenida de Tibidabo 32 and the Plaça de Sant Felip Neri. The former does not exist, but up on the hill-side below Tibidabo, there are many ghostly, huge houses — now mainly private hospitals. These two exceptions are the Gothic sites of Barcelona *par excellence*, Gothic in the sense of the Gothic novel of shadows, fog, coffins in crypts, mysterious beautiful women and tormented young men assailed by undefined guilt...

112

Most of the novel's characters are clichés: the very beautiful and haughty Beatrice, the arrogant womanising industrialist Aldaya, the long-winded (the weakest parts of the book) Romero de Torres or the incredible and non-credible Julian Carax, who works in twenties Paris as a brothel pianist protected by the Madame. Readers are asked to believe Carax suffers there for twenty years after being abandoned in love, but many of us might have enjoyed ourselves playing piano in twenties Paris. Ruiz Zafón is completely unconvincing on the reasons for Carax's misery. Not to speak of the appallingly evil Fumero! Fumero is the most evil policeman in Franco's evil regime. Once an anarchist murderer in '36, then a fascist cop, a sadist who loves to kill, victim of terrible psychological wounds in his childhood, Fumero is a comic-book cut-out.

So why has *The Shadow of the Wind* been so successful? The answer lies in its combination of a good story and a certain flattery of its readers. It flatters by impersonating a literary and psychological novel, though much of it is Brazilian soap-opera and one-dimensional psychology. Stevenson didn't just have Mr. Hyde running round foggy London streets killing women, he had Dr. Jekyll too — the terror is based on the conflict, the divided personality of the good doctor.

The Shadow of the Wind deals in the comfortable received wisdom of history: fascists and anarchists are nasty. It does not question anything or show us characters in conflict living and reacting in a turbulent society. Readable and well-made as the book is, it is pernicious because it obscures Barcelona's history, like the fog that swirls perpetually through Ruiz Zafón's fairy-tale city.

Disordered and Dissolute

Barcelona most approaches the weather of *The Shadow of the Wind* in February. Hunched, hands deep in pockets, I am walking with a friend through the narrow streets of the *Call* near the Plaça del Pi. Despite the cold, people are down in the street tonight. A man in red tights and a white T-shirt passes, his long black cloak splayed out behind him, its red lining catching the street light. As he disappears round one corner, three masked witches skip arm-in-arm round another, filling the narrow alley, which is as tall and thin between the flat-fronted houses as a pit sunk into the ground. They wear high peaked hats, long black skirts and diving cleavages. "Hello," they shout, "do you like us?" One squeezes a breast out of her bra, another sticks out her tongue between glowing orange lips and the third shakes her skirt in our faces. I stand with a fixed foolish smile. The witches dance round us, screaming and beating us on the head with their rush brooms.

It is Carnival, lost in Britain with the Reformation. The last echo of that licence to turn the world upside down is the tossing of pancakes on Shrove Tuesday. Carnival survives in Catholic countries, the few days of satiety and sin before the forty-day austerity of Lent. The mediaeval carnival was the day when masters were servants and servants masters, when men wore petticoats and women cod-pieces, old scores were settled behind dominoes and masks, and the devil's flashing red tail twisted through the streets. It is the most popular and subversive of festivals.

Four centuries ago, in its fight against Luther, the Church popularised dozens of saint's-day celebrations and rituals to hold its people in thrall. But the February Carnival, necessary as a safety-valve in a hierarchical society, yet with its pagan roots in the bacchanal, was the most dangerous and difficult for them to command. For centuries Barcelona's authorities have swung between regulation and prohibition of the Carnival. Franco banned it, as did the Consell de Cent, the Council of a Hundred burghers that governed the city, in 1558 because:

> *"The people, in a highly disordered and dissolute fashion, wander throughout the city, disguised and masked... leading to... numerous deaths and many other evils, crimes and dire deeds."*

Today Carnival is party time, a pale image of the inversion of morals and social status it was. Yet the sexual pulse still throbs quicker. Thousands dress with liberating licence; people can still hide their identities and act their opposites. In Barcelona the opening rites of today's Council-sponsored Carnival are official. Mounted police (not unlike the Buckingham Palace Horse Guards) pat the necks of their snorting black horses as a uniformed band pounds out a Brazilian samba. On a special stage at one end of the Plaça Sant Jaume, long-snouted devils with gargoyle masks cavort and caress, and the Prince of Carnival, *Carnestoltes*, Lord of Misrule, steps forward to deliver the opening speech.

With studied brio and pausing, he attacks the Town Hall on the right of the square, and mocks the Generalitat on the left, flinging his arms out towards the floodlit buildings. He finishes with a cry for everyone to strip off their clothes and renounce hypocrisy. In public, few do, but as the evening deepens, groups in disguise begin to move about, accosting passers-by or singing ribald rhymes. The Rambles is packed. Transvestite nuns strolling arm in arm bless the crowds. Profane priests kiss and swagger. Mockery of the Church is still a powerful tonic in a country so marked by Catholicism. People wear square dice on their middles, are masked as political figures or dressed as animals. They wear fruit on their heads and carrots round their waists. I am kissed by several tottering Margaret Thatchers (still popular after all these years) in miniskirts and hairy legs. A crowd gathers round three transvestite flamenco dancers performing a parody of that Andalusian dance, so corrupted by tourist cliché. They exaggerate the high wailing notes and castanet clicking, and wink lewdly during the emotional climaxes. Children laugh and clap. Children dress up as witches, as Superman, as cartoon characters.

The Rose and the Book

In Barcelona there are dozens of festivals throughout the year, though none so pagan as Carnival. None of its festivals are like the Easter festivals of Andalusia that so shocked Richard Wright in the 1950s with their Ku Klux Klan hoods, mass adoration of the Virgin and self-flagellation. Religion is despatched quickly in Barcelona today and people get on with the party.

An off-season trip to Carnival is cheap and takes you out of a bleak Northern mid-winter, but the best times to visit Barcelona are spring and autumn, when it is warm enough to sit out, yet you avoid the stickiness of July and August. Two major festivals fall in April and September: *Sant Jordi* on April 23 and the Mercè on September 24.

In England few people celebrate St. George's Day, though sections of the political right are trying to found a tradition. St. George is *Sant Jordi*, Catalonia's patron saint, and April 23 in Catalonia is a massive popular festival. St. George, in the words of Catalonia's major modern poet Salvador Espriu, "freed us from the dragon of anger and hate." The blood of the slain dragon is seen in the red roses of love traditionally given on this day.

To commemorate the date of Cervantes' death in 1616 and Shakespeare's probable birth in 1564, an enterprising 1920s book-seller turned *Sant Jordi* into Catalan Book Day. It is a local festival on the way to becoming universal, for in 1995 UNESCO accepted the Catalan Government's proposal to declare April 23 World Book Day. Stalls stacked high with books line the Rambles from the Plaça de Catalunya to the Columbus monument. The road is closed as crowds spill off the pavements. Gangs of children are let off school to buy books. Workers, shop-keepers, students, everyone buys a book. Middle-class Catalans in their Sunday best smile happily at the heaps of new Catalan-language books, proof that here at least, after the long night, the Catalan language has survived.

Sant Jordi is not just a city-centre festival. From the early morning, throughout the city and all over Catalonia, even the tiniest newspaper kiosk puts out on the street a table with books for sale. Catalan patriots hang the *seny-*

era, the four-barred red and yellow flag of Catalonia, from their balconies. On every corner odourless roses, force-grown in Maresme green-houses and wrapped in silver paper along with an ear of wheat, are being sold out of plastic buckets.

Some five million roses are sold on April 23. Bosses buy them for their staff, mothers for their daughters... The sexist tradition is that women are given roses; men, books. But now nearly everyone receives books, bought with a 10% discount at all stands. The Catalan Booksellers' Guild announced in 2005 that book sales were up yet again, to about five million, matching the roses. This is 20% of annual sales in just one day.

Sant Jordi is a Catalan festival, but the position of Catalan literature within a Castilian Spanish-dominated world is precarious. The titles published in Catalan are swelled to nearly 9,000 a year by the Generalitat's subsidies. Of six million Catalan speakers, though, a good 50% never read at all and many read mainly in Castilian. No commonly agreed figure exists, but there cannot be more than two million people who read at all in Catalan: and those who read regularly in Catalan are almost certainly fewer than 50,000[2]. Only TV tie-ins, a very few well-known writers or children's literature sell very much at all. All Catalan speakers, even if they don't themselves read in Catalan, want their children to do so.

The twentieth century saw little reading by the English in translations from foreign languages. There are hundreds of books a year translated from English into Castilian and Catalan; but in England, no more than ten to fifteen works of fiction per year from Spain are translated, by just a few valiant publishers, often with subsidies from the Spanish Ministry of Culture. Only two novels have been published in translation from Catalan in England since 1990: Jesús Moncada's classic *The Towpath* (1994) and Sánchez Piñol's *Cold skin* (2006). Matthew Tree reports in *CAT* that on a text of Manuel de Pedrolo offered, already translated, to a London publisher in 1979 was scrawled the (presumably unconscious) insult: "Simply no readership here for regional literature."

This means that Quim Monzó, one of the best European short-story writers (published in the USA, but not the UK), and a dozen other fine writers are overlooked. A Catalan living in London told me: "They talk about the fight to save Catalan, but when I see that the arbiters of British culture have dictated that no-one in England has a chance to have even heard of Quim Monzó, I fear Catalan culture is to all intents and purposes dead already."

Sant Jordi is a peaceful mass festival. All the clichés the Council loves to recite in its propaganda seem true on April 23: the city's civic peace, for huge crowds move good-humouredly and patiently; its cultured air, for books are everywhere, on the long trestle tables and under people's arms; and its national identity, expressed in the colour of the Spring roses and the *senyeres* draping those trestle tables.

The Mercè

Like *Sant Jordi* and Carnival, the Mercè, the festival of Our Lady of Mercy patron of Barcelona, can best be experienced in the *barri gòtic*, the mediaeval city between the Via Laietana and the Rambles. We get off the metro at Jaume I on the cloudless morning of September 24. The sky is deep blue; but the sun is tolerable at this time of year. The crowds push us up into the Carrer dels Llibreters (of booksellers), though now that the last second-hand book-shop on the street has been converted to a souvenir shop, there are no longer any books sold here.

We move off towards the right. Looking across the crowds shuffling round the Plaça del Rei, Barcelona's most noble square, you see the heads of children hoisted onto adults' shoulders and then the heads of the giants brought out today to walk the streets. These giants, made from a light wood frame and *papier maché*, have their origins in the Middle Ages. There are several dragon-like heads, designed to inspire fear, fear to be ritually tidied away by St. George. Children stare with wide-open mouths and eyes. A woman figure with a shapely face and half-smile has huge naked breasts. An eagle head with a harsh curved beak, an ox, a lion... these are the gargoyles on the church gables or bench ends brought to life. The tall figures bob lightly as they glide through and above the crowd. The setting is unbeatable: the galleries of the Rei Martí tower with its high, slim arches, and the great steps at the back of the Plaça del Rei where the Catholic monarchs received Columbus and his Indians, who would have seemed stranger by far to the *barcelonins* of the time than these familiarly frightening giants.

We are borne on the crowd towards the Government Square, the Plaça Sant Jaume. *Castellers*, all in white shirts and red cummerbunds, are preparing a human tower. Since the transition, *castells*, human castles or towers, have spread throughout Catalonia. This is not just the recuperation of Catalan culture (the case in Southern Catalonia, where *castells* go back centuries), but its expansion and invention. The *castellers* balance on each others' shoulders, sometimes up to eight storeys high. A child, five or six years old, the *anxaneta*, scrambles to the top and raises quickly his/her arm to thunderous applause: the tower is complete. Rapidly each floor scurries down before the edifice collapses, strong hands lifting the top storeys off the base as they descend. Below, dozens of people lean in to the tower to take the weight. Sometimes the tower tumbles, though injuries seem rare. At the Mercè at mid-day today, in the Plaça Sant Jaume, there are no high towers, just a simple five-storey one below the Ajuntament balcony. Alongside Mayor Joan Clos and various councillors on the balcony, a burly *casteller* drops a black sash. The tiny *anxaneta* is hauled over the balustrade. The crammed square applauds. It is an emotional moment, one of those moments of shared Catalan identity. Collective balance and aplomb are celebrated in these towers: that this is a people who works together and is balanced. The flags of Spain, Catalonia and

Barcelona flutter above the Ajuntament building. At the back of the square the youth of ERC stand silently with a long banner demanding the removal of the Spanish flag.

The Mercè is one of the few days in the year when the Palace of the Generalitat, facing the Ajuntament across the Plaça de Sant Jaume, is open to the public. The rooms at the back of the Palace are airy and spacious, nothing over-blown and grandiose. You are reminded this is not a castle, despite the city's violent history, but a set of administrative offices. The main feature of the Palace is the *Pati dels tarongers*, a court-yard of orange trees in soil among the flag-stones, on the second floor. This very special garden, with its scent in the flowering season and its bitter orange fruits, gives the palace an Arabic touch. It could be an inner garden of a walled house in Granada's Albaicín. A strange presence in Catalonia that, in its more chauvinist moments, boasts of the absence of Arabic influence.

The front part of the Palace, dating from the sixteenth century, has all the palatial pomposity that the back lacks. The main hall, *El Saló de Sant Jordi*, consists of three naves separated by tall pillars and illuminated by an enormous candelabra. Its hundreds of bulbs cast light and shadow over the wall paintings of the major moments of Spanish history. Spanish not Catalan history, because the paintings are not ancient but date from the early years of the twentieth century, when the Palace was restored after centuries of neglect.

Unlike the mountain fastnesses of Asturias, the Basque country, Navarre and Aragon, Catalonia a thousand years ago was a *terra de pas*, a thoroughfare through which contacts went back and forth between Christian Europe and Muslim Al-Andalus. Conquered in 801 by Charlemagne, then sacked in 985 by Muslims, Barcelona might resemble more a tug-of-war between north and south than a thoroughfare. It is round about the time that William of Normandy conquered England in 1066 that it becomes correct to talk of Catalonia as a political entity. With the disintegration of the caliphate of Cordoba into warring kingdoms, the Count of Barcelona Ramon Berenguer I (1035-1076) created a Catalan feudal state. In the twelfth century, Catalonia extended its power north into Languedoc and Provence, and west into Aragon, a union achieved in 1137. These were links through marriage and negotiation rather than conquest by war. The thirteenth century saw, however, the military conquest of Valencia, with the expulsion of the Moors and the colonisation of the luscious orchards of the irrigated Levante. This led to expansion across the Mediterranean; in the late thirteenth and early fourteenth centuries the Almogàvers, mercenaries in the service of Catalonia, conquered Sicily and Athens.

This period of consolidation and expansion saw Catalan replacing Latin as the language of the area. Its first great writer, the Mallorcan philosopher Ramon Llull, wrote his *Book of Contemplation* in 1272. After Llull, many other writers gave Catalonia a richer literature in mediaeval times than anywhere except Italy. This period of glory closed with the Valencian Joanot Martorell's *Tirant lo Blanc* in the fifteenth century, a novel of chivalry with vivid realistic passages which drew on the campaigns of the Almogàvers. This fifteenth century saw the start of Catalonia's decline. Despite the conquest of Naples in 1443 under Alfons the Magnaminous, a rising trading bourgeoisie became overstretched by the monarchy's imperial ambitions.

By the thirteenth century, the *Corts*, the Parliament of Catalonia, had developed. The relationship between the King of Aragon (also Count of Barcelona) and the other estates (nobles, Church and burghers) was based on balance and a certain curtailment of royal power. The Generalitat developed to defend the decisions of the *Corts* against the Monarch. Pierre Vilar, the French historian of Catalonia, whose work had a big impact on the generations recovering a Catalan identity in the 1970s, wrote:

"This [Catalan political] creation is remarkable... especially on account of its precocity. Language, territory, economic life, the shaping of a mentality, a cultural com-

munity — the fundamental conditions of a nation — are
already fully present as early as the thirteenth century."

Catalonia was fated never to become a modern nation-state, yet its early empire, prosperity and cultural development made the people living there different from both France and the rest of Spain, and tenacious in their identity. Here, in a hall like the *Saló de Sant Jordi*, you can breathe a real, existing history. Seven hundred years ago, Catalonia was more politically and culturally developed than the British Isles.

In recent years, the Mercè festival has mushroomed. Unlike Carnival, with its roots lost in history, or *Sant Jordi* dating from the '20s, the Mercè was 'invented' in 1977, yet another initiative due to the dynamism of Residents' Associations. In its first years confined to the *Ciutat vella*, and in particular the stage of the Plaça del Rei, in recent years the Mercè has swollen to an enormous week of entertainments. The Council estimated that, in 2005, 800,000 people took part in its myriad activities.

The most exciting part of the Mercè is the *correfoc*, or *fire run*. It starts at dusk. Devils and dragons with fireworks on poles dance into the crowd to a driving drum-beat. Young people wrap scarves round their faces like bandits, jam hats down over their ears and button up old long-sleeved shirts. No bare arms or necks, for sparks shower down from the whirring, crackling Catharine-wheels. Under the intense drumming and constant explosion of fire-crackers, amidst the acrid smell of powder whose smoke makes your mouth metallic and eyes water, and squashed against the wall in one of the narrow streets with the *correfoc* dancing past, you can feel overwhelmed, think you are going to be suffocated or burnt. There are screams of semi-panic. It is a relief when residents throw buckets of water off balconies, clearing the smoke and fire. When you get home, your damp steaming shirt is spotted with spark-holes. You smell of gun-powder as if you had returned from a mediaeval battle.

The Pigeon Girl

High summer brings two major festivals. The first is Midsummer Night, celebrated in Catalonia and Valencia on the eve of *Sant Joan*, St. John, June 24, and in this too the Mediterranean passion for fire burns. This is the night of fireworks and all-night bonfire parties with *cava* and *coca*, a light sponge with pine nuts and preserved fruits. Spanish fireworks are not usually sparklers or fountains, but loud, house-rattling explosives that the young like to hurl under your feet. Traditionally, revellers jump over the dying bonfire at the end of the night, to burn away the junk of the past. After too much *cava*, they are likely to burn their feet and need the last part of the rite: a dawn plunge into the sea, to purify sins. The combination of heat, *cava* and noise makes this the most wearing of festivals. It is one of the most enduring and popular, too, probably because it coincides with the end of the school year and students can let rip after the weeks of exams.

If you do visit Barcelona in mid-August, doze away the steamy afternoons and use the night for the week-long Festa de Gràcia, Barcelona's most bohemian and relaxed local festival. *La plaça del diamant* by Mercè Rodoreda (*The Pigeon Girl* in Britain), the best-known Catalan novel of modern times, opens at this festival. The Plaça del Diamant (Diamond Square), near the Fontana metro station on the green line, is of all Gràcia's dozen squares the least prepossessing. Restored in the 1990s, the Plaça del Diamant, "an empty box made of old houses with the sky as a lid," in Rodoreda's words, marks the geographical centre of Gràcia, though not its emotional heart, which beats further over in the Plaça Rius i Taulet, where the tower of liberty faces the town hall.

In an interview towards the end of her life, Rodoreda (1908-1983) described how she could barely remember Gràcia when she began the novel in her Geneva exile.

"I only remembered, when I was 13 or 14, that once during the Festival of Gràcia, I was walking through the streets

with my father. In the Diamante square they had put up a tent, just as they did in other squares of course, but the one I always remembered was in that square. I had been forbidden to dance by my parents, but as I passed in front of the music, I wanted desperately to do so, and I walked on like a soul in torment through the decorated streets."

She ascribes the rich, magical source of her novel to that adolescent frustration of being forbidden to dance at the festival. Gabriel García Márquez, resident in Barcelona in the late '60s and early '70s, maintains that *La Plaça del Diamant* is, simply, "the most beautiful" post-war Spanish novel. The entire novel is set in Gràcia, "in a secret corner of the very secret city of Barcelona" (García Márquez). *La colometa*, the pigeon girl, her fingers aching after a long day wrapping cakes and tying knots in the *pastisseria* where she works, goes after work to the Festival in the Plaça del Diamant. Quimet, a wood-worker with a ready laugh and monkey eyes, invites her to dance. *La colometa* is carried away by the music and Quimet's smell of sweat mingled with cheap cologne. They dance all night and are left in the square with the musicians packing up. Suddenly she runs. He chases her. She runs and runs through the summer night till the tight petticoat wire rubbing her waist sore snaps.

She marries Quimet. Her life is one of drudgery. She goes out to clean while the amiable Quimet loafs about. The Second Republic is bad for the wood business. He breeds pigeons, but gives them away, while she cleans the cages. The Civil War breaks out and he and his anarchist friends go off to fight. Quimet never returns. She hears he has been killed. *La colometa* and her two children are left destitute. She decides to kill them and herself. The subtle, surprising dénouement is not to be given away... read the book.

The strengths of the novel lie in the consistency of *la colometa's* narrative voice (I hope the quote at the head of the chapter gives some sense of its distinctiveness), the extremely detailed descriptions of objects, everyday life and feelings, and the way that the great events of the time — Republic, revolution, Civil War and dictatorship — are told through the mind of a young working woman with her feet on the ground, unlike her dreaming husband. When her friend Julieta discovers freedom with a militia-man, *la colometa* reflects:

> *"I said I'd have liked a lot to spend a night like her so much in love, but I had work to do, cleaning offices and dusting and looking after the kids and that all the nice things of life, like the wind, the living ivy and the cypresses drilling the sky and the leaves of a garden going from one side to the other, these hadn't been made for me."*

Rodoreda fiercely rejected criticisms that *la colometa* is simple-minded because she does not rebel. "She did what she had to do," the author affirmed. *La colometa* observes everyone around her rebelling or reacting to the great events of the day. Her unawareness of history reveals history lived by a working woman. Her voice is the counterweight to Malraux's images of those flurries of anarchists racing in their wild heroism across the Plaça de Catalunya against the machine-guns from the Hotel Colón. One of these will be Quimet, who is incapable of earning a decent living, but gives away pigeons in expansive generosity to everyone except his work-worn wife and hungry children. *Dreams of a new world should start at home* could be Rodoreda's motto.

Rodoreda's novel is not just a high-class literary *tour de force*, building tension throughout to its impressive climax, but the most important book in the history of post-war Catalan literature. Her novel became a critical, popular and international success after its publication in 1962. It was then becoming possible to publish in Catalan again: the pioneering publisher *Edicions 62* was launched that year.

Joan Sales, himself a considerable novelist, wrote of the 1982 première of the film of *La plaça del diamant*, by when Rodoreda's book had been translated into fourteen languages:

> *"A crowd of several thousand men and women packed the Rambla de Catalunya outside the cinema... When Mercè Rodoreda with difficulty crossed that tightly packed crowd, one of the longest and most deafening ovations I have heard in my life broke out... See, I said to myself, how forty years of the profoundest persecution has not been able to suppress our people... which knows how to thank an author who spreads beyond the limits of our nation a language and literature that implacable persecution has not been able to kill."*

It may surprise English readers, confident in the assumption without even being aware of the assumption that their language just exists, how a novel can so rapidly transcend its status as a mere work of imagination, and become a political symbol of the survival of a language. This moment of emotion for many Catalans, pinpointed by Sales, shows how a writer in an oppressed language becomes more than a writer, she becomes representative. It is reminiscent of Colm Tóibín's description of painter Joan Miró, aged over eighty, crying as people came up to shake his hand at his Fundació after being unable to show in Catalonia for forty years. Other such moments were the funerals of Gaudí in 1926 or of the disgraced poet-priest Jacint Verdaguer in 1902, both mass events because their commitment to the survival of Catalonia was recognised.

This feeling is sentimental and profoundly open to political manipulation. It is also deeply and genuinely felt. It is the feeling of endurance of an oppressed nation against the odds. *La colometa* touches a chord in Catalans because of her endurance. *La colometa*, because of the conditions of her life as mother and worker in and out of the home, is pushed down, yet is not crushed. Her indomitable spirit connects with the experience of hundreds of thousands of Catalans who lived through those times, felt buffeted by events they did not understand or control, and could only endure.

---

[1] *The synagogue, at Carrer Marlet 5, can be visited by appointment. Ring 93.3170770.*

[2] *This applies to the press, too. Most of the press sold is in Castilian.*

PASSEIG DE GRÀCIA

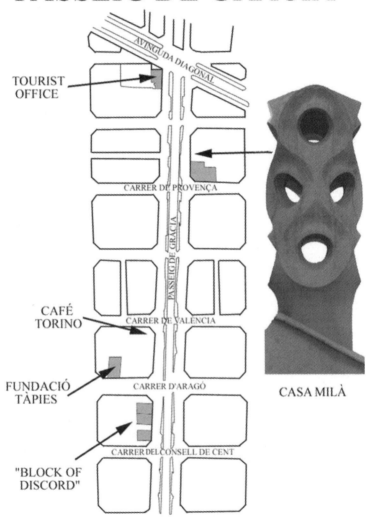

AVINGUDA DIAGONAL

TOURIST OFFICE

CARRER DE PROVENÇA

PASSEIG DE GRÀCIA

CAFÉ TORINO

CARRER DE VALÈNCIA

FUNDACIÓ TÀPIES

CARRER D'ARAGÓ

CARRER DEL CONSELL DE CENT

"BLOCK OF DISCORD"

CASA MILÀ

Chapter 7
A Palm Tree in a Country House

"—I will come back rich."
IGNACIO AGUSTÍ, *MARIONA REBULL.*

Music Palace

When the American writer James A. Michener was taken to Domènech i Muntaner's Palau de la Música Catalana (Palace of Catalan Music) in the 1960s, he was repelled by its "bewildering facade..., appropriate for the illustration to a Gothic fairy tale." Inside, the Palau's boldness won him over. It is designed as a dream, an allegory of music. The stage is presided by a bust of the nineteenth-century composer and collector of folk-songs, Anselm Clavé, on the left, representing Catalan music. On the right, universal music: who but Beethoven, with the winged horses of Wagner's Valkyries charging out above him!

The Palau was built for the *Orfeó català*, the Catalan choir whose home it still is, and was squeezed onto its site in the Old City because most of the choir lived there. Thus, though a world-famous tourist site, the Palau's origins are as a people's building, unlike almost all the other famous *modernista* buildings of the city. The other Domènech master-piece, the Sant Pau Hospital, is too. The Palau is also a Catalanist building: high claims are made for Catalonia when Clavé is placed alongside Beethoven. Ridiculous claims by any objective measure. Yet it is not idle boasting: it is the stubborn belief that asserts *we Catalans can be anything*.

This outlandish building, full of ceramic sculptures, multi-coloured mosaic, with its skylight "a hanging bell of stained glass with a choir of singing angels" (Robert Hughes), was the work of a conservative Catalan nationalist who belonged to Cambó's Lliga, the party wiped out in 1931 by Macià's landslide victory and then utterly ruined by its support for Franco. In art, all the extravagance and *rauxa* is expressed, while sober conservative business sense prevails in politics. In fact, you needed to be a good manager of money, as Domènech was, a good business person, to raise the wild Palau.

The Palau is not the stamping-ground of Catalan workers today. Yet it still has less of the upper-class vainglory associated with the Liceu. It is not an international opera-house, but what its name tells: a palace for Catalan music. It is a forceful reminder that Barcelona, despite the absence of great composers, is a musical city. Every neighbourhood has its popular choirs. The *sardana*, that rather restrained dance with complicated moves and music, is both popular and democratic. Anyone passing by can join in: the circle merely widens.

In the twentieth century, Barcelona has produced great singers. One of these, the soprano Montserrat Caballé, told Robert Hughes:

> "— My debut in Barcelona was in this Palau de la Música..., and I remember my father that day saying to me 'I am very proud because I believe you are going to do a wonderful career, Montserrat, but even more, that you have sung for the first time in *my Palau*'. The way my father said 'my Palau' fulfils me for the rest of my career, really."

These words that Caballé spoke in English on the BBC ooze sentimentality, but there is no reason to think that her feeling, combining her music and her Catalanism, is insincere.

The Palau has become one of the city's main tourist attractions, though photographers curse as they jostle each other on the narrow street because it is impossible to get a good long shot of its details. The same Catalanist impulse that built it a hundred years ago led to its magnificent restoration/ extension under Òscar Tusquets in the 1980s. Tusquets' rounding-off of Domènech's work fits perfectly; unlike poor Subirachs' derided continuation of the Sagrada Família.

It was in the Palau that a famous incident took place in May 1960. In the presence of Franco, a group of Catalan nationalists rose to sing the banned *El Cant de la Senyera* (Song of the Catalan flag). Dozens were arrested, among them Jordi Pujol, who was tortured and sentenced to seven years in prison as the ringleader, even though he had not been present at the Palau. Pujol became in the post-Franco period the dominant Catalan nationalist politician, President of the Generalitat from 1980 to 2003. Pujol is a Conservative banker formed in Christian circles, and his credibility, necessary to win a broader swathe of votes, was greatly enhanced by the events of the Palau.

The Palau, like most other *modernista* buildings, is a lived-in architecture. These are not the stern Imperial buildings of London and Paris. Because of its particular history, its own *Renaixença*, Renaissance, starting only 150 years ago, Barcelona is more comparable to Chicago or New York, where the skyscraping monuments of the nineteenth and twentieth centuries are used and lived in, not merely monuments to be scurried past by residents and scrutinised by tourists. In passing, note, as none of these cities are capitals, they escape the empty pomp of Ministries.

The Catalan Renaissance

So where did these incredible buildings emerge from? These *outré*, in Pevsner's puzzled word, masterpieces of *Art Nouveau*, like the Palau and the Pedrera discussed at the end of this chapter. These monuments to the self-confidence of a new ruling class, imbued with Catalanist feeling.

Before the great *modernista* construction spree from about 1880 to 1914, the *Renaixença* which gave rise to modern Catalan nationalism was literary. Throughout the eighteenth century educated Catalans tended to write in

Castilian, even though they spoke in Catalan. This was not just a question (though often it was) of obligation, but of a narrow layer of cultured people seeking a wider audience. The mass of Catalans were illiterate, and those who were literate were literate in Castilian, the language of their schooling.

Aribau's poem, *Oda a la Pàtria*, Ode to the Fatherland, was published in 1833. The Catalan Renaissance, after a century plus recovering from the decisive defeat of 1714 (see Ch. 8), is commonly dated from then, an arbitrary date like most starts of processes. One could hardly find a less likely paladin of Catalan nationalism than Aribau, a monarchist who for most of his life worked in the Civil Service in Madrid. His poem struck a chord by identifying homeland with language, a theme that has run consistently through definitions of Catalanism since then. In modern times, Jordi Pujol urged immigrants to learn Catalan in order to integrate into Catalonia. Catalans of the 1960s and '70s were urged to read in Catalan in order to 'fer país' (construct the country).

The other vital strand in Catalan nationalism was its embrace of modernity, in terms both of urban development and its industrial revolution; unlike Basque nationalism, theorised in the 1890s, which was originally a reaction against industry and modernity, a flight back to rural values. Barcelona's famous architects and their patrons were also on the whole conservative, but they were urban people, forward-looking in their outlook and European in their cultural desires.

At first, though, in the mid-nineteenth century Catalanists were cautious, after three centuries of decline then repression, and nostalgic. They looked back to Catalonia's golden Middle Age of great literature and imperial power, when the rest of Spain consisted of warring Muslim and Christian kingdoms. It took a couple of generations of enormous upheaval for the exuberant self-confidence seen in Gaudí's and Domènech's architecture to surge up.

The *Jocs florals*, Floral Games, an annual poetry contest of mediaeval inspiration and roots in Ancient Greece, were founded in 1859 (the year the walls came down) and nurtured a cultured literary tradition. The linguistic walls were finally to be blasted down in the 1870s, most famously by the appearance of a poet of genius, Jacint Verdaguer, a handsome young priest (as priests should be) who won the *Jocs florals* with his epic *Atlàntida*. Though Verdaguer's poetic language was dense and complex, and his epic style and subject matter were often archaic, he wrote directly about Nature. He showed his contemporaries that Catalan could be stretched to the full like any other language.

In the 1880s and '90s Àngel Guimerà was writing plays that are still performed. He developed from powerful historical verse dramas to his masterpiece *Terra baixa* (1897), a rural-romantic story, yet extremely realist in its dialogue and emotions. At the same time, Narcís Oller was writing realist novels, his most famous *La febre d'or* (Gold fever) (1893), an account of a society like our own, addicted to gambling on the Stock Exchange. At long last, for the first time since the sixteenth century, there was an audience for Catalan, not just writers in it. These three, Verdaguer, Guimerà and Oller, brought together the written and spoken language. Bridging the two is not automatic: it required major writers such as these, who were read and heard, to re-found Catalan, spoken by less than three million people then, against the power of a state and several hundred million Spanish speakers world-wide.

At a more popular level, during the liberating period of the First Republic (1868-73), in Republican Gràcia, papers sprang up in Catalan, such as *L'Esquella de la Torratxa* (see Ch. 13). None of the Catalan writers of the nineteenth century was a radical Romantic — no Shelley or Byron. Radicalism came in at the hand of Bakunin's agents in the 1870s with a non-literary bang. Yet the Gràcia workers and artisans showed that popular politics could be expressed in Catalan.

At the same time as Catalan was being re-established as an integrated spoken and written language, Catalonia was undergoing its Industrial Revolution (which maintained its position as the richest part of Spain) and the city of Barcelona was expanding. In the 1850s, 200,000 people were packed into the Old City. The over-crowding in this already smoky industrial city that maintained its mediaeval layout was such that cholera outbreaks and riots were common. Workers and bourgeois, doctors and speculators: all sectors of this diverse society agreed the straitjacket of the walls had to be burst open.

In 1854, Madrid finally gave permission to demolish the walls and citadel. Curiously, the plan for the Eixample (Expansion) of the utopian socialist Ildefons Cerdà was imposed on the city of Barcelona from Madrid. Originally, Rovira i Trias' plan was chosen unanimously by the jury of nine experts. Rovira is left for posterity as a statue sitting on a bench in the pretty Gràcia square named after him, ruefully staring at the unfulfilled plan at his feet, with the highly anti-planning slogan: "The layout of a city is the work of time rather than of architects."

Cerdà's visionary project fitted the needs of the day more than Rovira's apparently more grandiose one. It was a time of several city expansion projects in Europe, such as Vienna's, which in 1858 received 85 projects for its wall-demolition and expansion. Franz Joseph's Empire seems to have been forty times more democratic than the Spanish monarchy. Inspired by Haussmann's grid design for Paris, Cerdà yet sought to escape the monotonous tyranny of Haussmann's order. The Madrid bureaucrats did not prefer Cerdà's plan for its progressive ideas of blocks no higher than four storeys to provide maximum light, a ratio of 2:1 in building to green space, his insistence on poor and rich sharing the same areas, or his planning of schools, pharmacies and shops to be spread out at regular intervals and so be within everyone's reach. Madrid continued to look at Barcelona as the dangerously secessionist place it had been since the 1640s. Now the first Industrial Revolution in Spain was creating the added danger of an urban proletariat with its revolutionary ideologies. Madrid favoured Cerdà because of the squareness of his plan, the straightness and twenty-metre width of his streets. The cavalry charge could sweep such streets clear. Cannon could shoot straight along them. They were hard to block with barricades.

Cerdà`s plan was adopted, but then subverted by economic forces. This is almost a definition of utopian socialism: failure to realise that economic forces cannot be controlled unless state power is exercised to control those forces. State power was not opposed to the speculation spree that developed the Eixample. You will notice in walking around that every block is filled in on all sides: Cerdà's idea was to build only on two sides, thus leaving green space. You can also see, if you peer, that extra floors are often stuck on top. This building upwards was technically illegal: everyone knew they were there, but no-one objected as long as they weren't *seen*. Set back from the street, they are now nice pent-houses with roof-gardens. If you penetrate one of the blocks, instead of inner gardens, though some backwaters of peace remain, the insides of the blocks are stuffed with workshops and parking lots. The radical lawyer Eduard Moreno tells an odd story about Cerdà: in the 1950s, his remains, brought back to Barcelona, were transferred in a furniture van rather than a hearse. So strong was the feeling of the Barcelona property-developing class, Moreno suggests, that even a hundred years after his plan, it insulted this utopian who desired a speculators' nightmare — a green city.

Eduardo Mendoza's novel, *The City of Marvels*, covers the rise of Onofre Bouvila, an illiterate brute from a remote Catalan county who becomes prodigiously rich between his arrival in Barcelona just before the 1888 Exhibition and his death at the 1929 Exhibition. At one stage, Onofre buys a field on the edge of the Eixample. He then arranges for tramlines to be laid to his plot. With the promise of transport, he sells the land at a vast profit. The next day his workmen take up the tramlines.

Despite the distortion of Cerdà's ideals, the dividing-line between the *Ciutat vella* and the Eixample has remained palpable to this day. When the walls came down, the rich scampered out of the *Ciutat vella's* disease, dirt and over-crowding as fast as they could. Many residents of leafy Bonanova, Sant Gervasi or Sarrià never enter the *Ciutat vella* except on feast days like Sant Jordi or taxi excursions to the opera. The walls have gone, yet there is still an invisible curtain round the Old City.

This contrast, that can be savoured from Chapter One's early seat at the Zurich, is between old and new, between plebeian and bourgeois, between dirty and elegant. It is one of the principal reasons Barcelona is so attractive to tourists, who often say: "You get two cities in one." One full of excitingly malodorous shadow, the other of Gaudí's dazzling Mediterranean light.

Indianos and Industrialists

The development of the Eixample, the national Renaissance and the new wealth pouring into the city were the preconditions for the burst of creative architec-ture of Gaudí and his contemporaries. I have sketched above the type of gangster wealth accumulated by the likes of Onofre Bouvila. Another source of wealth, which flooded into Barcelona in the second part of the nineteenth century, was brought by the *indianos*. Not Indians, but those who came back from the Indies. All round Catalonia, you can see *masies*, or country mansion-farmhouses, with a large palm-tree shading the forecourt. The only palm native to Catalonia is the short stubby *margallot*, whose hearts are traditionally eaten. The tall palm by a *masia* is the sign of the *indiano* returned. The local boy who went to Cuba as a penniless adolescent and returned twenty years later fabulously rich. Most did not, of course, but enough did for the legend of the *indiano* to be real. "I've gone. I can't stand this life. I'm doing it for you and the

136

children. Wait for me. I will come back rich," read the rather confused note that Joaquín Ruiz left his wife before leaving for America, in Ignacio Agustí's *Mariona Rebull*. "I will come back rich," those mythical five words that expressed the legend of the *indiano*.

Josep Xifré was one of the first of these *indianos* to leave their mark on the city, a man who moved not only between two continents but between two historical times. Born in 1777 at Arenys, a fishing port on the Maresme coast North of Barcelona, he grew up in a world where North African pirates had raided the port three years before his birth and carried off young people into slavery and for ransom. Pirate raids were a regular feature of the Catalan coast up to the Napoleonic Wars: for this reason, many coastal villages have a safer inland branch where most people lived. Xifré's Arenys today still has a port, Arenys de Mar ('by the sea'), and a twin village two kilometres into the hills, Arenys de Munt ('on the hill').

At 21, his family ruined, Xifré joined his uncle's tanning business in Cuba. The key to his wealth was trade with the USA. So successful was he that he moved to New York and diversified from leather into property development. He returned to Barcelona in 1831 and continued to buy, sell and construct property. Right down to today, property developers have had an abnormal weight in the Catalan economy. It is quick and easy money, as Onofre showed. Xifré's lasting monument is Els Porxos (The Porches), built opposite the *Llotja* in 1835. Today, on one side of his block is a famous restaurant, the Set Portes; on the other, a bazaar for cheap electrical goods (where Picasso's family lived briefly). Originally the Porxos gave onto the Stock Exchange and the sea, the two sources of Xifré's wealth. Round the building, defying its tatty appearance today, are a number of carved reliefs celebrating the various activities of an *indiano*.

Barcelona's many family textile concerns, despite chronically low wages, were often not that profitable. The Spanish market was small and Catalan industry found it hard to compete on level terms with France and Britain. Despite this, there were a few very rich industrialists, though these exceptions are often wrongly seen as the quintessential nineteenth-century Catalan capitalists. The most famous was Eusebi Güell, whom we met earlier through his park and his association with Gaudí. Güell epitomises a certain rule of Barcelona family fortunes: the first generation emerges from a fishing-port/ remote village/ Pyrenean valley to found the fortune; the second turns wealth into fabulous riches. The third and subsequent generations decline: decadence sets in and the grand-children of the fisherman/ peasant/ shepherd who worked eighteen hours a day to make his fortune become *rentier* men and women of leisure, gracing the Royal Polo and Tennis Clubs, or presiding, like one of Güell's descendants recently, over The Equestrian Circle. But what else is money for, than not to have to work?

Joan Güell, grandson of a shepherd, came back from Cuba in the 1830s and founded a textile factory in Sants. He called it *El Vapor Vell*, The Old Steam Factory, because the *Vapor Nou* already existed. It was just one of the mills where women and children worked twelve hours a day that gave to Barcelona the tag "Manchester of Spain". Cotton-spinning, money-spinning.

The name of Sants may be familiar as the city's main railway station, a bustling new building with a hotel on top and the platforms underground. The front of the station leads onto a hard, functional square and neon high-rise city, with the Carrer Tarragona's tinted glass-and-cement business offices hoping to create Barcelona's Wall Street on the site where the POUM's, and Orwell's, *Lenin* barracks once stood.

The station is flanked on one side by the Parc de l'Espanya industrial, one of the best-known new parks laid out by the City Council in the 1980s – though only after the local Residents' Association had struggled long and hard for it. On the site of *La España industrial*, the most powerful steam factory in Spain when it opened in 1847, this park is a bold mix of styles that can be read as a requiem for the passing of the industrial age. At one end a huge metal dragon lets you walk up inside and hurtle down shiny slides if you're young. Its main function now, alas, is as a toilet for people caught short round the train station.

Holding your nose from the top of the dragon, a lake with stadium-like steps and seating on both sides opens out in front. Beyond the lake, trees and grass lead away to Council offices in an old *masia*. Along the top of the park is a row of ten imposing towers, looking like lighthouses. This park is a heady mix of a soft park (grass, bushes, trees) and the hard park of the towers and step-seating. It also mixes Catalan myth (the dragon), the rural past (house and garden), the recent industrial past (towers), and the present: the step-seats where the unemployed can sit on each side of the stagnant lake and watch each other. The leisure society. The grass is useful for the homeless to catch up on their sleep.

Walk on down to the Plaça de Sants. You are walking above the railway tunnels. To the right of the busy Plaça, heart of a bustling working-class area, is what was the first factory on the plain outside Barcelona: Joan Güell's *El vapor vell*. Restored, its lean chimney still behind and above it, it now houses the Sants public library on the top floor, which retains the strong wood gables of the original, high factory roof. Here the library assistant found me some books on the history of the plant. One book told me that Gaudí's patron's father (this is who Joan Güell was) made his money "in business overseas". Another more radical local pamphlet said "in slave trading".

These early industrialists did not have it all their own way. Several factories were burnt down by artisans thrown out of work by industrialisation, so creating a number of *vapors cremats*, as they were sardonically known: burnt steam factories. Joan Güell eventually fled to live in Nîmes (home of another textile, denim '*de*

Nîmes'), after the General Manager of the *Vapor vell* was killed by gunmen during the first Barcelona general strike, in 1855.

Before this sensible, or cowardly, self-exile, Joan Güell expanded his wealth by traditional means: he married the daughter of an Italian residing in Barcelona. She died giving birth to Eusebi Güell i Bacigaluppi in 1846. Joan then quickly married his dead wife's sister. Even today the relatively small Barcelona bourgeoisie is enormously endogamic, which can lead to surprising family connections and usually warranted suspicions of undue influence.

The Tenth Richest Man in the World

Eusebi Güell became the richest man in Spain when in 1871 he married Isabel López, daughter of Antonio López, the Marquis of Comillas, who had made his money out of Cuban sugar plantations worked by slaves. This took Güell onto the boards of his father-in-law's companies: various banks, the Philippines Tobacco Company and the Transatlántica shipping firm. He inherited his father's concerns, which included the most long-term money-maker: the Maquinista industrial machinery and locomotive factory, set up in 1855. Even today, if you look at the older carriages on the Barcelona metro, you will see MAQUINISTA embossed on them. Eusebi Güell then expanded his fortune with the Asland cement factory. He was said to be the tenth richest man in the world, a precision of number which gives a ring of truth to what is impossible to prove.

Eusebi Güell shared Gaudí's Catalanism, expressed by the architect in an extremely rigid, racist rejection of the rest of Spain:

> *"We Catalans are people in equilibrium with our qualities.*
> *Those of the centre [i.e. Castile] do not have our qualities,*
> *nor even our defects. They're just not soldered together."*

...and of Northern Europe:

140

"We who live in countries bathed by the Mediterranean feel beauty with greater intensity than people from the Northern countries."

The new industrialists had money, but no political clout. Barcelona was the wealthiest city in Spain, but Madrid ran the country. "For all its ridiculous vanity Madrid was a metropolis in name only. It was a bumpkin in a gentleman's coat buttoned over a torn, dirty shirt," Pérez Galdós, Spain's major nineteenth-century novelist, wrote scathingly in *Fortunata and Jacinta* (1887). Madrid did not appreciate the problems of Catalonia's developing industrial society. To add injury to insult, in 1898 the Spanish state reached its nadir by losing Cuba and the Philippines in the war with the United States. Catalan industrialists were keen to disassociate itself as much as they possibly could from this disastrous, backward, poorer, less developed state.

Thus for about fifty years, from 1875 to 1925, the new Catalan bourgeoisie poured their spare cash and energy into having their houses built, particularly in the Eixample. *Modernisme* was a style with eclectic origins: Moorish and oriental themes showing the influence of trade across the Mediterranean; the neo-Gothic of the earlier nineteenth century; ornate decoration, inspired in Arts and Crafts movements, but designed to declare: *The owner of this house is wealthy, sophisticated and loves art.*

The sheer amount of this artistic architecture means that any visitor should take a few hours just to stroll round the central part of the Eixample. It has been preserved so fully in the century since it was built (despite the Franco hiatus) for the same motives that inspired its construction: the desire to conserve a Catalan identity against the stifling power of Madrid. Glance into the doorways at the stair-cases, the iron-work on the lift cages, the plaster filigree of the walls. Look up to the curving bunches of grapes and sea-shells on facades, pineapples on roofs, here a Gothic turret, there a balcony that looks as if it is

141

growing a tumour which on closer inspection is a bunch of concrete fruit, the stained glass. In the 1990s, the Council undertook an ambitious programme of restoration of about 400 *esgrafiats*, delicate patterns carved and painted on the facades of many *modernista* houses.

The wealthiest of these *nouveaux riches*, such as Güell, reacted not just by building boastful houses, but by pouring their money into art sponsorship. Who knows today that Antonio López (the Marquis of Comillas) or Eusebi Güell made their money out of slave labour? It is like the Tates with their Caribbean sugar plantations or the Guggenheim family with its silver mines in Mexico. These millionaires became architecture and arts patrons under the same impulse as Maecenas in Augustan Rome or the Medicis in Florence: the desire for their names to live on after their deaths. As indeed they have: Batlló, Milà and Güell are now remembered for magnificent houses, for Art not Money.

Eusebi Güell financed the sumptuous Palace on Nou de la Rambla (restored for Gaudí Year 2002), where he savoured the pinnacle of his glory in 1889 entertaining the Queen Regent María Cristina on her visit to the Universal Exhibition. The investment paid off, for in 1908 he was ennobled like his father-in-law, becoming Count Güell. The story is told of Güell's steward who came to his boss, worried that Gaudí was over-spending on too much detail. The Count-to-be replied like the mediaeval prince he aspired to be: "Too much? Too much, you say? Tell Gaudí he's not spending enough." Güell also financed Gaudí's 'Capricho' in the Asturian town of Comillas (where Antonio López hailed from), the Park that bears Güell's name, and what most specialists consider Gaudí's masterpiece, the crypt at the Colònia Güell, at Santa Coloma de Cervelló outside Barcelona.

In short, this new Catalan industrial bourgeoisie was a frustrated class. They represented the richest, most dynamic part of Spain, yet they had no access to political power. That made many of them, like Güell, ideologues of

142

conservative Catalan nationalism. Conservative, because they were major capitalists in a period of intense labour unrest; yet nationalist because they felt that Madrid's backwardness and anti-Catalanism held them back.

The Pedrera

Gaudí Year in 2002 opened to the public for the first time the main floor of the Batlló family's house (now owned by Chupa-chups sweets) on the Passeig de Gràcia. It is worth a visit, for here you can see the extraordinary attention Gaudí paid to every detail: the door-handles moulded to hands' shapes; the perfectly fitting windows, despite the curves. He was an architect who worked with the crafts-men, following a building through every stage of its construction.

The Casa Batlló house is next door to the Casa Amatller by Puig i Cadafalch. You can walk into the lobby of the Casa Amatller and look up the stair-well, covered by a stained-glass roof: neo-Gothic, like most of Puig's work. The stairs are heavy, wide stone slabs. This is a more sober straight-lined *modernisme* than Gaudí's. On the same block is Domènech's Lleó Morera house, with Cartier on one side of the main door and Loewe on the other — the *Passeig de Gràcia* is Barcelona's Regent Street. Loewe vandalised the building, tearing out the stone sculptures and putting in plate glass to show their fancy goods. "No one," thunders Robert Hughes, "who cares for architec-ture should ever buy anything from Loewe, on principle." Their prices are another reason. The Lleó Morera is a house kept locked against all intruders, with ferocious keep-out notices in several languages and a caretaker who barks like a Doberman. For compensation, take a look next door (the number is 351 Consell de Cent) and you will see yellow flowers in green leaves in plaster round the top of the hall-way: one of the myriad small wonders you find in the Eixample. The three named houses form the famous Block of Discord, different styles by the three greatest architects of the period, which from the McDonald's tables on the other side of the street fall into harmony.

Walk on up the Passeig de Gràcia. Glancing left down the eight-lane Aragó, you will see the Tàpies Foundation, an early building by Domènech now dressed with barbed wire on top by Tàpies to resemble a prison. Follow up the Passeig de Gràcia to the corner of València and have a coffee after the exertions of the Block of Discord in the Torino, a *modernista*-style café opened in 1995. Despite its high chairs, that make you feel like a baby, it's a nice place, but it's not the original, designed by Gaudí, that was knocked down in the 1930s.

Refreshed, you are ready for Gaudí's last great civil contract, the Casa Milà, known as *La pedrera*, the quarry, an expressionist master-piece. This huge block of flats took six years to complete. Gaudí finished it in 1912, in dispute with the Milà family because they refused to accept the twenty-foot statue of the Virgin Mary he wanted to stick on the roof. The family feared, with some reason (though a deplorable lack of religious back-bone), that their luxury apartment block would become a target for anarchists. Gaudí undertook no more civil engineering work after this, but devoted himself to the Sagrada Família and a life of piety. It may not have been only religion about which Gaudí and his employers disagreed. The first thing the Milà family did on occupying their flat was to strip out the curving walls and install a French classical design.

Many things happened to Gaudí around the time he finished the Casa Milà: the *Setmana tràgica*, that so shook Catalan industrialists' confidence in their future, the growing strength of anarchism which argued the opposite world-view to Gaudí's, and the changing art fashions — the coming of neo-classical *Noucentisme* — that relegated his style to out-of-date. Other things we can imagine: his loneliness, the effect of the deaths of his father aged nearly 100 and of Rosa his niece (from alcohol abuse) who kept house for him. He withdrew from the world. He lost the panache that had made him build his vision of Catalonia in stone meant to last. He became the visionary hermit of his last decade. His most famous project, the Sagrada Família, the temple to redeem the city from its sins of atheist anarchism, represented a defeat, a withdrawal from the world.

The impact of the Casa Milà is different. This house is of the world, a rippling fantasy in stone at the heart of the business city. It is still a heart-stopper today, even when it has been seen so often in photos. The daring of such a building: people fumble for their cameras as their mouths drop open at, in David Mackay's words: "the wave-like rhythms of the irregular walls draped with sea-weedy balconies." Or a molten cliff with caves, as someone else wrote. It is called expressionist because it seems the expression of emotional force, inner feeling, through exaggeration and distortion of a simple line.

The Casa Milà was bought in 1986 by the *Caixa de Catalunya*, the second savings-bank of Catalonia. The first is called with majestic self-confidence *La Caixa*, The Savings-bank. *La Caixa's* logo of a blue starfish shedding a yellow and red tear[1], seen all over the city, was designed by Miró. Its annual calendar, issued free to clients every December, is a work of art. The *Caixa de Catalunya*, in buying *La Pedrera*, was running hard to keep up. Its bankbooks are adorned with a drawing of a Gaudí chimney from the *Pedrera* roof. Its calendars show scenes from their house. Why do these two savings-banks spend such money on art? One could suppose they gain customers because art softens the dirty feel of money. Yet Catalans, business people, have never felt money is dirty. Rather, the banks perceive that their customers like their art sponsorship, for it is associated with Catalan feeling. Miró, Gaudí. With them we can look anyone in the eye. We will put our money there.

The *Caixa de Catalunya* spent several years on restoration, cleaning the soot off the facade, replacing damaged bits of glass, stone and mosaic, recovering murals. Most of all, they restored the attic, which had been converted into thirteen apartments in the 1950s, to its former glory. It is

145

now the most comprehensive permanent museum to Gaudí in the city, its contents set off by the magnificent off-centre line of its curved brick ceiling.

In front of the Casa Milà in winter, the women ushers wear red dresses with red-fringed black capes like Iberia air hostesses. Do not be daunted by them, but as an appetiser look round the free exhibition on the first floor of the Casa Milà. From the exhibition rooms you can see into the inner patios of the neighbouring houses, the inside of one of Cerdà's Eixample blocks. Look too up the round stair-well with its curving iron-work; and observe the ramp leading down to the underground car-park, the first to be built in the city. Gaudí was perhaps inspired by the painter Ramon Casas, who lived next door to the Casa Milà and is said to have been the first *barceloní* to own a motor-car[2].

In the free part there is also a toilet, a valued find in Barcelona, and inside the men's toilet a Gaudí round stone pillar. Here, privately, you can run your fingers over the rough stone. Toilet-bowls and sinks do not fit in badly with the curving nature of the whole house, in which famously there is not a square wall or angle. "How can I fit my piano in, Mr. Gaudí?" asked one of the tenants in a famous satirical ditty by Josep Carner. "Take up the violin," the crusty genius replied.

Gaudí's name today adds value to all it touches. Two of his houses now have fancy restaurants, though in his last two decades he is reputed to have fed himself on lettuce dipped in milk. Spain's major fashion show is held in Barcelona, and it is called the *Passarel·la Gaudí*, the Gaudí Catwalk. No matter that the architect would have more in common with the Ayatollah Khomeini than with Claudia Schiffer. In a recent document, the Passarel·la Gaudí explained:

> "Renowned for its design and architecture, Barcelona is a world fashion city. Our aim is to use Barcelona's infra-structures and international position to add value to our Fashion Show."

The syllogism goes: Barcelona = great design/architecture = Gaudí. Our fashion parade (or restaurant, or hotel, or chupa-chups, or bank, or designer chair...) becomes more glamorous if it bears the Gaudí name.

The free floor of the Casa Milà is the aperitif for the paying part, which takes you up to the sixth floor attic and the roof. Even though you may spend most of your stay in Barcelona in bars, restaurants, wandering the streets or at the *Camp Nou*, you must grab a moment to walk round this attic and roof. The Casa Milà has no furtive extra storey, but a roof for strolling on, among the sentry or warrior-like chimneys, which like Moorish turrets are all the same bar slight variations you have to look for (Gaudí is imposing *and* subtle). The roof has an undulating floor. Like walking on the sea or the "landscape of a dream" (Robert Hughes). It is also like a visit to the zoo, with the visitors snapping pictures through the bars everywhere, uniformed supervisors (to stop visitors chipping off the *trencadís*) and the smooth ochre stone like the polished walls of the animal enclosures.

From the roof of the Casa Milà you can look across the Eixample to the Sagrada Família, its spires like extensions of these chimneys they wouldn't let Gaudí crown with a Virgin. To throw my pennyworth into what is an ongoing debate: the Casa Milà is both the peak of *modernisme* and its last great building. The Sagrada Família, surprising though it is, is pastiche, decadence and religious mania.

---

[1] *I write what I have always seen. I am told* La Caixa's *logo is actually a hand dropping a coin into a money-box!*

[2] *Casas' studio is conserved within the Vinçon store.*

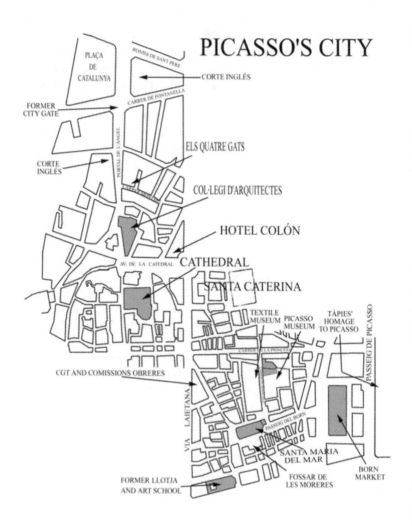

PICASSO'S CITY

PLAÇA DE CATALUNYA

RONDA DE SANT PERE

CORTE INGLÉS

FORMER CITY GATE

CARRER DE FONTANELLA

CORTE INGLÉS

PORTAL DE L'ÀNGEL

ELS QUATRE GATS

COL·LEGI D'ARQUITECTES

HOTEL COLÓN

AV. DE LA CATEDRAL

CATHEDRAL

SANTA CATERINA

TEXTILE MUSEUM

PICASSO MUSEUM

TÀPIES' HOMAGE TO PICASSO

PASSEIG DE PICASSO

CARRER DE LA PRINCESA

CGT AND COMISSIONS OBRERES

VIA LAIETANA

PASSEIG DEL BORN

SANTA MARIA DEL MAR

FORMER LLOTJA AND ART SCHOOL

FOSSAR DE LES MORERES

BORN MARKET

Chapter 8
The Mediaeval-Modern City

"...a dirty city... with the middle ages lingering on in many parts of it, and the streets packed with horses, mules, and asses, carrying paniers or pulling carts, drays, wagons, omnibuses, cabs; a city smelling not only of horse and humanity but of the port, the fish-markets, hot olive oil, and the countless factory-chimneys."
PATRICK O'BRIAN, *PICASSO*.

Not 9 to 5

When the French novelist George Sand, *en route* to Mallorca with Chopin in November 1838, entered the main gate of Barcelona, the Portal de l'Àngel, she wrote of: "...the formidable and massive fortifications of Barcelona, with a bewildering number of gates, draw-bridges, posterns and ramparts."

The stage-coaches left through this gate at 3am, when the night-soil operators also entered to empty the cess-pits (*pous morts*, dead pits in Catalan) and later cart out the city's excrement to fertilise the fields of the plain. After three o'clock the gates were shut again till dawn, for the countryside was in the midst of one of the two major civil wars, the 'Carlist' wars, of the nineteenth century. The city was no more secure than in Don Quixote's time. George Sand wrote in *Winter in Majorca*:

"Behind a triple ring of cannon, and cut off from the rest of Spain by banditry and civil war, the gay youth of Barcelona sunned itself on the rambla... — the women, beautiful, graceful and coquettish, preoccupied by the fold of their mantillas and the play of their fans; the men by their cigars, as they strolled along, laughing, chatting, ogling the ladies, discussing the Italian opera, and

seeming not to care in the least what might be happening
beyond the city walls."

Today the crowds are even bigger, and seem just as relaxed despite the rumbles of precarious employment, housing crisis and war bearing down on our lives. The gate George Sand entered and left by before the walls came down leads into the street with the highest shop-rents in Barcelona. You understand why on a Friday or Saturday evening. People from outlying neighbourhoods such as Verneda or Nou barris pour down "into Barcelona." Though the Portal de l'Àngel, pedestrianised in the '90s, is a wide street, at seven o'clock on, say, a week-end November night, it is packed. The shops are open, and really open, lights full on and doors flung wide despite the cold. Shoe shops, clothes shops: people who work all week are buying. Don't think these well-dressed consumers are well-off: many buy on credit. But appearance in public is important in Spain. People dress better than in the UK, whether they can afford to or not.

A brownish, turreted department store looking like Selfridge's dominates the Portal de l'Àngel. This was the *Galerías Preciados*, used by so few shoppers that it was hard to understand why the *Corte inglés* bought it in the mid-90s, unless it was for asset-stripping. On Friday and Saturday evenings, both multi-storey stores, the *Corte inglés* on the Plaça de Catalunya and the old *Galerías* 200 yards away, are full. No asset-stripping, just good old-fashioned selling.

This phenomenon contradicts the view expressed in Chapter One that the centre of Barcelona is dominated by tourists. Though by day this is true, especially in the Rambles, the Passeig de Gràcia, Park Güell and certain other sites, at week-ends *barcelonins* retake the centre. And the spectacle fulfils tourists' wildest dreams of a vibrating, busy, lively city. The crowds are peaceful too. Spaniards drink a lot, but they don't go out on a Saturday night to *get drunk*. It is one of the reasons architect

Richard Rogers believes that the quality of life in Barcelona is so superior to London's:

> *"For a non-Spanish person, it is amazing. The relaxed 24-hour life. It's not 9 to 5 and everything closed by 6, as it is in London. The sheer quality of public space is stunning. It's a most liveable city."*

The comparison is inevitable with the centre of British cities, where Friday or Saturday night means everything closed except for the pubs, and deserted except for groups of drunks tumbling and vomiting between pubs. The contrast with the Portal de l'Àngel is "stunning."

Central Barcelona is much more lived-in than North-American and many British cities, whose inner areas tend to house only the poor alongside office and shopping complexes where few live. In Marseilles, France's second city and just round the coast from Barcelona, the wealthy have abandoned the centre, creating what is known as a "doughnut effect": no-one is left in the middle. Some of that has happened in Barcelona, but life is still focused down-town by people of all sorts continuing to live there. Local shops still survive among the department stores, chains and fashion boutiques. The *Boqueria* market is both a tourist attraction and a local market. This quality is a point of attraction often cited by tourists: the places to visit are also where people are leading their daily lives.

Mediaeval-Modern

The second street on the left off the short fat Portal de l'Àngel is Montsió. Even on a busy Saturday night it is suddenly dark and ancient, with few shops or passers-by, one of those sudden contrasts that makes Barcelona *the great enchantress*. Just a hundred yards along Montsió is *Els quatre gats*, one of the legendary cafés of European bohemia. The gourmet menu is illuminated on a stand outside the door. The cover bears a design by Pablo Picasso, in the style of Toulouse-Lautrec. You can look back from the night and watch the crowds moving slowly down the brightly-lit Portal de l'Àngel.

In 1898 the seventeen-year old Picasso returned weak from a serious attack of scarlet fever in Madrid. He was invited by fellow-art student Manuel Pallarès to recuperate in his home village, Horta de Sant Joan. There Picasso and Pallarès spent nine months. The city-boy learnt to wield a scythe, watched and took part in the harvest of grapes and olives, and helped in the making of wine and oil. They became lifelong friends. "Everything I know I learnt in Pallarès' village," Picasso would repeat like an incantation in later years. To paint, they loaded their materials on a mule and then carried them up to a cave, where they stayed several weeks. Picasso learnt to cook and to speak Catalan, and continued to speak Catalan to Pallarès and other Catalan friends all his life.

Picasso was an early immigrant to Catalonia from Andalucía. Coming from Málaga with his family, he first saw the city from the sea in 1895. His father had found a job teaching at the Llotja Art School, in the *Ciutat vella*, and the family settled in a gloomy house at Carrer de la Mercè 3 (building demolished in the 1980s), only 100 yards from the school. The Art School was on the top floor of the Stock Exchange (*Llotja*) that claimed to be the oldest in the world. The main building is eighteenth-century, but it incorporates the original fourteenth-century Gothic hall, built just off the sea-front so as to conduct its shipping business. It seems odd to have an Art School on top of the Stock Exchange, anarcho-minded young artists sitting on top of all those suited traders. It reflects both the density of population of the Old City and how business during the nineteenth-century Catalan Renaissance did indeed patronise art, as the Gaudí story shows. Picasso was admitted to the Llotja school at the age of thirteen, even though the entry age was much higher. His father gave up painting. He was a good enough teacher to see how the talent of his adolescent son showed up his own mediocrity.

Picasso was to have studios in this Old City, all within a few streets of each other, in the following seven years: in the Carrers Plata, Escudillers blancs, Riera de Sant Joan, Nou de la Rambla. These were not studio-studios as we imagine them, airy rooms streaming with light, but small bare rooms where he could make the mess he wanted. He went to his parents' round the corner to eat. The Old City is so intimately associated with Picasso it is hard to imagine him outside it, though he often went walking in Collserola. The *Ciutat vella* is what he drew. In the words of one of his biographers, Patrick O'Brian, novelist of the Jack Aubrey stories and resident in Collioure, in French Catalonia, for fifty years:

> *"...he perpetually walked about Barcelona with Pallarès, drawing with scarcely a pause, filling albums and sketchbooks with street-scenes, horses, cats, dogs, whores, bawds, anarchist meetings, scores and scores of hands, paired and single, beggars, soldiers leaving for the unpopular Cuban campaign, soon to end in war with the United States."*

1890s Barcelona was "...a dirty city, upon the whole, with the middle ages lingering on in many parts of it." Picasso spent his formative years in this medieval-modern city, from 1895 to 1900, when at nineteen he first visited Paris. For several years after that he was still based in Barcelona, though spent longer and longer periods in Paris. In Barcelona, after many doubts, he adopted his name, which became a twentieth-century brand name: the dove of peace, a car, a perfume. Unusually, but like his master Velázquez, he took not his father's surname (Ruiz), but his mother's: Picasso.

Four Cats

Though Catalonia had little painting tradition, it was not a blank canvas. Catalonia's painting in the late 1890s was dominated by two wealthy bohemians, Ramon Casas and Santiago Rusiñol. Casas' father was an *indiano* and his mother a textiles heiress: thus combining the two main forms of nineteenth-century wealth. Casas himself, we have seen, had a house beside the Casa Milà on the Passeig de Gràcia. Both these lifelong friends could afford to dedicate their lives to art. Their Mecca was Paris, where they shared a spacious Montmartre flat above the *Moulin de la Galette* in the 1880s. The Barcelona art world was small and provincial; and Impressionism had to be imbibed at its source. By the same rule of thumb, when they returned to Barcelona, they had a huge impact on its art world, which was prepared to swallow without critical distance the latest trends from the north.

In the early 1890s, Rusiñol bought a house on the cliff in the old part of Sitges. Today this is the Cau Ferrat Museum, jumbled home to Rusiñol's collection of irons and brasses, many of his own paintings and two El Grecos, which in November 1894 Barcelona artists carried in procession from Sitges station to Cau Ferrat. Casas and Rusiñol were there; so was the poet Joan Maragall, grandfather of Barcelona's Olympic Mayor. The dishevelled Pere Romeu, manager of the *Quatre gats* a few years later, led the procession on horseback.

Financed mainly by Ramon Casas, the *Quatre gats* opened in 1897. There Barcelona's bohemia were marshalled by Rusiñol, able and affable showman. By day the most attractive approach to the *Quatre gats* is from Comtal under an arch into the Passatge del Patriarca, though the passage is closed after dark. On the wall there is a notice explaining how the street was called Espolsasacs, because here the monks of the former monastery shook the dirt and dust (pols) out of their habits (sacs) onto passers-by. A lasting habit, for even after the invention of vacuum-cleaners, people all over the city still shake from their balconies the dust, hairs and toe-nails off their rugs.

The *Quatre gats* was an imitation of *Le chat noir* and other bohemian hang-outs of 1890s Paris; and its name was down-beat, for *quatre gats*, four cats, means in Catalan *three men and a dog*, that is, hardly anyone at all. The *Quatre gats* today is re-opened and thriving: you can eat its quite expensive 'gastronomic menu' at mid-day, or take a coffee at any time. Or a glass of *orujo* (Spanish for '*grappa*') or *absenta*, as doubtless the Catalan Impressionists and their followers did. A reproduction of Casas' comic painting of him and Romeu on a tandem hangs inside the entrance on the left in the same place as the original did in 1897. The painting shows Casas pedalling hard in front, while the gangly Romeu free-rides behind: most likely, it is said, Casas' feeling about having to bear the weight of financing the *Quatre gats*. The building is a *modernista* building by Puig (pronounced *putsch*) i Cadafalch (architect of the Casa Amatller of the last chapter), in red brick with balconies and adornments in stone, and with a neo-Gothic door ("a general Teutonic air of phony mediaevalism," Patrick O'Brian). In the back room, in dark wood, with smaller-than-usual tables and chairs, there is a particularly delicate low gallery.

The teenage Picasso came into contact with Casas and Rusiñol, both by then in their 30s, at the *Quatre gats*. Here he would have heard the stories of Paris. Contemporaries report that Picasso said little at the *Quatre gats* sessions: he was younger, an Andalusian outsider, and an observer. What brought Picasso fully alive was the twelve hours a day he spent painting.

As well as a café, the *Quatre gats* was a cabaret, produced magazines and held exhibitions, and it was here that Picasso first showed, in February 1900, at the dawn of the century he dominated: about 150 drawings, many of his friends. Picasso was admired, but no more than Casas, who has as fine a set of drawings of the café's habitués. At the *Quatre gats* too, Picasso probably met his other equal at the time, Isidre Nonell, who painted the poor and Gypsies in dark tones and influenced Picasso's 'Blue Period' paintings. There is a certain myth that the *Quatre gats* was a hot-bed of anarchism. Anarchism, for sure, was in the air. At this time Casas combined his society portraits with three political paintings that caused a sensation: a public garrotting, often said to be of Santiago

Salvador the Liceu bomber; the *Corpus Christi procession* (1896), pregnant with emotion as the spectator knows it is about to be bombed; and *The Charge*, painted in 1899, but dated to 1902 to make it fit in with the General Strike of that year. Despite these impressive works, Casas was no anarchist. The painters of the *Quatre gats* were: "Neurotic dilettanti, only concerned with being different from the philistines and the bourgeois," in the words of Jaume Brossa, one of the few real anarchists of the *Quatre gats* circles. Rusiñol's expressed aim was to educate the philistine bourgeois, not kill or overthrow them.

What did Picasso gain from the *Quatre gats*? A world of outsiders he could feel at home in, a general free-thinking, anti-clerical, separatist attitude (all his life he supported Catalan independence) and something of an education with intellectual men and women of the world to fill in the huge gaps in his formal schooling. "The passion for destruction is also a creative passion," was one of Bakunin's refrains. Like him, Picasso was setting out to tear down the old order — in art.

Not all Barcelona's artists, of course, came to the *Quatre gats*. Gaudí never went there. His face does not appear in Ramon Casas' sketches. Nor did the other major architects of the time, nor Verdaguer, disgraced by this time for giving away too much of the Marquis of Comillas' money to the poor. Gaudí and Verdaguer believed in a Catholic, nationalist Catalonia and wanted nothing to do with the decadent internationalists of the *Quatre gats*, who were the very sinners Gaudí later sought to flee in the Park Güell and then redeem in the Sagrada Família.

Beside the door of the *Quatre gats* today a plaque commemorates the occupancy of the building by the Artistic Circle of St. Luke from 1903 to 1936. There is some irony in this, for the *Quatre gats* closed in 1903 and the Artistic Circle, which was the group to which Gaudí and other Christian artists belonged, took over the premises. Picasso and Gaudí did tread the same floor-boards, but not at the same time.

Demolition, Born Again or the Third Way

This chapter follows the thread of Picasso across the Old City. From the *Quatre gats*, return to and go down the Portal de l'Àngel. On the cathedral square the Col·legi d'Arquitectes has a frieze of figures designed by Picasso (there are more inside). From there, go on past the cathedral on the right and the current site of the Hotel Colón on the left. If you want an exotic haven to rest, this is it. Anyone (you do not have to be staying there) can walk in off the street and visit the carpeted lounge-cafeteria with deep arm-chairs, glass cabinets of white china and Stubbs reproductions of horses on the wall. It feels more like an English provincial tea-room than a five-star hotel right on Barcelona's tourist-packed cathedral square.

Going down the Via Laietana, after the Roman walls and monuments around the Plaça del Rei on the right, on the left a nine-storey triangular building rises. It is crowned by an open white dome on columns, rather like a summer-house in the gardens of an English country mansion. These are the offices of *Comissions obreres*, the major trade union federation (see Chapter Nine). Now this pioneer in assembly-led factory democracy is as bureaucratic as any other main-stream union in Europe. In the same building, occupying the top floor, is the anarchist-inclined CGT, result of an '80s split in the CNT[1]. It may seem odd that two unions of such different inspiration share the same premises. The reason is that the building belonged to the Ministry of Labour under Franco, and was then divided up between the newly legal unions after the transition.

The CGT's is the first door. Ride up in the CGT lift and walk round to the bar. Being anarchists, they have never thrown me out; though they might, if too many tourists abuse their terrace. They have serious political work to do: they not only organise workers, but are active in defence of immigrants. There are no Stubbs prints on the wall, but there is a wonderful terrace, where you can look out over the roof-tops of old Barcelona. This is a lay version of the similar view you get from the roof of the cathedral. From here you see the red-tiled flat tops of the houses, with improvised gardens of cacti and geraniums in old buckets and paint-tins, rickety railings, washing-lines and the hunch-backed little huts from which the stairs come out. On these roofs, people stretch out on cloying summer nights, pigeons waddle or illegal extensions are built, unseen from the street, to house a relative or immigrant without papers. From the CGT terrace, too, you can see the monuments of the Old City: the cable-car, Columbus, the cathedral. Turning, Santa Maria del Mar, in front of the twin towers of the Olympic village.

Back down in the mean streets, turn along Princesa. This area of the *Ciutat vella* between the Via Laietana and the Ciutadella Park is known as the Ribera district. Inland from Princesa is a rougher poorer Ribera. Plunge into these streets where Picasso padded, pencil in hand. Some are still crusty with age and dark, but most are touched by the fevers of restoration and demolition. The area, largely unchanged from Picasso's time till the 1990s, is changing rapidly now.

It is a good point to summarise the Council's controversial reform programme, which, round the Santa Caterina market, has raised a storm. The Council stands accused of destroying a quarter and its social fabric, moving people out, forcing shops to close and knocking down historic buildings.

On the seaward side of the Carrer Princesa, as if Princesa were a frontier, lies the Born area, Barcelona's Notting Hill, recently a slum and now the most gentrified part of the Old City. If your Barcelona is bars and nightlife, you'll find them here. Or the antique shops, art galleries, boutiques and delicatessens that accompany rehabilitated buildings (the 'benign metastasis' mentioned in Chapter Two on the Raval).

The contrast between the adjacent Born and Santa Caterina areas shows how the Council pursues different policies in different areas. The brilliant campaigning 'tourist' leaflet that the local Residents' Association and other organisations[2] have issued in English opens:

> "**WARNING**: *some buildings look awful. This decay is desired by the City Council. Many buildings could be perfectly well rehabilitated and do not need demolishing.*"

The above refers to Santa Caterina, a well-established old quarter, demolished; whereas the Born has been rehabilitated, with generous grants helping proprietors to value their properties upwards.

Rosa Gil, proprietor of the restaurant Casa Leopoldo, described in detail by Mandiargues and now a writers' haunt in the heart of the Raval, sees the Born as something of a model for the path down which the Raval should go:

> "*This is one of the ideas of the improvement plan: renew through an influx of new people, so that we could end up with something like the balance of the '40s, '50s and '60s. Vice and virtue lived in great harmony!*"

Rich and poor, residents and tourists, immigrants and natives... all living in harmony. Well, this rose-coloured view of the past would be nice, but it wasn't really like that in the '40s, '50s and '60s and it's unlikely now. The Council would like to see the tourist Old City done up like the Born, a prettified shop-window, its street structure maintained, the housing overhauled. Pere Cabrera, Council spokesperson for the Reform Plan, is particularly explicit in his desire to kick out the poor and conjures up a view of history to support his argument:

> "*Let's not forget that the great drama of the* Ciutat vella *began the day that the bourgeoisie and the city as a whole forgot the historic centre to move into the new city, the Eixample. The quarter's gone downhill since then.*"

It's clear that much of the Old City is evolving Bornwards, attracting a new young wealthy class, though not exactly Cabrera's *bourgeoisie*, who will continue to live in mansions in leafy suburbs. Much of the rest of it is going Santa Caterina-wards: a mix of demolition for multi-storey flats and striking new buildings, like the refurbished market.

The 'tourist' campaigning leaflet argues:

> *"A special feature of the neighbourhood of Santa Caterina is, or more precisely, was its intricate street layout and its wide range of architecture. Often, mediaeval basements were incorporated into posterior 18th century buildings which, in turn, were decorated with elaborate facade paintings. The city council... has inflicted demolition on a massive scale and eliminated many of the buildings which in any other European city would have been protected... Millions of euros destined as aid from the EU have been spent on converting a complex historical quarter of old Barcelona into rubble."*

In opposing this process, the protesters in Santa Caterina do not want their area to become another noisy Born, dominated by tourist businesses and with the poor driven out by price rises. They are positing a third way: neither demolition, nor conversion into tourist stage-set. The street lay-out can be maintained and housing rehabilitated without evicting the original, often ageing population. This is what Bologna did in its '70s heyday, pioneering urban renewal in an ancient European city. Of course, the Bologna way costs money. For rehabilitation with the original residents staying put, it would be difficult to find the private capital that, through public-private partnership, is making a killing on the Illa Robadors (Ch. 2) and in Santa Caterina.

In the cleaned-up Born, just behind the nineteenth-century iron-work market, stands the magnificently restored convent of Sant Agustí, used as a Community Centre. It is only 100 yards from the Santa Caterina demolition. The Council converts for tourism in one area, and demolishes next door.

The Picasso Museum

The Picasso Museum shows what can be done with a mediaeval slum. To reform a decaying old building, though, tends to cost a lot more than knocking it down. The Picasso Museum, the most visited in the city, apart from FC Barcelona's Museum, is just off Carrer Princesa, on the Carrer Montcada[3]. The Picasso Museum might have been in London. In 1960, nearly half a million people saw Picasso's exhibition at the Tate sugar magnate's gallery: an early example of the massive retrospectives of living artists and the enormous art crowds common today. Picasso came to set up the exhibition and liked London. He discussed a museum there with his friend, secretary and dogsbody from Barcelona days, Jaume Sabartés. Sabartés told Picasso he was intending to donate his 570 Picassos, all presents from the artist, to found a museum in Málaga as it was the artist's birth-place. "Why not Barcelona? I have so few ties with Málaga," said Picasso, according to Sabartés. And Barcelona, not Málaga or London, it was.

Picasso was a Communist, Catalan separatist and Republican. He never returned to Spain after the Civil War[4]. He didn't want Franco and Franco didn't want him: the negotiations, conducted by Sabartés, for a place to house the Museum were slow. But Sabartés, even in his great old age, was patient and stubborn. He had, too, a number of allies who saw that a Picasso museum would help promote Barcelona and the Catalan cause. Despite the 1960s and early 1970s being the dark years of Porcioles-encouraged speculation, both the Miró Foundation (elegant building designed by Sert on Montjuïc) and the Picasso Museum date from that time.

Eventually, Sabartés found and Picasso agreed on the Palau Aguilar in the Carrer Montcada, only a few minutes walk from where his family had lived in the Carrer de la Mercè. It finally opened in 1964. In its early days, it certainly didn't look like becoming one of Barcelona's greatest tourist attractions. It was based on Sabartés' collection and the few Picassos held by the Barcelona Museum of Modern Art. As the Fodor Guide for 1971 laments:

> *"As everyone knows, Picasso is not exactly on the best of terms with official representatives of Spanish culture. The result is that the Picasso museum in its present plight has about ten Blue Period paintings and a scattering of ceramics, plus a collection of lithographs. The name of the building discreetly diverts attention from its failure: it is called the Fundación Sabartés."*

After Sabartés' death in February 1968, Picasso sent a large number of new works. When the Museum acquired the next-door palace (it now occupies five!), he sent his 1950s series inspired by Velázquez's *Meninas*. Disappointment with the Museum is usually rooted in that it has none of Picasso's great early Cubist paintings, gives no overview of his development and is dominated by his juvenilia and early work. This is true, but it is fitting. Barcelona was where he was formed. The early work of a genius is interesting. And the maturer part of the early work, the 'Blue Period' as critics know it, was the immediate precursor of the Cubist revolution. It dealt with the poverty and misery of the *barri xinès*. Picasso was never part of bourgeois society despite his later wealth. Those early paintings in the museum remind you that this was a man sympathetic to anarchism in his youth and a member of the Communist Party for the last three decades of his life.

The Carrer Montcada was one of the noblest streets of Barcelona and its merchants' and aristocrats' palaces have mostly been conserved. The Textile Museum, with powerful outdoor heaters in winter in its court-yard café, is a good example: imagine the heavy wooden doors dragged back, the carriages turning in to the flag-stoned yard, the hens scattering, the nobles striding up the great stone stairs to their apartments, the snorting horses groomed and stabled on the ground floor.

The legend of Picasso has not faded in the thirty years since his death, despite the battering his personal conduct has taken. It is a legend based on many facets: his energy and hard work, his supposed sexual promiscuity (associated in the minds of many with his vast artistic output), his wealth. Money! The anecdote that best illustrates the nature of Picasso's fame is that he could move without money in the post-war years. If he scribbled a dove and signed a restaurant menu, his signature was worth far more than the bill for the expensive meals he and his retinue had eaten. In payment for a giant Easter Egg ordered from the famous Barcelona chocolate-sculptor and pastry-cook Antoni Escribà in the 1960s, Picasso grandly sent a picture in payment[5]. His art had become a commodity more valuable than money. Mediaeval merchant-princes' palaces are, in this respect, fitting homes for his work.

The Barcelona authorities are proud of their association with Picasso. He is not just a money-spinner. His link to the city makes it feasible to talk of an important Paris-Barcelona axis (theme of several exhibitions), of a close link with the paradigmatic city of modern art. It was Picasso who returned to Paris from Barcelona the baton of cosmopolitan modern art that Casas and Rusiñol had originally brought from Paris to Barcelona. Picasso went to Paris without complexes, took them on and won. For many Catalans, wanting to be more advanced than backward Spain, but fearing they were less sophisticated than France, Picasso was a wonderful adopted son.

No Traitor

From the Picasso Museum, down the Carrer Montcada of palaces you reach Santa Maria del Mar, the parish church of fishermen and their families, and originally beside the sea. Surrounded now by the upmarket Born area, it is by general consensus the greatest church building in Barcelona. The anarchist destruction of its altars and riches in 1936 left it bare, all its dark brick and harsh Gothic lines visible, its vaulting like the ribs of an upturned ship. It was built bare, though, in just 50 years in the fourteenth century, a relative speed of construction that assisted its purity of style. It lacks North European Gothic's pointed spires and ornate internal decoration. It is best inside. Like all mediaeval churches it is a cool haven on a summer day, a place to sit and admire the soaring brick walls and roof. The church is made to seem still more spacious by the distance between its columns. "It shows the dual tendency of Catalan architecture to conquer space and purify form," wrote the Catalan architecture critic, Alexandre Cirici.

Beside Santa Maria del Mar lies the *Fossar de les Moreres*, the Mulberry Tree Graveyard which I was encouraged to visit by the Generalitat tourist office instead of the Civil War Graveyard behind Montjuïc (see Ch. 5). This is the burial-place of the martyrs of 1714, when the Castilian forces, led by the Duke of Berwick, illegitimate son of James II of England and mercenary, reduced the city after a ten-week siege. Berwick had 40,000 soldiers, whereas the defenders had 5,000. After two months of siege, the hated enemy paid tribute to the *barcelonins*. Berwick's praise was presumably to justify his failure to take the city quicker, but has entered *barcelonins'* legends of themselves:

> *"Never before has greater determination been seen than that of the garrison and the inhabitants of Barcelona."*

On September 11, Berwick's soldiers finally poured through seven breaches in the walls. Allison Peers wrote:

> *"All through the day, to the clanging of the great bell of the cathedral, fighting continued in the streets, behind barricades constructed hastily by women and children, and even in churches, monasteries and private houses."*

Queen Anne, who had encouraged the Catalans to take up arms in what is known in English history as the War of the Spanish Succession, had abandoned Catalonia to its fate instead of fulfilling her pledge to support it with the Navy. Perfidious Albion.

Two representatives of the Generalitat came to Berwick on September 13 to submit. Berwick, insisting on unconditional surrender, replied he had no knowledge of any Generalitat. The Consell de Cent and Generalitat were abolished and Catalonia ceased to be even a partly self-governing entity. The *Ciutadella*, the Citadel, was built: Barcelona was a city under occupation. In 1939, those who surrendered the Generalitat to Yagüe felt the added despair that history was repeating itself, though not as a farce, and so, perhaps, was not and never would be on their side.

The noble inscription on the Fossar de les Moreres reads: "No traitor is buried here./ Even though our flags are lost/ this is the urn of honour." On September 11 every year, the national day of Catalonia and a public holiday, Catalonia's political parties and numerous associations vie with each other to render homage to the martyrs who laid down their lives rather than accept this final loss of Catalan power.

All peoples remember their mistreatment at the hands of other peoples, even if good manners prevail nowadays. If they don't remember officially, a memory is passed down, an instinct that underlies the hand-shakes. 1714 was only a year before the first Jacobite rising of 1715. Today, great play is made of Catalonia's parallels with Scotland, as an implicit rebuke to the Spanish Government for not accepting national differences as readily as the London Government supposedly does. The respective trade union federations exchange visits. The Scottish First Minister is received by the President of the Generalitat. The Catalan Enric Miralles designed the Parliament Building in Edinburgh. *Braveheart* is repeated endlessly on TV3. Scotland's own legal code, football side, dress, bank-notes and autochthonous sports are often remarked. These parallels are forced: the '15 and the '45 were the last gasps of a feudal Highland Scotland defeated by the English in alliance with the Lowland Scots, alliance that did not occur in Catalonia. Indeed, Scottish nationalism has been a less powerful force than Catalan, which was resurgent a century and a bit after the 1714 catastrophe (see last chapter). Much of Scottish folklore was re-invented by the English, who appropriated kilts, bagpipes and the Highland Games, with the help of Walter Scott. The invention of Catalan folklore, the recovery and development of ancient or more recent customs, has been achieved by Catalans against a Spanish Government which has never, except for a few years during the Second Republic, accepted Catalan national difference.

There is one more visit to round off this chapter threaded around Picasso. From the Born, cross what is now the Passeig de Picasso to Antoni Tàpies' *Homage to Picasso*, a pile of junk within a transparent water-sprayed cube defying all who see it to interpret it. As John Payne in his recent book, *Catalonia*, points out, it is just what it is: a pile of junk. "Painting," thunder Picasso's words on the cube, "is not made to decorate apartments, but is a weapon of war."

---

[1] *A note of clarification: the CGT has nothing to do with the French union of the same name.*

[2] *Available from the Residents' Association at Rec 27, ground floor.*

[3] *Though neither the Picasso nor football museums are as popular as Salvador Dalí's in Figueres.*

[4] *This was probably no great hardship. After his 1917 stay, when he painted his wife Olga in a mantilla and with five-o'clock shadow, looking like a Barcelona transvestite, Picasso hardly visited the city.*

[5] *Antoni Escribà died in autumn 2004, but his family still run two magnificent cake shops, one a* modernista *building on the Rambles and the other on the Gran Via.*

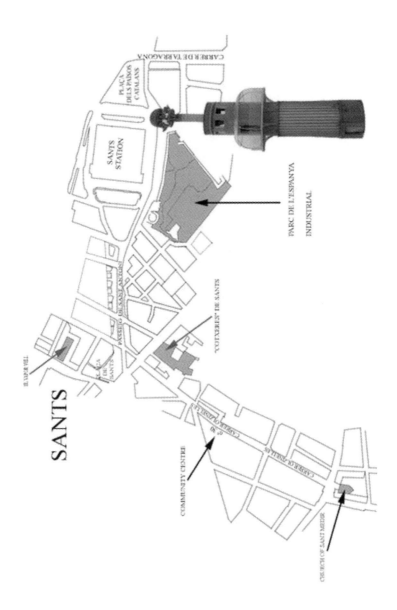

SANTS

PARC DE L'ESPANYA INDUSTRIAL

SANTS STATION

PLAÇA DELS PAÏSOS CATALANS

CARRER DE TARRAGONA

PASSEIG DE SANT ANTONI

EL VAPOR VELL

PLAÇA DE SANTS

"COLÒNIES" DE SANTS

COMMUNITY CENTRE

CARRER OLZINELLES

CARRER DE PUBILLA

CHURCH OF SANT MEDIR

Chapter 9
Transition

*"— You're right. We're not the desperate generation
any longer. We're just sad, because suddenly disappointment arrived. There was nothing complicated
about this. They talked to us of democracy, of the
King as arbiter, of the possible legalisation of the
political parties. They told us the best way was a
broad consensus, a pact, for if not the Civil War
would never finish. They convinced us. And it hasn't
been easy to get over this deceit."*
MARIANO SÁNCHEZ SOLER, *PARA MATAR.*

Spain was Different

Spain has changed more than any West European society
in the last thirty years. Anyone who knew Spain in
Franco's time will bear witness to the cloying atmosphere,
the nightmarish conformity of how people dressed, the
omnipresence of the black beetles — the priests — scurrying on their educational business, and the ubiquitous
sad-faced middle-aged women dressed in black. In one generation Spain moved from dictatorship to the most liberal
society in Europe; in two generations it has moved from a
predominantly rural to an urban society. 1960s Barcelona,
its crumbling buildings blackened with grime, its Old City
still pitted with Civil War bomb-sites, was transformed
into the 1992 city of design. If people visited Barcelona in
the 1960s, it was for the classic reasons discussed in the
opening chapters: it was cheaper than Northern Europe,
exotic, different. "Africa starts at the Pyrenees," was the
disdainful comment of French chauvinists (the Catalan
right added a variation: "Africa starts at the Ebro").
Disdain curiously echoed by the famous slogan of Manuel
Fraga's 1960s Ministry of Tourism: "Spain is different."
Sun, black bulls, yellow sand of beaches and bull-rings,

cheap wine: all intoxicating for Northern Europeans. Basically, though, Spain was different because the dictatorship put in place by Hitler and Mussolini lasted till 1977. That conveniently kept wages down and made the pound, dollar and mark go further.

On June 15 2002, *El País*, Spain's leading daily paper, devoted fourteen pages to the twenty-fifth anniversary of the 1977 general elections, the first democratic elections in Spain since February 1936. The front page of this supplement featured a photograph of Adolfo Suárez, Leopoldo Calvo Sotelo and Felipe González, the three Prime Ministers before Aznar during those 25 years[1]. Above them, the head-line:

> *"Spanish democracy is 25 years old today. Its main political actors celebrated it yesterday in the main chamber of the Parliament..."*

The way millions of people lived the transition, the period from a bit before Franco's death to after the 1977 elections, is radically different from this official version. The million people marching on the national day of Catalonia, September 11 1977, the more than 20% who voted for the PSUC (Catalan Communist Party) that same year, the tens of thousands who supported far-left parties, the millions who took part in strikes and protests — these too can claim to be the *main political actors* of the transition. It is because of their struggles that the more far-sighted representatives of the dictatorship, the King, Adolfo Suárez and Manuel Fraga, opted for changes in the political system. Their slogan was the Prince's famous paradox from Lampedusa's *The Leopard*: "If we want everything to remain the same, everything has to change."

This chapter looks at two main protagonists of the conflicts of these years: the Residents' Associations and the trade union *Comissions obreres* (Workers' Commissions). In Catalonia there was a larger mass movement than in the rest of Spain, with the exception of the Basque

169

Country; and a demand for national rights which was supported by Catalans and immigrants alike.

Resisting Franco

The first major struggle in Spain after the Civil War took twelve years to ripen, and when it did, it was spectacular: the 1951 Barcelona tram boycott. In 1950 a semi-skilled textile worker had to work eight hours to buy a dozen eggs; an unskilled worker, eight hours for a kilo of bread. Hunger was rife. Rationing created a thriving black market, run by *estraperlistas*, the equivalent of London's post-war *spivs*. The desperation caused by this situation combined with two other key factors to create the conditions for the tram boycott. In 1948 the Communist Party had abandoned guerrilla struggle to concentrate on underground organisation in the work-places; and in Madrid tram fares were lower, which was perceived as clear discrimination.

In this context, the announcement in February 1951 that tram tickets were to rise by twenty *céntimos* was explosive. In the first week of March the overwhelming majority of the population refused to travel on public transport. Historian Sebastian Balfour wrote:

> *"From the early morning long processions of workers walked into the capital. Empty tram-cars, protected by armed guards and occupied by a few Francoite fanatics, circulated through the packed streets."*

In various places police baton-charged protesters. Trams were stoned or burnt. On the afternoon of Sunday March 4, the authorities laid on special free trams at the Les Corts football stadium to take home the crowds after the Barcelona - Santander match. At the climax of his *Lizard tails* (2000), Juan Marsé describes this moment when thousands sensed the boycott was not just an act of desperate resistance, but could be won:

"Despite the pouring rain, not a single person gets on any of the numerous trams... the tram charges round the bend at you on its rails, the curtain of water giving it a spiky halo. All around it is the indifferent hunched-up crowd, a sea of heads ignoring its presence, men shrinking from the dreadful weather, some of them seeking refuge under umbrellas, others using newspapers, all the rest at the mercy of the rain."

On the Tuesday, the vertical union, membership of which was compulsory for workers and management alike, convened a meeting of 2,000 work-place representatives. According to a participant cited by Balfour:

"[The provincial boss] finished by singing Cara al Sol *[Facing the Sun — the Falangist anthem] then told them to go home: 'The meeting's over'. But no-one moved from their seats. Then the real meeting began... For four hours speakers stood up, one after the other... In the end they had to be removed from the premises by the Armed Police."*

The meeting called a general strike. The next day, Wednesday 7 March, the authorities cancelled the fare rise. But the protest did not end there: the following Monday some 300,000 workers struck in protest against arrests during the boycott, and paralysed the city for three days. As a result, the Civil Governor, City Mayor, police chief and the boss of the vertical union were all sacked.

Despite the hopes raised among the opposition, the Barcelona events did not augur the collapse of the regime, just about to be bolstered by the 1952 military treaty with the USA and the subsequent arrival of Marshall Aid. It would be twenty years before the opposition could muster again such broad mass protests. Organisation was going to be a very long haul, much tougher than it seemed right after the tram fares victory.

On March 12 1956, the large engineering factories of Barcelona, such as Pegaso, La Maquinista (Count Güell's locomotive plant now a shopping mall in Sant Andreu) and Olivetti, and its major textiles plants such as Fabra y

Coats and La España Industrial came out on strike. The regime responded by the classic combination of repression (arrests, beatings and prison sentences) and concession. Two wage rises that year led to the restoration of average earnings to the purchasing power of 1936! In 1958 the Collective Bargaining Act ceded the right to elect union representatives — within of course the state-run vertical trades union. The illegal opposition, particularly the Communist Party, seized its opportunity and many members were elected as representatives. "It went against the grain to participate in these state-controlled structures," said Cipriano García, the outstanding leader of the workers' struggle in Catalonia, "but I think we were right. We had to wriggle into every crack that opened in the system." And for Armando Baró, workers' leader in the SEAT car plant in the '60s, the vertical unions "gave you a certain legal gloss that allowed you to move."

On November 20 1964, while the dictatorship was still congratulating itself on "twenty-five years of peace and plenty," 300 workers met in the church of Sant Medir in the Barcelona quarter of Sants to formally found the *Comissions Obreres* of Catalonia. This was something more than a trade union: it was "a social and political movement to coordinate workplace struggles." The four central points of the platform agreed at Sant Medir combined basic economic demands — a minimum wage for eight hours work and a sliding scale of wages to defend purchasing power — with political demands: the right to strike and freedom to organise.

The use of churches as meeting-places was particularly painful for Franco. His attempt to eradicate left-wing ideology rested on an official doctrine of a united Catholic Spain. Now left-wing young priests and Christian organisations were working alongside the godless Communists. They were even meeting in churches, which had only recently been rebuilt after their destruction by atheists in the Civil War. Sant Medir itself was one such — re-opened in the 1950s. It's worth a visit, not just to contemplate a

172

key site of the anti-Franco struggle, but because it is a strikingly ugly building. Supposedly in a style influenced by Gaudí, it is a squat brown concrete building with Dalí-like eggs stuck on top. In the 1960s, after the liberalising Vatican II, the Sant Medir parish became a beacon of liturgical and social reform: where Negro spirituals were sung, guitars used, and priests took seriously the anti-dictatorial side of Christ's teaching.

The experience of the workers' movement in Spain in those years is a powerful demonstration of how History is not a force outside ourselves, like earthquakes or rain, but can be shaped by determined collective action. *Comissions obreres* leader José Luis López Bulla (the opera-lover from Chapter One) explained to me:

> *"It hardly needs be said that the workers' movement experienced its best and greatest development in big companies... where large numbers of people coincided in space and time... Under these circumstances, people began to take part in working out demands and how to fight for them. Assemblies became the general custom, along with what I would call social-political conversation in the form of a more or less permanent bush telegraph."*

Paradoxically, more advanced forms of participatory democracy were being created under the dictatorship than in the parliamentary democracies of Western Europe.

Residents' Associations

From the mid-60s, neighbourhood committees began to be set up to support people organising at work. From 1969 these local support committees blossomed into the *Associacions de veïns* or Residents' Associations, which became in the 1970s the biggest neighbourhood movement seen in Europe since Italy at the end of World War Two. I went to visit Carles Prieto, one of the organisers of the Residents' Association in the industrial quarter of Sants. A tall, lean man in his late fifties, he received me in his office in the town-hall of El Prat, a small industrial town that gives its name to the air-port, once part of Barcelona's 'red belt'. El Prat is still run by *Iniciativa per Catalunya*, the main descendant of the shattered PSUC (Catalan Communist Party). Here Prieto heads the Delta Programme, an ambitious project to re-develop the River Llobregat delta (see Ch. 16). He explained:

> *"You must remember that the same people working in factories and involved in struggles for higher wages had housing problems, or wanted to introduce into the areas where they lived the successful ways of organising they'd experienced at work. A SEAT worker earning good wages at the end of the '60s just wasn't going to go on living in a shack without running water."*

In 1969, a new law partly legalising Associations, a wave of workplace repression and "the influence of the Paris May," in Prieto's view, helped push forward the Residents' Associations. In Sants, a group of activists obtained from the local Church (Sant Medir, again) the keys to a run-down warehouse used to store *turrons* (the Valencian nougat devoured all over Spain at Christmas) and set up their neighbourhood centre at Olzinelles 30, still the local community centre (and there is still a *turró* warehouse opposite). From these first sweet-smelling meetings, the Associations spread very quickly throughout Barcelona and its surrounding industrial cities, in both workers' and more middle-class quarters, in both traditional Catalan areas like the former villages of Sant Andreu and Horta and the new immigrant-dominated sprawls across the plain and up the hills, such as the giant Nou (here meaning Nine) barris, Verneda or Carmel. Just as the factory Committees had been built painstakingly, often by taking up very basic questions such as the conditions of the showers; so the Residents' Associations focused first on rubbish in the streets and holes in the pavement.

Also like the Workers' Committees, they did not restrict themselves to bread-and-butter issues; not just because the main movers were political activists of the left, but because even the most trivial protest about a cracked paving-stone could snowball into a clash with the dictatorship's local representatives. Rapidly, the Associations posed wider demands, challenging illegal construction on green space or road projects, and formulating alternative plans for the city. Tying all these demands together was the call for a democratic City Council.

The Mayor of Barcelona from 1957 to 1973 was José María Porcioles. Porcioles was closely linked to the Banco de Madrid, which was connected with and protected by the Franco family: one of its main share-holders was the father of Franco's son-in-law. This bank, despite its name Barcelona-based, was founded in 1954 in Porcioles' office, when he was a notary before becoming Mayor. Porcioles and his cronies so enriched themselves in the speculative development of the 1960s that a new word was coined to describe corrupt building practice: *porciolisme*.

The workers migrating into Barcelona needed housing, which was flung up round the outskirts, often without electricity or roads. This is how the Falangist playboy Juan Antonio Samaranch, later President of the International Olympic Committee, made his second fortune, constructing Ciutat Meridiana in the 1960s. So blatant was corruption under Porcioles, riding roughshod over the regime's own urban planning laws, that he was finally removed by Madrid in 1973. The Residents' Associations, with their consistent exposures of building scandals, had helped create the climate for Porcioles' fall. Carles Prieto told me:

> "Before '73-'74, it was an uphill battle. People were often reluctant to sign petitions: 'Of course we agree with you, but we can't sign,' they'd say. Fear in Franco's Spain was ubiquitous. The fall of Porcioles gave people in Barcelona confidence. In Sants we had meetings of up to 150, most of them overjoyed just to be able to speak and hear Catalan in public. Masó, the Mayor put in after Porcioles, was a good-manager type, and a lot of the excessive abuses stopped. And in 1974 we won the battle with our alternative for the

Plaça de Sants. We defeated the idea for a fly-over and we got the old tram depot, the Cotxeres, *converted to a Community Centre. There was an inaugural parade in the square; over 150 local organisations were represented and the Mayor attended. After that, the tide turned. The mass of local people openly supported us."*

By the early 1970s, there were Residents' Associations in every *barri* of the city. As in Sants, these mobilised by focusing on particular local issues: a school in Can Anglada, a health centre in Santa Coloma, transport in Carmel, etc.. Many of today's public spaces, whether community centres or parks, were won then by local mobilisation. Residents' Associations were formed too in wealthier areas. One such was the *Left Side of the Eixample* Association. In 1974 this applied for legal registration, but was turned down because the word 'Left' in its name was politically unacceptable! The anecdote shows how the fearsome dictatorship in its dotage mingled farce with tragedy.

The Barcelona Federation of Residents' Associations (FAVB) pulled together the dozens of local associations. The FAVB was a powerful voice throughout the *transition* from dictatorship to democracy, opposing speculation and putting forward their own plans for the city[2]. Proper services, green spaces, community centres, fewer roads, controlled building, were the catch-words.

The Residents' Associations and *Comissions obreres* were the major forces organising mass pressure from below. However, a specific element of the transition in Catalonia was the demand for national rights. The trades union movement, dominated by workers who had migrated from other parts of Spain to Catalonia in the 1940s, 1950s and 1960s, driven by hunger and hope, took on board the demand for a Statute of Autonomy for Catalonia. In his book *Cuando hice las maletas* (When I packed my bags), López Bulla explains the joint struggle of the autochthonous and immigrant working-class:

176

> *"Two souls in Purgatory... one settled here all its life, with ancient Catalan roots; the other, we who made up a hotch-potch of varied origins and distinct codes and who had come to Catalonia hoping for better things."*

López Bulla exclaims to a friend over a beer:

> *"— But have you realised? The number of* charnegos *like you and me shouting Long Live Catalonia! and the like. Know what? Let's hold on to this country, because we haven't got any other."*

The uniting cry in Catalonia throughout the transition was for *Llibertat, Amnistia, Estatut d'Autonomia* — Liberty, Amnesty, Statute of Autonomy, culminating in the million-strong demonstration, the biggest in Spain in all those turbulent years, on September 11 1977. The powerful unity created made Catalonia the focus of struggle throughout the Spanish state during the transition. When the famous protest singers, Serrat, Raimon, Maria del Mar Bonet or Lluís Llach, sang in Madrid in the early '70s in Catalan, they were acclaimed.

From Hope to Disenchantment

The hopes of these heady years were soon dashed. The rest of the chapter looks at the disappointment of millions who had yearned for radical change through reference to the transition novels[3] of the best interpreter of modern Catalonia, Manuel Vázquez Montalbán. In *The Angst-ridden Executive* (1977), one of Montalbán's characters explains the basic reason for this disenchantment:

> *"—There's been a change of political faces, but in the financial and industrial worlds things have hardly changed at all, and what's more, the puppy-dogs inheriting economic power are tending to assume political power too."*

After so long a struggle to defeat the dictatorship, many found things had changed in form, but not much in content.

Chapter Two touched on Vázquez Montalbán's childhood in a Raval through which Falangists roamed with impunity to beat up anyone they heard speaking in Catalan or just didn't like the look of, years of misery and poverty. A few streets down from his home near the Plaça del Padró was the red-light district, where thousands of women worked because they had no other income. In his choice to join the PSUC in 1961 and in his writing, he remained faithful to the memory of that childhood where resistance and solidarity were needed just to survive. Though an internationally famous novelist, he remained a supporter of *Iniciativa* right up to his sadly early death in October, 2003.

"Programmed for poverty," in his words, Montalbán was one of the few to escape from the Raval to university. And then, against the wishes of his father, who had been a political prisoner after the war (and like so many refused to talk politics thereafter), Montalbán became involved in the student movement for democratic rights in the late 1950s. In May 1962 he was arrested, beaten up in front of his also-arrested wife Anna by the infamous Inspector Vicente Creix in the police station on the Via Laietana, and sent to Lérida (Lleida) jail. "It was my second university," he said, the one where he received his political education. This atheist was released after fifteen months in an amnesty occasioned by Pope John XXIII's death in June 1963.

> *"It was bizarre. We all lived the death agony of John XXIII as if it was a football match on the radio... We all wanted the Pope to die because we knew it would lead to a pardon."*

In the 1960s and 1970s, Montalbán made his name as a poet and a campaigning journalist with the opposition weeklies, *Triunfo* and *Por favor*. In these final years of the decaying dictatorship, such journalists were important. In Carles Prieto's words, "we in the Residents' Associations relied on friendly journalists to always manage to say a little bit more than what was allowed." Franco finally died on November 20 1975, eleven years to the day after that crucial *Comissions Obreres* meeting in Sant Medir.

Montalbán consciously started to write crime novels in the 1970s as a way of making serious political comment in a popular format. A sophisticated student of the communications media, he understood it was not enough to be a left-winger writing in left-wing journals. He was one of several writers who helped create a new reading public in the 1970s by writing more demotically and using elements of popular culture. His explicit aim, first formulated around the time of *The Angst-ridden Executive*, was ambitious: to denounce injustice through an ongoing social chronicle of the times. There was another underlying purpose: to recover the memory obliterated by Franco, and to show how historic injustices had not been rectified. He succeeded. By his death his series of sixteen Carvalho novels had sold over one and a half million copies in Spain alone, and won prizes throughout Europe. Montalbán contributed significantly to the image of Barcelona as a place of good living, an exciting city. This was paradoxical, in that, while the Carvalho novels have become part of the city's appeal, they form a coherent assault on the way Barcelona has been pulled down and re-developed.

Montalbán's detective novels have often been likened to Raymond Chandler's. In several ways, the comparison is valid. Montalbán strips off Barcelona's mask of democracy, as Chandler does Los Angeles', and finds that the real crooks are the capitalists. Like Marlowe, Carvalho is a 'common man' who talks and understands everyday language and life. Equipped with the wisecracks and pistol required to deal with an evil urban world, yet he is a moral man walking the mean streets. However, Carvalho differs sharply from Marlowe, the driven puritan, in his enjoyment of life: sex, drink, food, the pleasure of wandering round the city (all pleasures, of course, that the city's tourists also hope to find). He is something of a Mediterranean version of Marlowe: Montalbán was provocatively challenging a certain left-wing puritanism in his creation of the sybaritic detective.

The Angst-ridden Executive, set in 1975/76, is acted out against a back-drop of street demonstrations. In this intense period, full of hopes and anxieties, different currents and classes were fighting for their views of what Spain should become. Nightly, Pepe Carvalho notes sardonically from his dingy office window, the prostitutes withdraw from the Rambles for two hours while police and oppositionists battle it out.

The plot is simple. Antonio Jauma, womaniser and Spanish representative of a multinational, is found murdered smelling of women's perfume and with knickers in his pocket. Nearly everyone jumps to the obvious conclusion: Jauma has died because of some sex intrigue. Everyone, that is, but Carvalho — and in one of the subtle shifts in perception that Montalbán enjoyed, readers find that Jauma has been killed not because he is a Don Juan (though he is) but because he is honest. He was threatening to expose the illegal financing of the far right by the multinational company he worked for. This company, formerly involved in the 1973 Chilean coup, was interested in controlling the Spanish transition. As a character in the book explains, right-wing terrorism may not eventually be needed, but the ruling class likes to cover all contingencies.

The Angst-ridden Executive is a poor translation of the title. Its awkward, even comic timbre misses the gaunt directness of the Spanish title: *La soledad del manager*, The Loneliness of the Executive. Antonio Jauma is a man made lonely by his honesty. Thus friendship, the remedy to loneliness, becomes an important strand. Friendship made, between Jauma and Carvalho, and betrayed, by Jauma's old friends. "I only believe in my stomach," Carvalho grunts early on in the book. Carvalho is a gourmet who describes recipes in loving detail. He is a connoisseur of fine wines, yet in the dramatic climax of the novel Carvalho empties onto a priceless carpet a glass of 1966 Nuits St. Georges offered him by Jauma's killer. Carvalho is often called by critics a cynic, but he is not. He is the moral man, the man of honour: much as he adores his stomach, he will not drink with a murderer. Like his author, Carvalho is sceptical, as one must be before the lies through which the powerful govern, but not cynical. Vázquez Montalbán believed in the efficacy of political action; and his Carvalho believes in solidarity with the poor.

Carvalho is strongly placed in the *Ciutat vella*. Montalbán has him wander frequently through the area, just as tourists do; but for Carvalho the landscape is a trigger for memory. Three-dimensional viewing, whereas we tourists see more one-dimensionally, noting the exotic, the striking difference. Though nowadays tourists are so numerous in Barcelona that some areas have more tourists than residents, the tourist is the real exotic. Those elderly people in the bars and on the benches of the *Ciutat vella* are wondering why the hell you're taking photos of them. Their lives feel neither exotic nor photogenic. All tourists, who come from another place just to look, without responsibility or obligations, then go away again, have something of the *voyeur*, as described by the *voleur* Genet.

Carvalho can reason and remember from what he sees, whilst the tourist can only look, wonder and photograph. These details triggering the past are from *The Angst-ridden Executive*:

> "He had a beer on Plaza Real, and pined after the long-lost tapas that used to be the speciality of the most crowded bar in the neighbourhood — squid in a spicy black pepper and nutmeg sauce..."
> "The street was shared between delivery vans and ageing prostitutes in angora wool sweaters..."
> "He returned to his office on foot, mingling with the midday crowds on the Ramblas and bathing in the innocence of the sun: students, office workers, old-age pensioners..."

At the end of his working-day in the *Ciutat vella*, Carvalho goes off home, setting up a tension between places. The *Ciutat vella* is the landscape of Carvalho's earliest memories but, like his author, he has escaped:

> *"Carvalho knew these people and their ways. They made him feel alive, and he wouldn't have changed them for the world, even though at night he preferred to flee the defeated city and make for the pinewood heights."*

Where, however, Montalbán delves deepest into the transition is in his non-Carvalho novel, *The Pianist* (1985), one of the peaks of modern Spanish literature[4]. Here he sets up a direct contrast between the two main periods of class conflict in twentieth-century Spain: the Civil War and the transition. *The Pianist* is a choral novel in three parts: the first set in the Raval in 1983, the second in the same area in 1946 and the third in Paris in 1936 during the days leading up to Franco's rising on July 18. The first part portrays a group of middle-class *barcelonins* in their thirties. They are meeting up for an evening out ten years after their friendships were forged at university in struggle against the dictatorship. It is a disastrous evening, for the group is breaking up as each follows his/her separate path or career. Montalbán contrasts their disorientation with the solidarity of the neighbours in the Raval after the Civil War, in the richly lyrical second part. This takes place on the roof-tops, a *Rambles* in the sky, the only partly free space in the occupied city. The fascination with which the 1940s young listen to people's memories, to history, contrasts sharply with the world-weary scepticism of the 1980s friends. Though in the 1940s, the residents of the Raval "carry the post-war on their backs like a corpse," they show the elementary solidarity that the 1983 group, living in the same area of the Raval forty years on, has lost.

The Pianist is an elegiac tribute to the defeated side in the Civil War, but it is more than that. *The Pianist* of the title is an old revolutionary, Albert Rosell, in the 1980s playing the piano for drag acts in a night-club frequented by the new Socialist satraps of Spain. Over seventy years old, Rosell lives in poverty caring for his invalid wife. The hopes of the 1936 Revolution described in the third part of the novel have been totally destroyed. The isolation of Rosell is thrown into sharp relief by the failure of the 1983 group, the former leftists who should have been Rosell's heirs, to establish any connection with him or the struggle he lost. Rosell, through his love for Teresa and his unwavering commitment to a better world, becomes the ethical reference of the novel, while the socialists and Doria, a Dalí-like scoundrel, charge without the burden of memory into the future. The 1939 victory of Franco is effectively repeated in 1983 by the silencing of the past.

Montalbán's is a profoundly pessimistic view: a not illogical response to two major defeats such as the Civil War and the transition. At the same time, his pessimism of the mind does not affect his optimism of the spirit. He does not cede in his excoriation of the powerful and the struggle to recover historical memory, as a precondition of building a better future.

Bitter-Sweet

The Carvalho books are attractive companions for cultural tourists, who are often well-attuned to the conventions of detective fiction and keen to tramp the city pavements. Montalbán offers a dialectic of nostalgia and rage, of pleasure in the city and anger at how it is. Later I will return to this social chronicle of Barcelona to illuminate the time elapsed between the transition and the Olympics.

The importance Montalbán placed on recovering memory is not an individual quirk. Many other fine Barcelona novelists of Montalbán's generation, such as Víctor Mora, brought up like him in the *Ciutat vella*, or Juan Marsé from outlying Guinardó, concentrated on recording the lives of those defeated in the Civil War. Conserving the memory of a rapidly vanishing past is a common concern everywhere at this time of accelerating global change. In Spain, recovery of officially forgotten history has a particular urgency because the dictatorship ruined so many lives. Then, in the transition, politicians took advantage of people's longing for peace to sweep the dictatorship under the carpet.

It is only now, a generation after the transition, that the media are beginning to acknowledge the sufferings of millions under Franco. A number of books about the repression have been published. The popular radio journalist Iñaki Gabilondo collected and broadcast numerous testimonies in 2001-2002. Aged relatives have called for mass graves to be opened. Fear is lifting 25 years after the end of the dictatorship. Popular pressure and the threat that the same United Nations teams that had investigated massacres and mass graves in Kosovo might intervene in Spain even pushed the Conservative Government to condemn Franco for the first time, on November 20 2002. Better late than never. In Germany and France, conservative parties condemned the Third Reich and Vichy in the 1940s.

In Spain, cases such as that of Pilar Vaquerizo, widow of Joaquín Delgado an anarchist executed in 1963 for a crime he did not commit, are still not uncommon. In 1998 the Supreme Court ruled, as is standard in these cases, against a review of Delgado's case because the verdict was given "in line with the legislation then in force." Nor can Pilar receive the compensation paid to political prisoners and their families because her husband was not in prison long enough. He was executed too quickly. Ironically, she receives a small pension from the French state for being "widow of a political victim of Francoism." The Spanish authorities have still a long way to go, but at least now much of society, traumatised too long, is beginning to move. The election of the Socialist Party Government in March 2004 has helped along this process.

In the pact between the Communist Party and the *ancien régime* that lies at the heart of the Spanish transition, a deal was done to forget the past. The Communists were legalised and their leaders obtained parliamentary seats and mayoral chairs. In exchange, torturers such as Vicente Creix were not tried or even sacked. Officials of the dictatorship continued in their posts. The Communists, who had been courageous fighters against the dictatorship, now argued for the pact with the dictatorship's heirs. This was as terrible a blow to the Communist Party rank-and-file as the 1939 Hitler-Stalin pact. Ana Briongos, the Communist worker in the SEAT car factory in Montalbán's novel *Southern Seas*, explains bitterly to Carvalho:

> *"No-one swallowed this pact and we, with all the good faith we were capable of, had to go out and defend it... that in the long run it benefited the working-class, in short, we said what they had told us to say. Afterwards, it became clear it was a swindle, like all the rest."*

This pact, known as the Moncloa Pact (December 1977), in which all partes agreed wage restraint, tore the Communists apart to the delight of the Socialist Party and the US State Department (the theme of *Murder in the Central Committee*, another of Montalbán's Carvalho transition novels), leading to the PSUC's collapse in 1981 and reducing the Communist Party to only four parliamentary seats in Spain at the 1982 elections. *Southern Seas'* description of the transition's effect on worker militants parallels *The Pianist's* later evocation of its impact on university militants.

Montalbán's view of the transition as betrayal leading to subsequent disenchantment is not the establishment's view. Nor does the eminent British historian, Paul Preston, agree with Montalbán. Here, acting as political commentator rather than historian, Preston told *Catalonia Today* in 2005:

> *"Although some people nowadays claim it was a scandal that a 'pact of forgetting' occurred, I think it was absolutely necessary... Some way had to be found of calming the likely*

backlash from Franco supporters who would be outraged by any movement towards democracy."

The transition driven from below was settled from above. Change is impossible, we are told today. There is only one world order possible, that of multinational-led globalisation. The history of the mass movements of the transition suggests that another Spain was possible. Much of the bitter-sweetness of Montalbán's novels comes from his pleasure in post-Franco Barcelona ("All said and done," he told me in an interview, "for those of us with money, it's a pretty good place to live"), underlain with his melancholy that no better deal for the moneyless majority came out of the transition.

---

[1] *Suárez was Prime Minister from 1977 to 1981; Calvo Sotelo, in 1981 and 1982; González, from 1982 to 1996; and José María Aznar, from 1996 to 2004.*

[2] *The FAVB still thrives today and publishes an excellent monthly journal denouncing speculation and corruption,* La veu del Carrer *(Voice of the Street). Available free from any Community Centre or Obradors 8, in the* Ciutat vella.

[3] The Angst-ridden Executive *(1977),* Southern Seas *(1979),* The Pianist *(1985).*

[4] *This assertion is designed to stimulate some enterprising publisher to re-issue in English Vázquez Montalbán's greatest novel.*

FRANCE

Argelès-sur-Mer

ANDORRA

CATALONIA

ARAGON

Blanes

Mataró

RIVER EBRO

BARCELONA

TERUEL

RINCÓN DE ADEMUZ

BALEARIC ISLANDS

VALENCIA

VALENCIA

CATALAN-SPEAKING
LANDS

Chapter 10
Your Own House

"Like those cities of the Orient that are surrounded by hungry dogs trying to get inside the city walls, Barcelona is under constant threat of invasion by an army of parasites."
JOSEP PLA, *BARCELONA*.

Harsh Land

The *Rincón de Ademuz* belongs to the province of Valencia, but is an enclave surrounded by Aragon and Castile. I am spending the summer in a village at about 1300 metres — the height of Ben Nevis. "This is a harsh land," Señor Aurelio tells me, "and it breeds tough people." His own gentleness belies his comment, as we walk uphill towards a plot of almond trees. He carries on his shoulder his *azada*, a mattock that you bring down with the swing of an axe into hard earth. He moves in a steady loping step. He wears faded blue overalls and *alpargatas*, rope-soled shoes. He has a full head of wavy white hair. His thick-lensed glasses are bound at one joint with selotape. I offer to carry his *azada*. "My spade is like a soldier's rifle," he smiles. "I never put it down." In truth he should carry mine. Aurelio is eighty years old and much stronger than me, half his age. When we work together digging or cutting wood, his rhythm has me sweating and gasping within five minutes. He quite likes that and smiles with friendly malice while his *azada* rhythmically rises and strikes.

This is a harsh land. The English are accustomed to see land dressed; even hills are covered demurely by trees and grass. Naked rock is a shock. "Spain changed my life," V.S. Pritchett wrote. "Here one could see the bare flesh and bone of the earth." When you drive across central Spain, wave after wave of bare eroded hills roll down towards the main roads. But the hills are not so empty as they seem at first: in among them lie hidden valleys, with orchards, fields, streams lined by poplars and villages like the one I am visiting. Nor are the naked and pitted hill-sides quite so bare. They sprout hardy bushes of brambles, lavender, spicy savory, wild rose, thyme and gorse, all of which the tough-mouthed sheep chew.

It's not just a harsh land to look at, it's harsh to live off. The soil is thin; the corn it produces is not tall or abundant. Though its hills are not empty, the *Rincón* is still losing population, as it has for the last fifty years. Of the 300 people in Señor Aurelio's village immediately after the Civil War, there were no more than twenty left by 1992, when I first visited. By 2006 eleven remained. As we climb the hill, the effects of mechanisation and emigration become more visible. The old foot-paths have been widened for tractors and combine harvesters: the dry-stone walls have fallen and the dividing banks between the small plots are clotted with weeds. The strips of land formerly cultivated on the most inaccessible points of the hill-side have given way to flocks of EU-subsidised sheep. This abandon pains and infuriates Aurelio, who stops and sweeps the hills with a gesture: "*Me cago en...* Before, every single plot was cultivated and every path was carefully maintained. But now, there's no-one to do the work..."

As the *Rincón de Ademuz* belongs to Valencia, it is formally part of what Catalans call the *Països catalans*, the greater historical-linguistic area where Catalan and its associated dialects are spoken. However, the *Rincón* has much more in common with Aragon than plump fertile coastal Valencia. The *Rincón*'s closest provincial capital is Spain's smallest, the beautiful Mudejar Aragonese city of Teruel[1]; its original settlers came from Aragon in the thirteenth century when the Moors were driven out.

In 1926, the year Gaudí died, Aurelio aged 14 set out after the harvest to walk from his village, the only world he had known, to Barcelona. It was a journey out of a barter economy into the world of money. His mother pre-pared him some food wrapped in a cloth. He walked the more direct mule-tracks along the ridges rather than the newer roads in the valleys. He slept in the tick-ridden, dung-strewn *corrales*, shelters for confining sheep during a night far from home or at mid-day while the shepherd slept. His food lasted three days and then he stole fruit. An owner of an orchard threatened him with oaths backed by a shot-gun. A farmer invited him to eat one evening. In a week he reached Barcelona.

That first winter in the city Aurelio worked in a *granja*, a dairy with its own cows, just below the Park Güell. He slept on straw in the loft above the cows. Though there were no cows in the *Rincón*, he learned quickly to milk them. He also swept out the byre, replaced the straw and delivered the milk round Gràcia from churns on a horse-drawn wagon. One day, one of the rare cars in the neighbourhood sped round a corner and knocked over his cart, spilling the milk down the hill. Despite his fears he would be blamed, his boss supported him. Aurelio told me: "He took my side because he knew I was a good worker."

By March he was back in the village for ploughing and sowing. He worked on the land throughout the spring and summer before returning to Barcelona in the autumn. Now he travelled by a combination of bus and train, using money saved from his winter wages. Work was easy to obtain in the late 1920s. Aurelio worked one winter on the Gran Via, being resurfaced near the Plaça de Espanya for the 1929 International Exhibition. Another year he worked on the building of the underground.

He continued the pattern of summer on the land and winter in a factory or on a building-site throughout the '30s until the Civil War. Conscripted into the Republican Army, Aurelio fought on the Ebro front in 1938 and saw a man shot dead beside him while a bullet grazed his own neck. He showed me the near-fatal mark, no more now than the sort of white scar on your knee from falling over as a child. When he fired he shut his eyes because he

190

didn't want to risk killing anyone from his village. The *Rincón* was a frontier zone, as it had always been in wars, and relatives and people he knew had been conscripted into Franco's armies. On the Ebro he fought alongside the International Brigades and told me that the Swedes were terrible, they squeezed the unripe grapes to try to get drunk. His daughter explained later that he had always told that story, but saying it was the English. He had changed their nationality out of politeness to me.

In the chaotic Ebro retreat he crossed the wide river, though he had never swum before, and ended up in Barcelona. He continued with the remnants of the Army, riding to Blanes on a lorry and when the petrol ran out walking to the French border. Two months later, when Franco's envoys came to the refugee camps on the freezing beaches at Argelès in France to say that all Republican soldiers who were not members of political parties could return to Spain without fear of reprisal, he believed them. On his return, he was at once imprisoned while being investigated. He got out after a couple of months and made his way back to the *Rincón*.

After the Civil War, the subsistence economy of smallholdings in which Aurelio had grown up broke down. Hunger flayed Spain, and the huge emigration to the cities began. Aurelio married in 1945 and once again lived in Barcelona in the winter. He and his wife sub-let a room in the rented flat of his brother's family. He worked every hour he could: tanneries, building-sites, factories. Often he did additional work at week-ends: gardening, building. In the Spring the couple returned to care for his in-laws' land now, rather than his own parents'.

> *"For myself, I would have stayed here in the village. I like it here. It's peaceful and I've always enjoyed working the land. But it was no place to bring up children."*

They moved to Barcelona permanently, where by his retirement in 1980 they had brought up three children and managed to buy two flats. When he retired, he went back to the pattern of his youth: returning to the village for the planting, growing and harvesting seasons and spending the winters in the city. They did up the house in the village. The bare threshing-floor in front of the house was turned into a lush garden.

Land of Welcome

Between 1945 and 1970, about one and a half million people from other parts of Spain came, like Aurelio and most of his village, to live in Catalonia, the great majority in the Metropolitan area of Barcelona. Today about 45% of Catalonia's seven-million population are fruit of this immigration.

The first wave of workers to work in Barcelona's nineteenth-century industry came from rural Catalonia itself. Jobs in the city beckoned. The phylloxera plague that devastated grape-vines pushed country-people out, as did the *hereu* system, which meant that land was inherited whole by the eldest son instead of being sub-divided into greater and greater poverty, as happened in Galicia. Onofre Bouvila, in Eduardo Mendoza's *City of Marvels*, was one of these immigrants who fled "the rural, sombre and brutal Catalonia", to work on the Universal Exhibition in the great spending spree of the 1880s.

The twentieth century, up to about 1970, saw immigration from other zones of Spain, especially post-1939 landless labourers fleeing famine in Murcia, Andalucía and Extremadura. After 1975 a smaller, but important, influx from other continents began: Latin Americans and in the '90s Africans. In the last decade of the twentieth century and the first five years of the twenty-first, this new immigration added three million people to Spain as a whole, while the native-born population hardly increased in that period. Perhaps a third of these have ended up in Catalonia. It is common now to see the features of the Andes on the streets of Barcelona.

Ex-President Jordi Pujol argues that Catalonia has always been a *terra d'acolliment*, a land of welcome.

Indeed this was the title of a 2001 exhibition in Madrid designed to explain Catalonia to the rest of Spain "in its reality and in its dreams." At the exhibition's opening ceremony, before the King and Queen, Pujol explained that Catalonia had been for decades "a land that welcomes people from other lands... yet without its own identity being fractured."

You often hear it said by Catalans that Catalonia is a *land of welcome*. They differentiate themselves from the Basques, a people whose roots are lost in pre-history, whose pre-Romance language is as impenetrable as the Basque country's deep valleys and whose nationalist ideology has often been based on a flight from modernity into an idealised rural past. Catalans like to be Spain's 'good nationalists,' not the bad ones like the Basques. It was not always so, of course: it was Catalans who were known as bomb-throwing anarchists a hundred years ago. For Catalans, their language is their distinguishing feature and their nationalism has signified an embrace of modernity. Thus, runs the orthodox view, second-generation immigrants, duly welcomed, learn Catalan and themselves become Catalans.

Francesc de Carreras, a Law Professor at Barcelona's Autonomous University and an anti-nationalist, asked rhetorically:

> "The question is... what is the authentic reality of Catalonia: are we a land of welcome or simply a land of immigration?... Are we a society that needs cheap labour power and, in accord with the laws of the market, finds it?"

A journalist friend, who I had always supposed was Catalan because he speaks and writes habitually in Catalan and has a Catalan fore-name, is the son of immigrants from Málaga. He exploded in response to Carreras' question:

> "Land of welcome! This really pisses me off. My parents came here and set to work like slaves. They, we two children, my father's brother and his two daughters lived

193

in a flat measuring 49 square metres. You know, my
father used to say — 'Sure, there was plenty of work
about, but money was another question'."

Pujol's line of Catalonia as a land of welcome takes no
account of the harsh reality of twelve hours work a day
under a dictatorship, poor housing, poor nutrition.
Francesc de Carreras answers his own question:

*"This mystic entity 'Catalonia' does not exist... There are
racist and non-racist Catalans, there are villains who
exploit misery and misfortune, and there are others who
try to help others in difficulties. We're a normal country...,
not a homogeneous whole."*

The arrival *en masse* of immigrants after the Civil War
meant that ghettos formed where Catalan was hardly spoken. Immigrants entered a Barcelona whose native Catalan
was banned by the regime and whose residents could all
speak Spanish. It was hardly surprising that most of them
did not learn to speak Catalan. Imagine a Somali emigrant
arriving in London and finding that English was prohibited
and nearly all Londoners knew how to speak Somali!

It was in the struggles of the 1960s that a certain unity
between Catalans and immigrants was forged, as the
quote from López Bulla in the preceding chapter shows.
Views of course were not uniform: it was common for
immigrants to the new ghettos to only know Catalans who
were bosses or shop-keepers, and so feel either hostile to
them as exploiters or resentful of them because they had
more. Common, too, to argue that we were in Spain anyway, so why couldn't everyone just speak Spanish and
understand each other. There was an area of L'Hospitalet
called La Torrassa that reputedly put up a sign after the
Civil War:

"Catalonia ends here. Here starts Murcia."

The reverse feeling was common, too: people felt exces-
sively grateful to the Catalonia that had put food in their

mouths and educated their children. Many of these immigrants, coming from a rural pre-industrial world, identify with Catalonia because it has signified their entry into modern urban life. No longer washing clothes in a stream, but with washing-machines; no longer going to bed at dusk, but having electric light.

Immigration meant the clash of two worlds. From the starving bare-foot towns of Andalucía in the 1940s and '50s, Catalonia seemed fabulously wealthy. *Dogs in Catalonia*, it was said in a famous catch-phrase, *are tied up with pork sausages*. The only Catalans the Andalusían poor might have known were traders or bosses talking in a language they couldn't understand. When the young López Bulla reached Mataró in 1965, a light-bulb lit up in his mind. "This language is for real," he said to himself. Speaking Catalan wasn't just a trick bosses used so that workers couldn't understand what they were saying. What's more, not just bosses, but poor people used it, too. On first arrival in Catalonia, López Bulla was amazed at a place where people walked quickly through the streets, ate meat, wore wrist-watches, and put on shoes not just on Sundays but every day. In López Bulla's home town of Santafé in Granada province, people hung around the main square all day doing nothing, waiting to see if the local estate boss might come by looking for casual labourers, whereas through Mataró's Plaza de Santa Ana people strode briskly about their business. Everyone had something to do.

Languages

By the time Franco died, the Catalan language was in deep crisis. More than half Catalonia's population had Castilian Spanish as their first language and for nearly forty years no-one had studied Catalan at school. Thus many Catalans spoke their own language but were functionally illiterate in it. If they read books or newspapers, they found it easier to read in Castilian. After 1980, the Generalitat introduced a programme of *normalització lingüística,*

195

linguistic normalisation, a process which commanded widespread consensus among nearly all sectors of the population of Catalonia. This consensus was helped along by the Generalitat's non-exclusive approach, expressed by Pujol's famous *Everyone who lives and works in Catalonia is Catalan*.

All government, administration and official business was to be conducted in Catalan. Street-names were changed, shop signs in Catalan were subsidised, restaurant menus, film tickets, adverts, leaflets were all written in Catalan. Most importantly, the education system was changed so that children were not just taught Catalan, but taught all subjects *in* Catalan. A newspaper in Catalan *Avui* (Today) was supported; radio stations and two television channels, TV3 and Canal 33, were launched. By the year 2000, roughly 90% of Catalonia's inhabitants claimed to understand Catalan, whilst some 64% could speak it. Given the figure of 44% native speakers, 64% is a significant figure. It means a large number of immigrants and children of immigrants have learned Catalan. Some of these learned Catalan during the transition as an act of solidarity; others learned it as a way of fleeing a backward past; most perhaps learned it for work purposes. In the smaller towns of Catalonia, children of immigrants learned Catalan naturally because there it was dominant.

These optimistic figures imply that the use of Catalan is extending and that the future of the language is secure. This is the view of John Hooper, the former *Guardian* correspondent in Madrid, whose *The New Spaniards* is an excellent general survey of 1990s Spain:

> *"It is certainly not difficult to imagine that within, say, a quarter of a century Castilian in Catalonia could occupy a position rather like English in Scandinavia — a second language which people are able to speak exceptionally well, but a second language nevertheless."*

The novelist Matthew Tree, in his witty travel book *CAT*, is also optimistic. He started his journey round Catalonia *to find out whether it really existed* in l'Hospitalet (where the famous notice was put up), now a working-class overwhelmingly immigrant city of 250,000 people adjoining Barcelona. There people tell him:

"— We feel just as Catalan as anyone else, we change the language we speak at the drop of a hat, you can use Catalan with anyone in l'Hospitalet, everyone understands it... All us children of the immigration know how to speak Catalan."

I went to check out the state of Catalan with linguist Pere Comellas of the University of Barcelona. His diagnosis of the chances of survival of Catalan was much more pessimistic. He pointed to the steady loss of minority languages under the impact of globalisation, the strength of Castilian as a world language, the difficulty of a language without a nation-state, the continuing preference of Catalans for reading in Castilian, and the minority presence of Catalan in TV programmes watched in Catalonia.

"Nearly all linguists think that Catalan is doomed to extinction unless a miracle occurs: that the children of immigrants in Barcelona start speaking to each other in Catalan... Our days as a linguistic community are numbered. What luck you have, that your mother tongue is English!"

The miracle does not seem likely (but there again, miracles by definition never do), for the Catalan school system is itself in deep crisis today. 2004 figures put the school failure rate at 34%, one of the highest in the EU; and education spending is 3.26% of GNP, lower than in Spain as a whole and way below the EU average. Private education accounts for 42% of education (60% in the city of Barcelona), the highest figure in any region of Europe, and is generally subsidised by the state. Increasingly the state system is becoming the preserve of children of new and old immigrants. Within these schools, despite years of schooling in Catalan, students continue to talk the language of their homes.

Does it matter?

"I would argue," says Pere Comellas, *"that it does matter. The steady elimination of languages is like the elimination of species: it leads to less variety, less precision in the world. When they lose their local language, people lose their ability to express themselves so clearly."*

Juan Marsé wrote a rather bitter satire on linguistic normalisation: his 1990 novel *El amante bilingüe,* The bilingual lover. Here nearly everyone is schizophrenic, most obviously Marsé's near-eponymous protagonist Juan Marés, a Catalan who adopts the personality of an Andalusian to win back his lost love, Norma. She works for the Generalitat's campaign for linguistic normalisation. Every local reader will have recalled the cartoon character Norma, used in the early '80s on posters and stickers to insist *El català, cosa de tots* (Catalan is everyone's business). Norma, the normaliser, in the novel is also schizophrenic. While her job is to promote Catalan in all respects, she continuously hunts for sex with non-Catalan immigrants. Indeed, if your job is to promote Catalan, it's clear you are going to spend your time with non-Catalans. Marsé revels in double meanings: the word *lengua* tongue, for example, is the language you speak and an organ used in sex. As in language, so in sex, the two linguistic communities need each other.

The satire has a serious purpose. For Marsé, Catalonia is dependent on the input of immigrants, just as Norma's job and sex-life is. To deny their influence on Catalonia is to deny a major part of its history, personality and identity.

Marsé's novel is a sharp attack on the pomposities and linguistic correctness of the Catalan political establishment. He is also a signatory of the *Foro Babel*, a manifesto opposed to legislation in favour of Catalan and calling for bilingualism. Pere Comellas explained the opposing viewpoint:

"The problem is that nearly everyone wants bilingualism, but Catalan speakers are always bilingual, whereas Castilian speakers aren't always. And where Catalan has not been legislated for, such as in Valencia and the Balearics, its use has declined. In fact, the battle for Catalan has already been lost in those two communities."

Murcians and Africans

Many remember the waiter Manuel in the oft-repeated 1980s sit-com *Fawlty Towers*. The traumatised Manuel, frequent butt of John Cleese's rage and victim of his incompetence, would say in strongly accented English: "Yays, ee yam from Barcelona." A Spanish waiter in Torquay is far more likely to be from Galicia, but Ourense doesn't have quite the ring of Barcelona. Great comedy though *Fawlty Towers* is, the image of the foreign dumb waiter is a painful stereotype. It certainly wouldn't do when *Fawlty Towers* was dubbed into Catalan. TV3 had Manuel saying instead: "I am from Murcia." In symbiosis with the fiercely protective gesture of the inhabitants of La Torrassa putting up their notice *Murcia starts here*, Catalans have often looked down their noses at Murcians. "Murcians all belong to the FAI," was a common tag in the 1920s. The FAI was the Iberian Anarchist Federation, and needless to say not all Murcians were anarchists, though some may have joined up when they heard what some Catalans said about them. The comment reflected racist fear of the darker-skinned Southerner. For canny peasant Josep Pla (1897-1981), the revered official writer of deep Catalonia, Southerners were *hungry dogs... threatening invasion*.

No longer so. Now the 'threat' is from black immigrants. In 1992 it was rare to see a black face on the streets of Barcelona. Many Spaniards would happily boast of their open non-racist society, forgetting the Gypsies. And forgetting that if there was little prejudice against Jews and Arabs, that was because there were very few around. They'd been kicked out 500 years before. The absence of black people was an aspect of Barcelona that made it seem extraordinarily provincial in comparison with Paris or London. Spaniards who went to London would nearly always remark on their amazement at seeing, not just a few blacks as door-men of hotels or selling trinkets in the streets, but black people as bus drivers, museum officials or bank workers. The reason was simple: Spain as a whole has been too poor a country to attract foreign immigration until very recently. Indeed, the waves of migration that filled Barcelona were only part of a more general emigration that took hundreds of thousands of Spaniards to Germany, Holland, France and other European countries in the 1950s and '60s. According to Juan Goytisolo, the Parisian upper class in the 1950s hired Spanish maids ("so clean") and the word for a maid is still today, when Spanish maids have been replaced by Moroccans, *une espagnole*:

> "Where does your espagnole come from?"
> "Morocco."

Africans, whether Moroccans or from countries South of the Sahara, have not had an easy time of it in Spain. Papers are hard to come by and jobs insecure and ill-paid. In January 2001 around 700 Africans in danger of deportation occupied eight churches in Barcelona (including Sant Medir) to protest against restrictive new immigration legislation. Many of them embarked on a hunger strike. In response, thousands of *barcelonins* contributed practical solidarity: money, blankets, food and water.

The reply from official Catalonia was not so generous: ex-President of the Catalan Parliament, Heribert Barrera, thundered that "immigration endangered the survival of Catalonia" and praised the Austrian ultra-rightist Jorg Haider. What was worse than this 83-year old's views was that his party, the party of Macià and Companys, the ERC, did not expel him. The Barrera controversy followed hot on the heels of racist statements from Artur Mas,

Convergència's candidate to succeed Pujol at the 2003 elections. Mas said he agreed with Marta Ferrusola, Pujol's wife, who spoke out against the building of mosques, warning that immigrants sought to impose their religious and cultural practices on Catalonia. Ferrusola's view must also have permeated Barcelona's Socialist Council, who refused permission for the building of a new mosque – extraordinary, when Paris, London or Madrid have mosques as a matter of course.

The fear of *murcianos* fifty years ago is easily transferred to fear of Arabs and Africans today. Perhaps pointless to remark that Catalans themselves have often been emigrants, and that the very same people who have parts of their family living in France or Argentina and whose heart-strings are torn by Verdaguer's famous song *L'emigrant* reject these new immigrants.

In the summer of 2001 about seventy black Africans slept rough in the Plaça de Catalunya under the trees opposite the *Corte inglés*. They had no legal papers, no housing, no work and no sanitary or washing facilities. For several weeks different authorities blamed each other for the situation. The Socialist Council did nothing. Everyone hoped the squatters would just disappear as mysteriously as they had appeared. The presence of these young black men at the heart of the tourist city was like a crack in the walls of the museum through which the slum street can be glimpsed. Finally the Council had the police expel them from the Plaça de Catalunya to a less visible square, and then arrest them. In June 2004, during the Forum of Cultures, two of whose three themes were "Multiculturalism" and "Creating conditions for Peace", over a thousand immigrants occupied the cathedral in protest against restrictive immigration laws. Mayor Joan Clos agreed to the police kicking them out. Though Clos is an anaesthetist by profession, fine words on multi-culturalism from his Socialist City Council and on "land of welcome" from the nationalist *Convergència* are unlikely to put protest to sleep[2].

In 1994 Señor Aurelio died in a car accident on the long emigrants' journey he had made almost every year from 1926 between the *Rincón de Ademuz* and Barcelona. A few days before his death, I asked him how he was. He grinned a broad smile, his eyes crinkling with vitality, and he replied *Inmejorable*, Never better. He wasn't a person to complain about what, by any objective reckoning, was a tough life: leaving school at eleven, walking to Barcelona at fourteen, working from before dawn to after dusk, wounded in the war, brief exile and imprisonment, factory work, emigration. He was clear about the cost of migration, even though he had willingly migrated, an ambivalence common to nearly all who have gone on that to-and-fro journey. He told us one day:

> *"Try to have your own house. It's very difficult to live in other people's houses."*

Land of immigration, but not land of welcome.

---

[1] *A Mudejar was a Moor living in Spain under Christian rule. The word is applied to a style of Moorish art produced under the Christians.*

[2] *See too the comments on the murder of Wilson Pacheco in Chapter Sixteen.*

Part 3

Re-inventing
Modern Barcelona

Chapter 11
More Than a Club

"Barça, the football club was ...founded at the turn of the century, and quickly became a crucial factor in the city's culture, a vehicle for integrating the new immigrant workers into the life of Barcelona. In times of political difficulty it took on all the force of a political party, an unarmed army. Its victories were political victories, its games mass meetings."
COLM TÓIBÍN *HOMAGE TO BARCELONA.*

The President Núñez Museum

Barça és més que un club — Barça is more than a club. This proud cry, which became a cliché down the years, described not just that FC Barcelona is the football club with the largest membership (some 106,000) and stadium (98,000 capacity, all seated) in Europe, but that the club transcends sport. It is so weighty an institution that people joke in Catalonia: who's more powerful — the President of *Barça* or the President of the Generalitat? Federico Mayor Zaragoza, former secretary-general of UNESCO, wrote in the more-than-a-club's official centenary commemoration book: "The role of FC Barcelona at the heart of Catalan society goes far beyond sporting boundaries. *Barça* is an instrument of the cohesion of Catalonia."

Quite a statement about a sports club. Zaragoza is referring to how FC Barcelona is not only identified by Catalans as representative of Catalan national rights, but has won the support of the *other Catalans*, the emigrants from other parts of Spain discussed in the last chapter. This year, as every year, in the local derbies between FC Barcelona and Espanyol, the city's two First Division

205

clubs, you could hear people screaming obscenities round the theme of "anti-catalan" at the few Espanyol supporters who venture to the Camp Nou. Espanyol, which only recently changed its name to the Catalan spelling from the Spanish *Español*, is traditionally the club of centralists, those who see themselves as Spanish rather than Catalan. What is interesting in these ritual exchanges is that many *Barça* supporters are screaming their insults in Castilian: they themselves are from immigrant families, and their identification with *Barça* is a vital part of their integration into Catalonia.

Barça inspires almost as much hyperbole as the saintly Gaudí. If Zaragoza's claim seems exaggerated, try the following comments for size. City historian-journalist Lluís Permanyer in a recent guide-book:

> *"...it has played a surprising political role, championing Catalan nationalism and liberty; it is the city's army, opera and ballet all in one and all Barcelona celebrates with its victories and weeps with its defeats."*

Or Vázquez Montalbán: the "epic weapon of a country without a state or an army."

A pre-Olympic purple passage comes from the normally understated Colm Tóibín's *Homage to Barcelona*:

> *"Barça, the richest football club in the world, was the most potent symbol of the city's greatness and of Catalonia's destiny... And when it won, then the whole of Catalonia, its great traditions, its glorious future, would win as well, would shine like a light."*

You approach the FC Barcelona President Núñez Museum across a springy wooden walk-way over a car-park to the monstrous and now slightly old-fashioned sports stadium. Among the old posters, replicas of trophies, programmes, photos of stars, magazines, books on football, auctioned-off pieces of Wembley stadium and laced leather balls on exhibit inside the museum, there is a scrap of paper bearing notes in the hand of Antoni Tàpies, Catalonia's most famous living painter. He had jotted these down after a meeting with club executives about the 1999 centenary poster, which he had been commissioned to design. Tàpies noted the four required themes: a football boot, 100 years, the club's connection with the city of Barcelona and: "In some way [the poster] has to combine Barça and Catalanism." Tàpies was instructed to make the explicit political point that Barça was Catalanist. The wits commented that Tàpies had finally made a boot to go with the notorious twenty-metre holed white sock he proposed in 1992 for the National Museum of Catalan Art (MNAC).

The museum at the Camp Nou is the most visited in Barcelona. This could mean that Núñez, boss of a huge building firm and President of FC Barcelona from 1979 to 2000, is more popular than Picasso, whose museum comes in a close second. It could well be taken as evidence of the club's undoubtedly profound roots in Catalan society. In fact, though, the museum on a normal working day is packed with the British.

The car-park on an off-season Thursday in May held half-a-dozen coaches, including one from Bolton. These are not the cultural tourists on their long week-end breaks, but the beach tourists who come for a fortnight to Lloret or Calella on charter flights or the long haul down the French motorways. The cultural tourists come too, for the tourist bus stops here in between visits to Gaudí buildings.

The museum's success means it is to be expanded and re-vamped. The re-design will feature an Art section alongside the History section. Joan Miró designed the 75th anniversary poster. Dalí will also be featured in the museum. FC Barcelona, conscious of its position as standard-bearer of Catalonia, takes itself very seriously and is fully attuned to the marketing properties of fine art. "We are a city of art and culture," insisted Núñez's successor Joan Gaspart, just in case anyone had missed the point.

That is why the design of the poster makes both the Catalan and the Barcelona city connections, and employs Catalonia's most famous living artist. To the match spectator or museum visitor all these associations — art, football, the city of Barcelona, Catalan identity — seem natural and seamless. Tàpies' scrawled reminder to himself shows how carefully they are manufactured. "Football," wrote journalist Margarita Rivière, "is a factory of feelings and goals. In that order."

How did this football club, founded 100 years ago by a Swiss, Hans (or Joan, to which his name has been catalanised) Gamper, come to represent Catalan aspirations? The following story from its early years tells a lot. In 1925, during the dictatorship of Primo de Rivera, a band from a visiting English ship was invited to play before a match. It appears that the English musicians were listened to with respect until they played the Spanish national anthem, at which point sections of the crowd hissed. For this crime, and for referring to the Spanish championship, which Barcelona had just won, as the peninsular championship, Milans del Bosch, Military Governor of Barcelona, closed the ground for six months and obliged the founder-President Gamper to resign. When representations were made in Madrid, Catalan folklore has it that the appropriate Minister said: "Sooner ask me to pardon a man condemned to death than reopen Barcelona Football Club."

In the 1920s, the "Havana cigar smokers of the conservative Catalan League in the stands and the anarchist *caliqueño* smokers on the terraces" (Vázquez Montalbán), industrialists and syndicalists who were engaged in the factories and streets in a struggle often waged pistol in hand, sat in the same ground and cheered the same team. This muting of social conflict has, of course, always been a function of sport. In Catalonia it took on an extra twist, because of the loathing felt by both conservative nationalist bosses and anarchist workers for the Madrid Government.

At the end of the Civil War, fourteen years after the club's closure under Primo de Rivera, *Barça* had only 3,500 members left, its President Josep Sunyol had been shot by Francoist soldiers when his car strayed across enemy lines near Guadalajara, its offices had been destroyed (March 16, 1938) by an Italian bomb, and its team was scattered over Europe and America. As the club was one of the institutions identified with the sin of separatism (for Franco all Catalan nationalists were separatists), there was real doubt whether it would be allowed to survive. But it did, and in its rebirth, despite the imposition of Government nominees as Presidents and of course the complete prohibition of any Catalan symbol, sign or word, reasserted itself as a pole of Catalan opposition to the regime, now much more ruthlessly ultra-centralist than Primo de Rivera's in 1925.

All Heart

The person who did more than any other to create the modern *Barça* was not a Catalan at all. He was a Hungarian, Ladislao Kubala (1927-2002). Born in Budapest to a working-class family, Kubala was scoring goals for Ferencvaros at the age of eighteen. He moved to Slovan Bratislava in what is now Slovakia. Uniquely, he was a triple international: for Hungary and Czechoslovakia — and later for Spain, too. Kubala's story was entwined with the politics of the day. In January 1949 he fled the Communist regime to Austria, then Italy, but Hungarian protests led to him being banned by FIFA. He could only play by forming a touring side of all-star exiles, called Hungaria. In 1950 they visited Spain, where Pep Samitier saw Kubala play in Madrid. Samitier was Barcelona's greatest player of the '20s and, after blotting his copy-book by moving to Real Madrid and showing his sympathies with the Franco regime, had returned as *Barça's* manager. Legend has it that Samitier, offering the heavy-drinking Hungarian constant refreshment, enticed Kubala onto a train to Barcelona before he could sign the contract offered him by Real Madrid. In Barcelona Kubala, who was despite his drinking no fool, drew the Madrid draft contract from his pocket and told the President: "I want this." In 1950 he became Barcelona's highest-paid signing to date, though he did not play for a further nine months because of the FIFA ban.

Samitier solved this by going right to the top. Franco, whose only leisure activities apart from having people executed and shooting animals were watching football and films, was negotiating at the time Cold War recognition from the United States to break his international isolation. He saw the advantages of a defector from Communism. His Government supported the lifting of the FIFA ban and gave Kubala Spanish nationality in 1951. It arranged for an anti-Communist propaganda film to be shot, *The Stars Search for Peace*. I have not been able to find the film, but in his fascinating book *Barça, a People's Passion* Jimmy Burns wrote:

> *"The film reproduces a somewhat romanticised old Hollywood-style version of Kubala's escape from Hungary, sanitising his drinking bouts, and transforming the world of football into a glossy fantasy made up of sickly condescending saints."*

Kubala became the leader of a team that won five Spanish Cups, four Spanish League titles and two European Fairs Cups between 1951 and 1960. He was extraordinarily strong and fast, and had unrivalled ball-control based on constant practice. He introduced new football skills into Spain: sheltering the ball with his body, bending free-kicks hit with the instep or outside of either foot, feinting with his body. Like most sports figures who become more than sports figures, a household name known beyond their game, Kubala had a recognisable personality. He was generous, explosive and on the pitch both tough and an artist. His legend includes countless stories of all-night drinking bouts in clubs, after which he would go straight to the ground, take alternate hot and cold showers, and drink

210

black coffees before trotting out onto the pitch to be the best player. He was generous to a fault, paying a *pensió* for a family he found sleeping in the street, supporting several Hungarian refugees for lengthy periods and throughout his life giving away money, clothes and personal possessions. One of those from a poor background who *really* do not forget their origins. Combined with these excesses, he was a meticulous professional footballer: warming up properly, polishing his boots, laying out his kit neatly, always practising. Vázquez Montalbán quoted a popular song: "He was this foreigner tall and blond as beer, who arrives in a boat without a name and bears a heart tattooed on his chest," to express how Kubala lit up the life of a 1950s kid from the slums. Real Madrid's Alfredo di Stefano, his only equal on the pitch in 1950s Spain, said: "Laszy was one of the greatest footballers. And in human terms he was still greater."

This larger-than-life Hungarian was a major factor in the rebirth of mass Catalanism, or Catalan nationalist feeling, in the 1950s. The victories he inspired restored pride in the club's achievements. When people danced in the Rambles to celebrate a victory over Real Madrid or one of the cups or League titles, many of them were also celebrating a victory over the regime. In years when political protest was not permitted, political feeling emerged in the guise of sporting celebration. *Barça* was more than a club: *There are six things on earth that glitter more than the sun/ the five cups of Barcelona and the shit of Español*, sang the fans (sun being *sol* in Catalan and Spanish, so the chant rhymes). In 1957, the Camp Nou was inaugurated, the New Ground with 100,000 capacity. Kubala became known as "the man who built the Camp Nou," for it was his talent that brought in the crowds that created the need for the new ground and the income to pay for it.

After the fierce disappointment of losing the 1961 European Cup final to Benfica, a match in which Kubala hit the post twice, the '60s '70s and '80s were not successful decades for a club geared to great achievement. Too

211

often, the justified perception of centralist discrimination against a club that represented Catalonia became an excuse. Matches were not *always* lost for political reasons. The resigned slogan *Aquest any sí* (This year we will) was trotted out year after year to animate the club's disgruntled following. Disappointment at not winning Leagues, Cups or the elusive European Cup — and, even worse, seeing Real Madrid win them instead — led to a defensive losers' mentality that blamed the referees, the machinations of the Government, the pitch... Anything. If you identify a football team with the fortunes of a nation, it is especially galling to accept you are second-best.

Dutchmen

Three foreigners marked the peaks of *Barça*: Gamper, Kubala, who brought light into the darkest years, and Johan Cruyff, who like Kubala a generation before him became in 1973 the club's most expensive signing. In 1988, the lanky Dutchman who had won them a League title in 1974 was re-hired to coach the club. Cruyff arrived with all the authority of being considered the greatest player of his generation, shrugged, said "This is just a club" and as manager proceeded to win — with outrageous luck at times — four successive leagues and the European Cup in 1992. Luck, but it was winners' luck. Cruyff changed Barcelona's self-image. No longer neurotic victims of injustice, but winners — and almost as important, an attractive side that enjoyed playing open, attacking football.

Barça still reflected Catalan society's view of itself, but that view, too, had changed. Prosperity was growing among Catalonia's middle layers. Self-confidence replaced doubt and feeling wronged. Instead of sneaking across to Perpignan in Seat 600s to watch *Last Tango in Paris*, Catalans arrived there as rich neighbours in big cars to buy up local delicacies. Alongside his own attractive panache, Cruyff's team echoed the charm and art of the Olympic city.

FC Barcelona's centenary celebrations arrived in 1999 after twenty years of Josep Lluís Núñez's presidency — the President Núñez of the Museum. *El centenari de tots*, The centenary of everyone, proclaimed the huge banners that hung down the grey concrete outer walls of the Camp Nou like messages from a spaceship. But Barcelonism was deeply divided. The 100,000 devotees who packed the stadium on March 10 1999 for the homage to Cruyff and his *Dream Team* were turning their fingers in the wound of Núñez's pride. For Núñez's sacking of Cruyff in May 1996 opened a deep breach in the club. Núñez would never be so loved as Cruyff. And his revenge was the petty revenge of the powerful man who is not loved. Though by contract the club had to put on the March 10 homage, Cruyff and the oddly named opposition group he allied himself with, the Blue Elephant, were excluded from the *centenari de tots*.

Despite their marriage of convenience for eight years, Cruyff's seductive arrogance is totally distinct from Núñez's... well, unseductive arrogance. The latter married money and then made more money through property development, like many Spanish big club Presidents. All over Barcelona, the utilitarian blocks of flats and billboards of *Núñez i Navarro* flaunt his wealth. Also like other autocratic club Presidents, Núñez did not take kindly to criticism. Without the politician's talent of not making enemies, he had the dictator's gift of casting his enemies into outer darkness. Thus, it was the centenary celebrations of those loyal to Núñez.

The President to succeed Núñez was his deputy, Joan Gaspart. The President's father appeared in Chapter Four. He wanted in the '60s to develop the Park Güell as a private garden to his fourteen-storey hotel, trying to use his close friendship with Francoist officials in the Porcioles administration. The present Gaspart continues to preside HUSA and its hundred or so hotels, which in its brochure is "proud of its family character." "Family character" here means the same family continues to own the company.

The school of Dutch football which Cruyff can be said to have started persisted at the Camp Nou, but under the martinet Louis Van Gaal, and taken to extremes, with eight Dutch players in the team, and not playing attractive football. The *pedrera*, 'quarry' or young-player, policy Barcelona were so proud of was buried, as Núñez and his cheque-book sought to buy success. "You can buy players, but not a team," said Cruyff succinctly, the phantom hovering permanently just out of view but making everyone nervous.

For several years after the Cruyff era ended in 1996, FC Barcelona was cast back into the purgatory of self-doubt. From 1999 to 2004 it won no trophy at all, not even the derided Catalan Cup. When Núñez resigned in 2000 after 21 years as President, the coach Van Gaal resigned with him. In his farewell statement Van Gaal insulted Catalonia — "a good place to live, but not to work", a crude comment which hit deep at Catalan pride that they were different from other Spaniards precisely because they *did* know how to work, in healthy equilibrium with the Mediterranean good life. Van Gaal then went on to fail to qualify the talented Dutch national side for the 2002 World Cup finals. As a reward for insult and failure he was rehired by Gaspart in May 2002 – symbolically arriving on the day of the artist Kubala's death. The second Van Gaal didn't last six months.

2003 saw a fresh start. A younger President, Joan Laporta, was elected with the support of Cruyff, and a new trainer, Frank Rijkaard, the seventh in seven years, was appointed. Laporta and Rijkaard are the urbane and courteous antitheses of the visceral Gaspart and disciplinarian Van Gaal. How long they last depends on results, for the pressure to win is suffocating and what is called the *entorn*, i.e. the press, the fans, the internal politics, everything that surrounds the team, is intense and destabilising. Despite his success, Laporta has never been free of the plots and accusations that are normal at *Barça*.

Laporta was lucky. He had promised to hire the dismal David Beckham in his election campaign, but Real Madrid got there first. Instead, he found Ronaldinho, who has become the great star of a resurgent Barça that won the 2005 League title. The supporters will accept a team that wins championships, but only love a Kubala, a Cruyff, a winner with style and flair. The Brazilian Ronaldinho is one such. A happy player, a fantasist on the pitch, he inspires the fans as no-one has done since Cruyff himself.

Glorious Failure

Why is *Barça* as interesting to the British as it seems to be? There are obvious reasons: one is that more football being available on television in the UK since the '90s means fans watch foreign games more frequently. But that does not explain why *Barça* — why not Milan, Ajax or Real Madrid (though this may be changing, because of Beckham)? Another reason has been the recent presence of British players and managers, Terry Venables in the 1980s, known as *El Tel* and bringing with him Steve Archibald, Gary Lineker and Mark Hughes, and the managers Vic Buckingham before Venables and the popular Bobby Robson after. Yet that does not supply the whole answer, either. The answer has to lie in the romantic aura surrounding the club, evoked in those over-blown quotes cited earlier in the chapter: the aura of fine players, an attacking creative style, huge support, identification with a cause. But this begs a further question: where does this aura come from? Partly from history, but it has also been carefully created. The businessmen who have controlled the club have polished its international reputation. They have sold the club as glorious, artistic and creative, whose very failures were noble because the dice were always loaded against them: a romantic image of Catalan underdogs against the odds. And they also assiduously link the club with the charms of the city of Barcelona (remember Tàpies' instructions) and with Art (Tàpies himself, Miró, Dalí...).

The politics of FC Barcelona are complex, with a number of contradictory dynamics at work. Franco was astute enough to understand how football could be used as a means of mass control during the decades when Spain was very rapidly becoming both an urban and a television society. These processes occurred at the same time, whereas in France and Britain urbanisation happened a century before TV. Spanish nationalism meant that Franco's regime more or less openly favoured Real Madrid — something perceived not only in Catalonia, but all over Spain, where the 400 *Peñas barcelonistas* (Supporters' Clubs) group the more anti-centralist forces. At the same time, however, the regime sought to create competition. The great rivals coincided in what was most important: maintaining their rivalry. Permanent victory of Real Madrid would be useless: crowds would drop, unrest would flourish. Permanent competition was what was required. *Barça* was thus both a rallying-point for Catalanist sentiment, sharpened by love for a sports artist like Kubala; and a way in which that sentiment could be diverted off the streets and into hatred for Real Madrid. At the same time, the opposite, anti-barcelonism, was a way of rallying adherents to Franco's national-catholic patriotism: when *Barça* beat Real Madrid in the quarter-finals of the 1961 European Cup, several papers lamented "Spain defeated..."

Another dynamic was the regime's anti-communism, which was seen in its support for the refugee Kubala. Catalan nationalists have at times felt uneasy at Franco's support for Barcelona's greatest star. A more comforting story of a Catalonia united in its opposition to Franco would have been preferable.

In the '90s, money rained on football like men in the song. Season tickets, television rights, exploitation of players' images, sponsorship contracts, all spiralled upwards. *Barça* was frustrated at its inability to achieve the property deals of Real Madrid in the late '90s, by which the Madrid club, helped by its sympathetic City Council to trample over all sorts of urban planning regulations, jumped from near-bankruptcy to fabulous wealth. In successive years Madrid bought the services of Figo and Ronaldo (ex-Barcelona players), Zidane and Beckham. *Barça* tried a similar property deal with its own prime building land a few years ago, but mass demonstrations organised by the Les Corts Residents' Association, to Núñez's shock and rage, prevented the speculative operation.

Barça does not just stare obsessively into the distorting mirror of Madrid. The club watched enviously Manchester United's enormous 1990s take-off, the wealth generated from merchandising — shirts, balls, books and pens. It is running hard to catch up, with constant development of its facilities and spin-offs. The team has followed Madrid on successful off-season tours of the Far East. The exit from the Josep Lluís Núñez Museum guides the visitor ineluctably through the glittering new shop, where among the mementoes, shiny bric-à-brac, Barça wine, Barça biscuits and designer clothes, you can have your photo taken and computer-imaged onto a print beside your favourite player.

"Just look at this ground," sighed a Londoner sitting in the stands with an eight or nine-year old son wearing an Arsenal shirt. A few dozen people were scattered across a small cordoned section of the red plastic bucket seats. They were resting from the coach journey, the tour round the Núñez museum and the warm day. This is the best part of the museum visit: you can sit and look out over the empty pitch. A man was painting the black balustrade below. As on bridges, this is a permanent job: once you've got right round, it's time to start again. "It's so big, and you can imagine it full, all the great games, the wall of noise," Chris the Londoner was saying. He was expressing the magic of a mass sport, communal passion, however sullied and manipulated by business interests. The pitch, beautifully mown in parallel lines, was an empty stage on which you could imagine or recall any performance. No boring bad-tempered match to interfere with your dreams.

Chris was wrong, though. If he actually got to a Barça game, he'd be amazed at the quietness of the Camp Nou. He was picturing what Highbury would sound like if it was twice as big. At Barcelona, by comparison, the noise is slight. The fans do not get behind their team. It is perhaps the only club where the players actually have to encourage the supporters. If the team goes a goal down, the crowd falls silent, or boos and whistles players. If the team is on a losing streak, the crowd gets out white handkerchiefs and shouts obscenities at the trainer. An English fan told me:

> "Barça *fans are crap. There's no comparison with Manchester or Liverpool. At even your average lower Division side in the UK, there's more noise. Obviously if they do get behind the team here it's noisy — since there's so many of them."*

The only time you could talk of a "wall of noise" is in each season's ritual confrontation with Real Madrid. For several years now, whenever Madrid's Brazilian scurrying power-house Roberto Carlos touches the ball, thousands of the 98,000 filling the stadium start making monkey noises. No-one in liberal progressive Barcelona criticises this. Not the press, not the club. Racism and the presence of fascist gangs within supporters' clubs have not, until very recently, been seriously challenged in Spain. Indeed, the far-right fan-clubs, *boixos nois* (Wild kids) in Barcelona and *ultrasur* in Madrid, were traditionally sheltered by the clubs, with offices inside the stadiums and free tickets to away matches.

Soon after his election, in late 2003, Laporta moved to curtail the privileges of the *boixos nois*. This gang of a few hundred members at most, who had called Gaspart their 'godfather', could no longer use a room in the stadium, receive free tickets to games or travel free with the team. Violence in and outside the stadium by supporters was not acceptable, affirmed Laporta. So far, to his credit, Laporta has sustained his position, despite death threats against himself and his family. It is a position that dovetails with a new business approach to football. As has happened in England over the last fifteen years, the stand against violence is associated with all-seater stadiums, steep rises in admission charges and a more middle-class audience.

Laporta's opposition to the *boixos nois* is unlikely to be for anti-racist reasons. It is not encouraging that he won the Presidency against the Jewish front-runner Lluís Bassat, after Bassat was subjected to a campaign of anti-Semitism. On election day, this climaxed with a group of *boixos nois* shouting 'judío de mierda' ('fucking Jew') at Bassat as he arrived at the ground to vote. This was not a campaign that originated in the Laporta camp, but it was strikingly depressing that the other candidates failed to show solidarity with Bassat.

It remains to be seen if the *boixos nois*, or their successors, will continue to be ostracised. Few fans travel in Spain: partly because of the distances involved, but also because of their passivity — only about two or three hundred Espanyol supporters will attend a local derby in the Camp Nou, and the reverse is true when Espanyol host the derby. The *boixos nois* are valuable because they turned up day-in day-out and made a noise. And if some of them wear fascist insignia and lead racist chants, well wild boys will be boys, won't they? ...and weren't we all like that in our youth? They are the shock troops of the club directors, politicians and millionaires up in the Directors' Box. The Directors' Box, or rather the sumptuous heated rooms with bars and arm-chairs behind it, of the Camp Nou is what the private rooms of the Liceu were 100 years ago. Under Laporta, the rooms are being extended and redesigned in maximum luxury. It is here that a land developer can have a quiet word with the Mayor without the compromise of setting up a formal meeting. It is here deals are agreed which the lawyers will formalise afterwards.

The interesting books about football are not Roy of the Rovers stuff, which take the hero through countless difficulties to the pinnacle of triumph. Vázquez Montalbán's *Off Side* portrays its hero ten years after glory on the pitch, in a lonely room smelling of liniment in a *pensió* run by a retired prostitute in the *Ciutat vella*. While Palacín, approaching forty, is trying to keep his knees going for one last contract with a non-League club, Jack Mortimer, a Gary Lineker look-alike, is the new signing of Barcelona's richest football club (it is not difficult to grasp which club the author is talking about). As the stars on the field rise and fall, the club directors "minor Caesars... who use your centre forward to make yourself feel like Gods who manage victories and defeats" remain the same, using their power to fix property deals.

Like the politicians and builders who throng the hospitality rooms behind the Directors' Box, the fans remain the same too. I mean, those fans who follow football, not those with enough spare cash to attend. In front of the Chinese restaurant on the corner of the suburban Barcelona street where I live, there is a spot of pavement touched by the sun even on chilly winter days. Invariably a man is standing there reading *Sport* if he is alone or talking about the contents of *Sport* with other middle-aged unemployed men. Among the biggest-selling daily papers in Spain are *Marca, As, Sport* and *El Mundo deportivo*, the first two published in and supporting Madrid; and the last two, Barcelona. On match days, my neighbour is listening to the commentary on his transistor squashed against his ear. This man, who is an immigrant to Barcelona from another part of Spain, has been prematurely chucked out of the labour market. He is on the street because it is cheaper than sitting with his friends in a café and his flat is too cold and dismal in the winter to stay in all day. His pleasure lies in his identification with the fortunes of *Barça*.

Chapter 12
Family Life, Sex and the City

"In families, feeling and cohabitation have that fatal and instinctive coherence you see in a bird's nest or ant-hill."
JOSEP MARIA DE SAGARRA, *VIDA PRIVADA.*

Authentic Pleasure

In 1999 Pedro Almodóvar's *All About My Mother* won the Oscar for best foreign film. It was a typical Almodóvar film, replete with the trademarks of Spain's most famous living film director. *All About My Mother* has a complicated story-line explained in thoroughly visual terms, over-the-top characters, a well-nigh unbelievable plot, rapid-fire wise-cracking worthy of Billy Wilder at his peak, actresses performing at the height of their powers and meticulously designed sets rioting with metallic colour. More than all these, it has the Almodóvar flare of passion and freedom.

All About My Mother is Almodóvar's first film set in Barcelona. He is one of the main icons of early-80s Madrid, when Franco's fascist *movimiento* gave way, in just a few years, to a grass-roots explosion of youth culture known as the *movida*. For the first time Madrid became a youth capital, and gave Spain a sophisticated, witty, gay-inspired culture.

Yet Barcelona seems perfect for Almodóvar. We first see the city in a breath-taking wide-angle, the camera rising like a wave up and over the Collserola hills to show the Eixample spread out below, the music swelling like a shot inspired in Olympic publicity. It would not be out of place to see hairy-chested Freddie Mercury in a frock chant *Barcelo-o-o-o-o-na*. We cut to Manuela, played by Cecilia

Roth, passing the Sagrada Família by night, the facade of the cathedral in a blaze of shimmering light. Though this is an ordinary orientation shot, like the Eiffel Tower to show you're in Paris, it also shows the exoticism of the city. The Sagrada Família is cut to typical urban waste-land, vacant lots under a motorway. Cars are circling. Their head-lights pick out, not the fantastic curves of Gaudí's cathedral, but transvestite and transexual prosti-tutes in all their sculptured glory.

The film tells how Manuela comes from Madrid to Barcelona to search for the estranged father of her eigh-teen-year old son, killed in an accident. Her grief propels her on a complex journey into the past. The people she meets are the normal Almodóvar *pot-pourri*, including a pregnant nun, a lesbian junkie and an elderly man with Alzheimer's. The father, a transvestite dying of AIDS, first appears towards the end. Late for a funeral, he staggers down some steps in the Montjuïc cemetery, looking rather like Quentin Crisp on a bad day. Several friends think the film falls apart at this juncture, the bizarre melodrama of its characters crushing any serious intent. While they are choking back laughter, others, myself included, are near crying with the rawness and intensity of the emotions expressed. Almodóvar teeters on the dangerous edge. Director of improbable melodramas with impossible char-acters, yet his films work (when they work) because the emotions expressed are authentic.

The Barcelona shown by Almodóvar includes little con-cession to Catalan, even in the background. It is modern: there are black people everywhere and the rebuilt Hospital del Mar is prominent. Yet its tone is 1980s post-Franco *Ciutat vella* drugs and transvestism. The main Barcelona character is a transvestite prostitute called Agrado, mean-ing Pleasure, who is kind, spontaneous and attractive: "You know why I'm called Agrado? All my life I've tried to make life pleasurable for others." Agrado makes a central speech, in which she lists all the expensive cosmetic surgery she has had, and ends with the paradox:

"It costs a lot to be authentic, and you shouldn't be mean, because the closer you resemble what you have dreamed of becoming, the more authentic you are."

She is a self-made woman.

All About My Mother is a film of people trying to be what they want to be and the kindness, the solidarity of perfect strangers. Manuela and Agrado are both 'authentic' and that brings out the best in others, even at the toughest moments.

Since before Genet's time, when the *Carolinas* marched down the Rambles at dawn to lay their red roses, *travestís*, transvestites, have been a feature of Barcelona life: in the music hall, in *Ciutat vella* bars. José María Carandell, in his *Secret Guide to Barcelona*, even dates the start of Barcelona transvestism to a Paral·lel music-hall act of the first decade of the twentieth century. Its roots, though, lie deeper in the overturning of order, including sexual order, in the Carnival (Ch. 6). In times of dictatorship, transvestites are submerged, but as more liberal times approach, they presage change as they rise into visibility like dolphins leaping to announce the spring.

Ocaña, performance artist and painter, was a symbol of transition Barcelona. Ocaña was permanent Carnival. When homosexuality was illegal, he openly proclaimed he was gay. In the still used to advertise the 1978 film *Retrat intermitent*, Intermittent portrait, that Ventura Pons made of his short life (he died after an accident in 1983 at the age of 36), Ocaña looks the spitting image of Carmen Amaya, the great flamenco dancer of the 1950s from Poble Nou. In this film, Ocaña, himself an Andalusian immigrant, took on all the clichés of Andalusian women. His life became a performance as he strutted up and down the Rambles in mantilla, flowers in hair, veil, lace gloves and fan, occasionally raising his dress to show his arse and penis.

In the film Ocaña explains how he loved the colour, incense and beauty of the church, though he hated religion. He both felt part of Andalusian religious processions and parodied them. An aesthetic challenge to propriety, he was political too: "My aim is to break the mould, make things change."

Daniel Asensio, who was a friend of Ocaña, told me:

> *"He was a constant provocateur. Usually he dressed as Charlie Chaplin, walking up and down the Ramblas, or in the Plaza Real where he lived, or most of all in the Café de la Ópera. He was very vulgar and quick-witted, openly homosexual. What he did brilliantly was mix it with people in the street, or people would have a go at him and he was always so quick and sharp that he'd come off best and win the support of passers-by."*

Ocaña's subversion of traditional family values were a part of the outburst of freedom that the transition brought. Forgotten now, Ocaña neither fits the image of cool, modern Barcelona; nor a sophisticated, non-provocative, less politicised gay scene.

The fictional Agrado and real Ocaña exist in Barcelona, but they are not representative. Anyone who thinks the city is packed with gender-bending polemicists is in for a disappointment. Nevertheless, it is part of Barcelona's image. There's probably no more transvestism than in London, where Danny La Rue and Boy George are household names. I remember a thousand people packing the Wellington on Shepherd's Bush Green thirty years ago to acclaim a drag act singing *Hey, big spender, hey, big spender... spend — a little time with me*.

Transvestites are relatively popular as prostitutes, judging from newspaper adverts in the daily press and, in the late '80s and early '90s, remarkable scenes of men with perfectly designed breasts (*Why have real breasts when you can design such perfect ones?* as Agrado might say) and micro-skirts showing their bodies to the slowing cars round the *Camp nou*. For years, these prostitutes did a roaring trade with the football crowds. Mourners bearing flowers to the neighbouring Les Corts cemetery regularly stumbled over used condoms and sex among the tombs.

Sex. How can one know people's sexual habits? Surveys assure us that the puritan North-Americans have more sex than anyone else. One assumes sex in Spain has evolved since the dark days Richard Wright found (Ch. 2). Certainly, if you watch Spanish films — and the Catalan directors Ventura Pons, Vicente Aranda and Bigas Luna lead this trend — you'd conclude there's an awful lot of sex about. Female nudity and at least fifteen minutes of sex per film that would have been too strong for 1970s *Emmanuelle* are imperatives for these commercial directors. This was understandable during the transition, as a reaction to the censorship and repression of the Franco years, when the *destape*, sudden explosion of freedom, took place. But its persistence makes you wonder — they're talking so much, do they ever do it?

Despite Ocaña, there is very little ordinary visibility for gays and lesbians in Barcelona. Though the vast majority of Catalans seem liberal and not at all hostile to homosexuality, gay foreign visitors find that Barcelona lags behind other European cities in its practical acceptance and openness. In most jobs and families it would be very hard to come out; and lesbians in particular are almost wholly invisible. Clearly, as the guide-books indicate, there are clubs, saunas and organisations: the gay and lesbian scenes exist in a parallel world, a ghetto.

The exception to this is Barcelona's 'Brighton,' Sitges, the sea-side town twenty miles south. Sitges, for over a century an artists' colony, has become an international gay resort. Sitges has conserved its beautiful old centre and church on a headland rising from the sea between two beaches. It is a town where many wealthy *barcelonins* have second homes; and doubtless the rich, as happened at Cadaqués on the north of the Costa Brava, prevented unbridled high-rise development. Gay or not, don't miss a day in Sitges — and stay or have a drink in the amiably decadent Hotel Romàntic with its garden and frescoes.

Gay and lesbian invisibility, combined with a certain generalised *tolerance* (see below), is due to the absence of a strong gay movement at the time of the transition – the Ocaña swallow made no summer. Madrid is a little different: the early '80s *movida* challenged many straight men's conceptions and laid the foundations for a bigger gay scene and movement.

Family

In Spain, and Catalonia is no exception, the family comes before everything. The extended rural family has survived the move to the cities, though its shape has become more nuclear. The family, above all, is a buffer for the lack of a welfare state in Spain. Unemployed or precariously employed young people live with their family; old people live with their family; students, separated men and separated women live with their family. Of 25-29 year olds, 62% live with their parents; while in the UK and France, less than 20% do. In Spain one in ten people lives alone; in Europe as a whole this is in one in four; in Paris, nearly one in two.

You will recall the *okupas* living below the Park Güell. They are part of a sizeable squatters' movement. Housing is very expensive in Barcelona. Not as dear as London, yet wages in Spain are lower. Little rented accommodation is available. If you don't want to occupy empty property, you live with your parents. Despite this, nearly everyone under thirty will tell you that they think very differently from their parents, there is little real contact with them, they don't talk about anything. That is not too surprising, given that they have grown up in a liberal consumer democracy, while their parents grew up in a dictatorship. Yet even when the young do move, after saving up to buy a flat (and in most cases needing parental help), they nearly always end up living close to their parents. The surprising thing is not that the young are forced to live with their parents because of expensive housing and lack of jobs or insecure employment, but that a great many *like* living with their parents. And when they don't live with their parents, they live three streets away.

For long I thought that this mutual acceptance of life together in a small flat meant that in Spain problems between parents and children, which in Britain are often avoided by the child moving to the other end of the country, would be tackled and sorted out. However, this is not generally so. All polls and personal experience show that mutual incomprehension is the norm. How then can such cohabitation work? Generally, by "tolerance." Twenty-to-thirty year old children lead their own lives, come and go when they like, may have boy or girl-friends, treat their parents' flat like a free hotel. Tolerance is a loaded word: it implies putting up with what you don't like too much.

Spain is still very traditional in its division of labour within the family. As recently as 1995, a survey found that both men and women affirmed that 75% of men never do domestic work. Women, who as in other Western countries generally work outside the home, are almost wholly responsible for running the home too. I know a family in which the sixty-year old father and thirty-year old son never do anything at all. The wife and mother is not especially upset at this. She likes the situation, she keeps her useless husband and son dependent on her. I know this family well enough to have rebuked on occasion the thirty-year old. He smiles tolerantly at my concern: why should he do anything? Both his parents and he are happy for him not to do anything. If he did do anything, he would disturb the equilibrium.

Divorce is very low in Spain: running at about 10% of all marriages (40% UK, 60% US). In all polls, the family comes at the top of the most important things in people's life. Most young people think of eventually getting married and having a family. Indeed, weddings in the '90s were on the increase, after dropping sharply immediately after the transition. Church weddings are on the up, too. Barcelona's *Noviaespaña* is the biggest wedding-clothes trade fair in the world. You can well believe this when you walk up the Passeig de Gràcia: there are three wedding-dress shops in high-rent premises within two blocks of Gaudí's Pedrera, including the wedding multi-national *Pronovias*. In most cases marriage means moving directly from a parental home to living with your partner, with the same expectations and division of labour passed on to another generation.

Spain missed out on the great cultural revolution of the 1960s. Formal equality of women was accepted by most men at the end of the dictatorship, because it was thought to be just part of what happened when democracy returned. Yet no struggle had taken place to make men change. In Britain in the early '70s the impact of the feminist movement, though always a small minority, was enormous: mass-circulation papers such as the *Mirror* and *Mail* ran polls and articles on what domestic chores men did. The message was: if women were to accede to the work-place on equal terms, men had to start to change.

In the thirty years since its first post-Franco elections, Spain has had little debate on the roles of men and women. Only now is public recognition starting of the extent of domestic violence against women. There is one unmistakable signal, however, that women are suffering the pressures of entering the labour market whilst still being wholly responsible for the family. The birth-rate has fallen. In Catalonia the birth-rate is one of the lowest in the world, since 1995 at 1.1 per woman. Only the much smaller countries of Bulgaria and Lithuania have lower birth-rates than Spain. The population is only growing at all because of immigration. There are several reasons for this decline, common throughout Europe but greater in Spain. Job insecurity (in Spain 80% of contracts for the under-thirties are short-term), lack of cheap housing and lack of confidence in a world plagued by famine and war undermine people's confidence in the future. The low birth rate is often put down to selfishness and hedonism: the young want more time to do their own thing. Rather, it is women's response to the demand that they be paid workers, home organisers and mothers all at once. They cut out one of the three jobs.

No-one protests about the family, but the realities of family life throttle women. The woman at the chicken stall in the market tells me, moving from foot to foot to relieve her varicose veins: "I'm on my feet for eight hours here. Then when I get home I have to look after my mother and cook the meal for my husband."

She's lucky. Some women look after their husband's ageing mothers, too. What else can you do? State old people's homes are rare and private homes are dear. More than that, there is no custom of the old living in old people's homes. Both the parent and the child feel bad about it. In *The New Spaniards*, John Hooper ends his chapter titled *Women on the verge of a nervous breakdown*:

> "*Ironically, it would seem that the longer Spanish men cling to traditional attitudes towards women, the greater the damage they will do to that most traditional of Spanish institutions, the family.*"

One of the features of Spanish life that people from Northern Europe find most attractive is the way children are treated. The attitude of "No children or dogs" is unimaginable in Spain. The frowning disapproval if a child shouts or runs about in a public place is impossible. If you have children, come and live in Spain. If your child starts to cry, there are numerous people on hand who see it as their pleasure and responsibility to step forward and distract him/her. Children are the centre of life. A friend tells me that one of the early scenes of Fellini's *Roma* reminded her of her infancy in 1950s Barcelona: on a summer's night, the whole family and the neighbours come down into the street and eat at improvised long tables while the trams rattle by. It is unthinkable that the children should be put to bed, while the adults feast. Everyone is present, generations mixed: babies, grandparents, teenagers, relations and friends.

Barcelona is not Los Angeles, with houses scattered over the desert valleys, connected by freeways. This is the city where everyone lives on top of each other and if your daughter moves half a mile away it feels like abandonment. Even the town's most famous fictional private eye Pepe Carvalho acquires a family of sorts. Yet this society so genuinely devoted to its children and addicted to living in nuclear families is having hardly any children. This lack of fecundity is saying something. It seems like a mass passive protest strike of the young. Protest perhaps against the family itself: young women are not wanting to repeat their mothers' lives of service.

In all this talk of the dominance of the family and the burden women carry within it, there is an important point to signal about women. In famously macho Spain, young women are not at all down-trodden. In studies and in jobs to which you accede by public examination — judges, civil servants, teachers — women have been doing better than men for the last fifteen years. And look around in the metro: women's heads are more often buried in a book than men's.

The family is a two-edged institution. Even those of us who have fled conventional life would love to have been brought up in an affectionate, big family, to have sat at the table in the street on a Fellinian summer's night. The family is supportive, stable, cocoons its members against a rough outside world.

Yet it can also be like the family drawn by Rosa Regàs in *Luna lunera*, Moony Moon, one of the best Catalan novels of recent years. It is written in Castilian and Regàs, born in 1933, explains in this autobiographical novel precisely how she was forbidden to speak Catalan as a child. In Regàs' story, the family is a fascist dictatorship in which the children are imprisoned, reflecting Franco's world outside the walls of the house on the Carrer Ferran. The grand-father of *Luna lunera* exercises absolute power and drives everyone either mad, to crime, to their deaths or to chronic suffering. Such a novel brings home how a dicta-

230

torship is not just a regime affecting public institutions, but enters deep into our family life, our intimate life. As such, it is not removed by the coming of democracy, but lasts in hearts and minds for several decades.

Another great novel of Catalan family life dates from before the dictatorship, but is also entirely negative: Josep Maria de Sagarra's *Vida privada*, Private life (1932). Sagarra's portrayal of a decadent upper class only confirms the view that the revolutionaries of 1936 were absolutely right. This *roman à clef* chronicles three generations of the aristocratic de Lloberola family. They decline from snobbery made more ridiculous by poverty to moral disintegration, represented in blackmail and pathological selfishness, to, in the third generation, murder and inability to feel anything at all. The Lloberola family is a nightmare, worthy antecedent of the grand-father's family in *Luna lunera*. The epigraph from the poet Salvador Espriu used by Regàs could just as well serve Sagarra: "my poor, dirty, sad, unlucky country." Sagarra sums up his view of family life:

> "It's pretty hard for a brother and sister to break out of the shell of family intimacy, which is precisely the least cordial, the least communicative, least human thing in existence."

The quote is not isolated, but consistently expresses Sagarra's ferocious assault on the upper-class Catalan family, and by extension 1920s and early '30s society. *Vida privada* was the only novel of Sagarra, more famous as dramatist, translator and poet. Indeed, until recently, there have not been a great many novelists in Catalonia. Caterina Albert (who published as Víctor Català), the maximum exponent of the rural novel with *Solitud* (1906), also published in this, her most productive decade, three volumes of short stories — but never published another novel. Catalonia's famous twentieth-century prose writer, Josep Pla, wrote no novels. His best-known books are a huge diary and travel sketches. His writing is best summed up by the title of his 1925 *Coses vistes*, Things seen. It is generally argued that the Catalan predilection for short stories and poems over novels is due to the historical problems of Catalan as an oppressed language. Plays, which are spoken, overcome this. And poems and short stories do not require the nuances and linguistic stamina of a novel. Commentators too will argue that this historical lacuna has now been overcome, with the post-Franco 'normalisation' of Catalan. They will name a string of fine recent novelists: Montserrat Roig (feminist author of a family saga), Baltasar Porcel, Imma Monsó...

I wonder though, as the novel is the means of writing about family life *par excellence*, whether the suffocating emotional closeness of family life, the shell Sagarra remarks on, inhibited the novel in Catalonia as much as historical and linguistic problems did. The best-known more recent writers in Catalan, such as Pere Calders, Jesús Moncada or Quim Monzó, also favour short stories. Monzó's great stories deal with the deracinated city dweller, and thus jump over family life. His wit and ferocity focus on sex life in a modern world where people are not having children. That is Barcelona today.

Chapter 13
So Many Murders

*"Catalonia is the melting-pot of Spain, with pasta
from Italy, rice dishes from Valencia, hearty country
food from neighbouring Aragon and saffron-hued
fish soups straight out of Provence."*
JANET MENDEL, THE BEST OF SPANISH COOKING.

Untrustworthy

Pepe Carvalho, Vázquez Montalbán's detective-guide to
Barcelona, is a gourmet: "ex-cop, ex-marxist and
gourmet," as he puts it. Carvalho's gourmet tastes are not
just a gimmick: as early as 1974 in *Tatuaje*, Montalbán
explained the detective's ideology of food. When the detective meets Teresa Marsé, a young woman in a hurry who
suggests going "—somewhere we can grab any old thing to
eat," the author comments lugubriously: "This was what
Carvalho never wanted to eat."

Earlier in *Tatuaje* Carvalho had reflected: "Really no
human being indifferent to food is trustworthy." Teresa's
trivial attitude to what she eats is part of a critique of her
superficial character. She does not treat her food well: she
does not treat people well. Food, like sex, wine and walking down the Rambles, is part of Carvalho's appreciation
of good living. It should not be gobbled down with indif-
ference. It is part of savouring the present, treating
yourself well. Especially important if one realises the
world is a mess and no-one else is likely to do so.

Unlike other traits of Carvalho, love of food was one
shared by the author. A health warning, though. One would
absolutely not recommend following with any regularity the
recipes scattered throughout the Carvalho novels. The contents are rich and the portions are huge: Carvalho is
gourmand as well as gourmet. Montalbán had known

hunger in his childhood. This is a powerful motive for eating a lot when you can. Such eating is not to be confused with the *healthy* Mediterranean diet widely lauded today.

English food is so often derided that the badness of English food has become a cliché. In Carvalho's terms the English are thoroughly untrustworthy. The lack of an English *cuisine*, the tasteless slough of a certain tradition of English cookery, is often reflected in enormous confusion among English people arriving in Barcelona. A friend of mine visited Barcelona seven years running in the 1980s. She raved over the beauty of Barcelona. If you pointed out a great building, though, she'd say *Oh yes* and hurry on. Her Barcelona was its wonderful bars and restaurants. When she took me to one of her haunts just off the Carrer Ample in the *Ciutat vella* to savour the food and drink, this consisted of red *xorisso* (pork sausage) fried in rancid reheated oil, *patates braves* wild potatoes (sautéed potatoes doused in chili sauce and mayonnaise), and a rough red wine drawn from the barrel. "Isn't it great?" she sighed, waving her hand round the smoke-filled bar. And it was. It was completely different. You could feel the excitement of a place only two hours out of Luton and so completely different. You just signalled for what you wanted and the fat bearded proprietor brought it at once. "And cheap...". It was cheap, too. It is like eating sausage and chips in a holiday caff. It's a great greasy experience, but the food is neither healthy nor good.

If you want to avoid this Spanish version of the fry-up, a second option is the bland international café-restaurants all over the centre that are common to every major tourist city. Here you can eat a respectable pizza or steak from a menu written in English. But you could eat much the same in London without the expense of an air ticket.

A third option is to eat *tapas* and *racions* (smaller and bigger portions, respectively) at one of the big open cafeterias that have opened over the past few years throughout the central area. These attractive cafés have long wooden bars. The pungent aroma of coffee pulls you in the always open door. Often, coarse sacks of coffee beans are piled in the entrance. Here too, for in Spain there has never been any strict line between a café and a bar, there are beers, spirits and wines arrayed enticingly along the shelves behind the bar like the prizes in a tombola. Where there is space, as on the Passeig de Gràcia, the pavement is covered by the café terraces. One can while away the day, or rest between the visits to the *Art Nouveau* buildings of the boulevard, watching the crowds saunter under the Gaudian lamp-standards.

These cafés, which seem so traditional and intrinsic a part of Mediterranean life, are a modern invention, only opened in the early 1990s. In the '70s and '80s most of the bigger cafés dating back 100 years or so were destroyed. They were done up in Formica and neon, converted to pizzerias or just closed down. The speedier pace of life after the transition could not afford people lazing round in cafés all day.

At much the same time, in 1980s Britain *tapas* bars, serving expensive exotic *tapas* and red wine, began to appear, using Spanish style to popularise the traditional English wine bar among a new generation. The large café has returned to Barcelona in the form of this *posh* version of a *tapas* bar. Many of these attractive new cafés are international chains, with names evocative of good coffee or *la dolce vita*, such as Il caffé de Roma with soft-green wooden chairs and rough red-brick walls, Caracas, Bracafé (Antillana de Cafes S.L.) or Jamaica. Just as *tapas* bars in Britain brand a vague Spanish idea, so these cafés brand Italy or the Caribbean. With the tourism industry now king, modernity includes vast numbers of people with the leisure and money to sit in cafés.

Old-style Barcelona cafés still exist, classy ones like the Velódromo in the Eixample, the Quimet in Horta, the Salambó in Gràcia or *Els quatre gats* (on *The Shadow of the Wind* route: see Ch. 6) and rougher ones like the Òpera on the Rambles or the Marsella discussed in Chapter Two. The gay-friendly Schilling on Carrer Ferran is beautifully decorated so that no casual customer would believe it is not several decades old. It was a gun-shop closed in 1997 and re-opened, not this time in imitation of a Bristol or Manchester *tapas* bar, but of an old *tertúlia* café — where groups of (mainly) men would sit around, doze and talk.

These modern café chains are part of the globalisation of consumption. In 1981 the first McDonald's opened in Barcelona. Throughout the '80s those hoping against hope to see Barcelona's Rose of Fire, its anarchist tradition, re-flower post-Franco were encouraged by regular smashing of McDonald's windows, especially when Catalan nationalist feeling ran high after a *Barça* victory over Real Madrid. In both Catalan and Castilian, a hamburger is a *hamburguesa*, word that conjoins neatly with *burgesia* and *burguesía*, bourgeoisie. Victory over Madrid, crowds milling at the top of the Rambles, smash the foreign hambourgeoisie's ugly plate glass!

False hopes. A new generation set to eating fast food with relish and it wasn't till the very end of the '90s when farmers' leader José Bové drove his tractor into McDonald's across the border in Millau, that people in Catalonia started to wonder just what they, and especially their children, were eating. McDonald-smashing was no longer an anecdotal last fling of a defeated post-transition left: Bové was part of a new movement. Nowadays, local anti-globalisation campaigns in Barcelona often picket McDonald's outlets, explaining the role of food multinationals and offering instead *pa amb tomàquet*, which is, in Alastair Boyd's words:

> "...the real national snack. It is made by rubbing a doorstep of bread with half a fresh tomato and adding a pinch of salt and a good dollop of the best olive oil. In its simple form it can accompany any meal but is often used as the foundation of a sort of open sandwich of ham, tuna, cheese or anything else you fancy."

Fast-food chains are now installed throughout Metropolitan Barcelona. *Pizza-moteros* (delivery bikers) roaring along pavements are customary perils. *Pan's & Co.* (owned by Avecrem, see below) introduced Mediterranean-style fast food with their tasty *entrepans* (filled bread rolls) and half of lager. Spain is now fully integrated into the world economy, represented by its membership of NATO, upgraded in the '90s to full membership, and of the European Union. Food, what we put inside us, what shapes our bodies, is not immune to the contradictory dynamics of globalisation.

Smoke Chupa Chups

It's not all one way: food and drink multinationals are among Catalonia's most successful companies. Avecrem pioneered fast food in hungry 1940s Spain, with its *Gallina blanca* (White hen) stock cubes. In 1959 *Gallina blanca* opened Spain's first battery farm, producing some 200,000 chickens a month. Chickens were becoming the food of the poor, not just luxuries for the rich.

Cola-Cao, a chocolate drink using cacao from the former Spanish colony of Guinea, was publicised by jingles with the excruciating *negrito* (little black man) from tropical Africa, that became part of the collective memory of Franco's Spain. Then imagine taking a word such as 'sandwich' or 'croissant' and registering it as a brand name: that is the trick Andreu Costafreda, founder of Panrico, brought off in Spain with 'doughnut,' registering it as *donut*.

Chupa Chups, manufacturer of a sweet on a stick, the children's lollipop of the same name, broke into the adult market by linking itself to anti-smoking campaigns. When Johan Cruyff had a heart attack in 1991 he gave up smoking, a habit he had indulged even when he was the world's greatest footballer in the early '70s. Instead, he chain-sucked the onomatopoeic Chupa Chups (Suck-sucks) on the bench during *Barça's* championship-winning seasons. By the late 1990s Chupa Chups had got into Australia, with Government backing for the brilliant advertising slo-gan *Smoke Chupa Chups*. A few years ago it bought Gaudí's *Casa Batlló* on the *Passeig de Gràcia*. We will look forward to seeing computer-generated adverts of the ascetic Gaudí sucking lollies.

The best-known Catalan multinationals are Freixenet and Codorniu, manufacturers of *cava*. In 1982, when they lost the fight to call their sparkling wine *champagne*, it seemed a decisive defeat. Yet both companies have triumphed internationally — particularly in the American market — selling *cava* as a quality, cheaper, less snobbish alternative to champagne. In 1998 the more downmarket Freixenet exported 73 million bottles, including 5.3 million to the UK, a figure expected to have doubled by 2007.

All these successful companies[1] have known how to adapt to the new global competitiveness of the past two decades. Curiously, these multinationals are family-owned companies. This is not so strange in Catalonia, though, which has a long tradition of the family company, not just in big companies, but right down to small workshops. The family is not just strong at home, but structures business and employment, too.

Mediterranean Diet

Greasy caff, international bland, heart-clogging blow-outs and *tapas* are four categories of what you can eat in Barcelona. There is a fifth, the *'authentic'* choice, *cuina catalana*, Catalan cuisine, an outstanding example of the today very fashionable Mediterranean diet. Despite civil war, post-war famine, forty years of dictatorship, the highest proportion of smokers in the European Union and extensive alcoholism, Spain's life expectancy is higher than Britain's. Women have the highest in Europe, with an expectancy of 82.8 (in Barcelona, 83.3); though the men are only at 75.8, seventh in the list. Combining men and women, Spain is the European country with, after tiny Iceland, the longest life expectancy[2].

Though these statistics might indicate that longevity is due to excess smoking and drinking, it is generally attributed to the Mediterranean diet. The term covers a multitude of variations, though the use of olive oil, wine, pulses such as chick-peas and lentils, fresh vegetables and fruit, and abundant fish from Spain's long Mediterranean coastline are defining characteristics. The classic diet has much less red meat than in Northern Europe.

Fish is a passion in Spain. In the markets, the fish with their huge eyes and gaping mouths are piled high on dripping ice and the *peixateres*, the fish-women, in their eye-liner, starched pinafores and expensive coiffures, hail passers-by as if they were selling trinkets or sexual services. The dead fish, frozen in their last drowning gasp, evoke one of Vázquez Montalbán's hyperboles: "... *cuisine*, this alibi for so many murders." Fish represents more than 10% of Spaniards' total expenditure on food — a much higher proportion than in Britain; and fish in Spain is dearer than meat. The *peix de platja*, beach fish, meaning it is caught by local fishing fleets, is not so appealing as once it was, given the sharp deterioration in the quality of water in the Mediterranean. The inland sea is overloaded with the pollution poured into it.

A cult of Catalan food has developed over the last decade. Numerous good, expensive restaurants offering inventive cooking based on Catalan cuisine have opened. Young star chefs are treated like artists. Some become T.V. stars. You can spend fortunes eating at *Can Gaig* in Barcelona or going North to *El Bulli*, Ferran Adrià's restaurant near Roses or *El Racó de Can Fabes* at Sant Celoni (with two, three and three Michelin stars, respectively).

The heartland of traditional Catalan cuisine is the Empordà, a plain between the Pyrenees and the sea to the North of Barcelona. Between sea and hills, between Provence with Italy not so far and Valencia with Castile nearby, the Empordà is the melting pot where Catalan *cuisine* was mixed. Lashed for a fifth of the days of the year by the *tramontana*, the wild wind from the north tearing across the mountains, its inhabitants have time confined indoors to cook. Among Josep Pla's 45-volume *Collected Works*, there are lengthy treatises on fish, kitchens and eating. If the *tramontana* doesn't drive you mad, as it did Dalí's grand-father, who fled from the gales lashing Cape Creus only to jump to his death from his windless Barcelona apartment, it can make you a cook.

Mar i muntanya, sea and mountain, is what defines many Ampordanese dishes, a mix of the products of the sea and the hills, like the paella. This, in Catalonia, is often made with rabbit or chicken as well as shell-fish, unlike the traditional Valencian dish. Look out for other Catalan versions of paella: *arròs negre*, rice blackened with squid ink instead of golden with saffron; or *fideuà*, the paella ingredients cooked with noodles not rice.

Mar i cel, sea and Heaven, is another Ampordanese dish, combining shrimps and rabbit. Rabbit and plums or chicken and pears are other combinations that cross normal boundaries. The Roses restaurant and laboratory of tastes of the now world-famous Ferran Adrià is in the Empordà. Though Adrià is a one-off eccentric of the food world, his roots are recognisable in the mixes of tastes and of categories of food that are traditional in the area.

If Catalonia's sea is full of polluted fish, its land is full of polluting pigs. Even the Dutch send their pigs to Catalonia for fattening. This has the advantage that pig slurry is contaminating water supplies in the area around the city of Vic, and not the flat lands of the low countries, where it could not even run away down the hill to the sea. In Catalonia pig is eaten in every conceivable way. Rich sausages — white, red or black; raw or cooked; *fuet, bisbe, bull, xoriço, sobrassada, llonganissa,* just some of their many names — are available everywhere. Pig's commonest form is *botifarra*: *botifarra amb seques*, sausage and beans, is a simple national dish that can be terrible or perfect.

The main dangers on holiday, apart from extreme exhaustion and a desire to recover your equilibrium by getting back to work, are diarrhoea (mainly solved by keeping out of the greasy bars and taking care with *tapas* left enticingly uncovered on the counter for everyone to breathe over) and constipation. The latter can be solved in Barcelona by the Catalan penchant for big salads that can often serve as a whole meal, not just a first course. Try *esqueixada*, with onions, peppers, black olives and salt cod; *xató*, with bitter endives, tuna, anchovies and the spicy *romesco* sauce of peppers, tomatoes and almonds; *amanida catalana*, salad with cold pork products; or *empedrat*, with chick-peas, boiled egg, tuna, peppers, tomato, onion.

Despite salad diversity, vegetarians do not have it easy in Spain. Vegetables are widely eaten, often in season, but usually flavoured with ham or sausage. Catalan salads often have bits of meat, vegetable soups are often spiced with a piece of pork sausage. Boiled vegetables by themselves are not embraced. The *samfaina* is a basic dish, though: it is like French ratatouille, a stew of aubergine, courgette, onion and tomato in olive oil. As another variation on *mar i muntanya*, eat salt cod stewed with this inland dish: *bacallà amb samfaina*.

To eat in Catalonia, you need to adapt to the local rhythms: lunch at two and supper at nine. Then you can take advantage of the best restaurant bargain in Europe, Spain's mid-day *menú del dia*, set-price menu. Try not to go too low in the price range, because the *menú* can be grim. But for eight to ten euros, you can often eat a good three-course meal, with wine thrown in if you don't mind sleeping afterwards. There is rarely a *menú del dia* in the evening, which makes the evening meal dearer. Evening can be the time to try *tapas* or the greasy caffs. There's choice enough: there are a huge number of restaurants in Barcelona. Most show their menus and prices outside; you have to try your luck.

On Sunday mornings in the Eixample, you will see queues in the very frequent cake-shops, *pastisseries*. The *barcelonins* going to lunch with the family will bear cakes, often a variety of individual cakelets, placed on a card tray with a card-board band placed over to prevent them being squashed, then wrapped with glossy paper tied with a ribbon. In the coloured ribbon a ring is formed and the dinky packet is dangled from two fingers along the street.

Puddings, like cakes, are good in Catalonia. If you ask for *pudin*, though, you will get sponge-cake. Try the simple desserts: *Mel i mató*, curds with honey; *Música*, fruits and nuts with muscatel, so called because they were given to musicians in the intervals of their performances; or *Crema catalana*, custard with burnt sugar topping.

Gràcia

Before 1992 it used to be possible to go to Barceloneta, the eighteenth-century seafarers' quarter on a promontory just North of the main harbour and eat magical fish lunches in sand-strewn shacks that gave onto the beach (see Ch. 16). Their demolition, in the name of getting rid of insalubrious dives now that Catalonia was becoming European and Olympic, gravely damaged Barcelona's culinary reputation. Instead, visitors are encouraged to go along the shore to the restaurant complex at the Port Olímpic. This is a sort of modern imitation of the most spoiled Costa Brava resorts: here you can eat under the twin towers of the Olympic village almost anything at all. Of the five styles defined in this chapter, it definitely tips towards international bland.

The best counter-point to the Port Olímpic is Gràcia, an area to stimulate your eyes, taste-buds and nose. Tranquillity, not bustle; traditional squares, not new plazas. In the side-streets you can still find the "dark little wine shops with a sweet-smelling counter frequented by solitary drinkers," in Juan Marsé's nostalgic words. For sure, Gràcia is changing constantly too: most notably in the number of North European foreigners now living there. These are known as *guiris*, possibly from the Catalan word *guirigall* meaning *confused babbling*. Yet, in comparison with much of Barcelona, its attraction is the constancy of its village atmosphere. If you stroll into Gràcia from where the Eixample ends by the Diagonal at the top of the Passeig de Gràcia, at about 7pm, the urban village is at its best. The tree-lined, pedestrianised Carrer Torrijos, say: follow it up from the Travessera de Gràcia. Its shops are open: African goods and food shops, furniture stores, a bike shop run by a Dutchman, small wood workshops (reminiscent of Rodoreda's Quimet in Ch. 6), ordinary local grocer's and veg. shops, and all sorts of bars and restaurants. Torrijos runs past the Verdi Park, complex of cinemas where you can always find a film in English (*versió original*) and ends in the Plaça de la Virreina, to my mind the most beautiful of Gràcia's dozen squares. It is a "hard square," without flower-beds, and it works. Kids play football, teenagers sprawl over the benches, *okupas* roll joints, bicyclists cross, an old couple wander arm in arm. The mixed architecture feels settled: the flat-faced apartment houses with their wiggly or bulging-out cast-iron balconies, not flat and stern like Parisian ones; the great church of rough stone at the top of the square; and on the corner of Torrijos, palatial houses, one with a spire.

The old town of Gràcia is the place to eat at night. In the elegant Salambó, you can savour a big, old-style café-restaurant, its decor of rare woods ransacked from Brazilian jungles and benches of rounded wooden slats like the ones on cross-channel ferries. The Salambó is on Torrijos, and beside it, on the corner of the Virreina square, is the restaurant called the Pas de Virreina, specialising in the wild mushrooms that are a passion in Catalonia. Even if you don't want to eat them, in spring or autumn look in the door at the baskets full of several varieties, reeking of the damp secret smell of upturned moss and rotting leaves.

The squares, the Plaça de Rius i Taulet, the nearby Plaça de la Revolució or the Plaça del Sol, are all ringed with restaurants and cafés where you can get full meals or *tapas*. In these outdoor cafés, the tang of marijuana hangs in the air on humid summer evenings, like orange blossom in Valencia.

Gràcia retains the alternative, libertarian and bohemian

atmosphere that can be traced back to the nineteenth century. With its barrel-making and corset industries, it was early a centre of working-class activity and agitation: the Republicans and Federalists of the 1870s became in later generations the anarchists of the 1920s and '30s. It was also a centre of free-thinking ideologies. Vegetarianism, Protestantism, theosophy, Esperanto were just some of the currents of thought that left their mark. In 1897, when Gràcia was swallowed against its will by Barcelona, it was a town of 60,000 inhabitants, the ninth largest in all Spain.

In the late nineteenth century, six journals were published in Gràcia, one of them feminist, and another the famous *L'Esquella de la Torratxa*, The Bell of the Tower. This Republican weekly was named after Gràcia's most striking emblem, the 33-metre clock-tower facing the Town Hall in the Plaça de Rius i Taulet. The clock-tower was symbol of Liberty, its bell ringing out to summon the *gràciencs* to revolt or defence of their town. Barricades went up repeatedly in Gràcia: in 1870, 1874, 1909, 1917 and 1936.

Smoke

You are likely to find yourself, in this pursuit of café life and Mediterranean cookery, sitting at the next table to people smoking. Usually tobacco, though soft drugs have been decriminalised and are smoked in public, especially in Gràcia. Spain has today the highest proportion of tobacco smokers in the countries of Western Europe. 36% of the population, fourteen million people, smoked in the year 2000. Richard Ford's nineteenth-century observation that a Spaniard without a cigar "resembled a house without a chimney, a steamer without a funnel" still holds. Smoking reached its peak in 1986, but the steady drop in male smokers since then has been nearly made up for by the increase in women smokers. By the turn of the century, reported the Catalan Institute of Oncology, 45% of women between 15 and 24 smoked, as against 43% of men.

Why is this? Are Catalans more easily overwhelmed by the seductive power of multinationals? One of the tobacco companies' most enticing half-truths is that smoking keeps you thin. Thus, people happily consume enormous portions of junk food plus cakes, then light up as often as possible to defend their waist-line. In 2006, in Barcelona restaurants, people look at you in amazement if you make the request, standard in Britain now for at least twenty years, to the people at the next table: "Excuse me, would you mind not smoking?" Such words are considered close to fascism, an undue interference in individual liberty. And there lies one of the keys to smoking. Catalonia, and Spain as a whole, came late to democratic consumer habits. Women rarely smoked in public before 1975: and it still seems a sign of freedom, and not of addiction or sub-jection to multinational propaganda.

Alcohol consumption in Spain is near the top of EU lists: usually placed second only to France. Lack of drunkenness disguises the extent of drinking, which may start early in the morning with people on their way to work downing an *anís* or *conyac* to 'matar el gusanillo' (kill the little worm), i.e. stave off hunger. Beer with mid-morning breakfast, late-morning *cigaló* (small black coffee flooded with brandy), wine with lunch, a liqueur with the coffee, after-work *gin-tònic*[3], wine with supper, a night-cap... So it goes on. If Spanish society has especially high levels of addiction, it may well be that it is extraordinarily stressed. The Civil War, famine and migration from country to city that Spaniards have lived through in recent generations are comparable to the pressures that Irish or Caribbean migrants to Britain have faced. Pressures that lead to higher rates of alcoholism and mental illness.

There are contradictory dynamics at work, for Spain is also famous as the country of relaxed living. Catalonia, in particular, prides itself on knowing how to relax and enjoy life, as well as work hard. As so often with national gener-alisations, they are applicable to a relatively small and more visible or vociferous layer of the population: a prosperous middle- and upper working-class. If you work hard in an office and then relax in a nice flat or a second home at the week-end, it may well be true that you have a good balance between hard work and leisure. Yet increasingly insecure jobs are undermining this balance, even for high-earners. If you are one of the over-50% of the population that lives in a small flat, very possibly with parents or adult children still there, in an underpaid job with difficulties making ends meet, cheap alcohol and tobacco are attractive props.

So Spaniards live longer than Britons. But for how much longer will they live longer? Work is becoming much more stressful, as multinationals press for greater productivity; the Mediterranean sea is dying; and the Mediterranean diet is being eroded. Young people are suffering the diseases of greater prosperity and addiction: already their cholesterol intake is higher as they consume fast food. In response, Ferran Adrià ran a *Fast Good* campaign to introduce the healthy Mediterranean diet to the young and the work-stressed junk-food consumers. However, this commercial gimmick is not going to help people savour their food. To become trustworthy in the way Carvalho suggests, eat slowly, preferably on a square in Gràcia. Try not to be a British cannibal, bolting down your food as if you hated it.

---

[1] *Except, perhaps,* Chupa Chups, *which had to retrench in 2003 after over-extension in Russia and China.*

[2] *OECD data for 2003.*

[3] *Spirits are poured in famously generous measures, bottle upended, often spilt to Brits' dismay over the counter: no silly arguments here about fifths or sixths of gills.*

Chapter 14
The Greatest Show on Earth

"We need victories. They cover over all defeats."
JUAN ANTONIO SAMARANCH.

The Best Games in History

On 25 July 1992, a middle-aged archer drew back his bow and fired the Olympic torch into the evening sky. The arrow, tipped with flaming pitch, curved into the Mediterranean sky revered by Gaudí and dropped into the bowl on top of the Montjuïc Stadium. The whirl of dark smoke at once erased by a puff of fire from the bowl opened the 1992 Olympic Games. That spring, after its travels round the world, the torch had come ashore at Empúries, the Greek and Roman ruins by the Bay of Roses, on the upper Costa Brava. Women in sandals and white tunics bearing wreaths stood on the sand before the round-topped pines to receive the small boat bearing the athlete with the eternal flame in to the beach. The symbols reminded the world's T.V. viewers of the Games' roots in the ancient Athenian ideal of the physical beauty and strength of youth. Or the Roman dream that a healthy body would house a healthy mind. For those who had seen Leni Riefenstahl's film *Olympia*, it might have conjured up too the Nazi perversion of this ideal. The Olympics, the "festival of youth and fair play," had returned to the shores of the Mediterranean for the first time since Rome in 1960.

In summer, a lot of *barcelonins* come down onto the street: the consequence of small flats, hot weather and a tradition brought from country villages. And people like to look. At anything going on in the street, at the beautiful or ugly passing by. There are always people watching people work (often offering advice) on the very frequent building-sites. The day before the Olympic opening ceremony, the torch was due to pass along the main road near where I lived at about 11.30 on a muggy evening. The street was packed. We had to wait an hour. Then the glow of the torch and the whiff of tar passed in a flash. The event in itself was nothing, like a 100-metre final: the talking up and the race post-mortem is all. The hour spent listening to the neighbours chat brought home the real popularity of the Olympic Games among the city's residents. Six years of disruption due to perpetual roadworks; six years of spending on stadiums, the Olympic villages and a new highway circling the city, while most of the population struggled to make ends meet, had not affected masses of *barcelonins*' pride in their city being projected onto the world stage. Several factors combined: passion for sport, satisfaction at getting one-up on Madrid, the fact that Catalonia's existence was being proclaimed round the world, and pleasure in the physical changes of the city. In 1991, on the first Sunday the Olympic village was open to the public, about a quarter of a million people went to see it. Tens of thousands of Olympic volunteers, working unpaid as guides, drivers, secretaries, ticket-checkers or translators, reflected this broad support.

Thus, the Games were popular among residents, or those who remained. In Barcelona in August, half the population leaves, the rich off to their second homes, and the poor too, though the poor's second homes are their *first*: the remote villages from which they emigrated. The Games attracted numerous visitors, too. After the dismantling of the Berlin wall and the fall of the Soviet Union, Barcelona's was a peaceful Games. For a brief two weeks people could even believe that the Games augured a post-Cold War world without war. Many a visitor discovered a city packed with people, yet hassle-free. The streets were full of open bars, pedestrians and street musicians and the pitted stone of the mediaeval city was bathed in soft electric light till the small hours. As visiting friends of mine did, you could climb the Sagrada Família towers in the afternoon, stroll down to the Diagonal to join the crowds applauding the women's marathon in the early evening, then wander up to have a drink and *tapas* on a bar terrace in a Gràcia square. Security, safety, relaxed atmosphere — no drunks, no bombs, no heavy cops, little hassling of women in the street, few muggings — are absolutely crucial factors in the re-birth of Barcelona as a tourist destination. Of course all these nasty things occur, but not so much as elsewhere. Or they are not perceived to happen so much. It is part of what Richard Rogers called, comparing London negatively with Barcelona, "the quality of the street — the whole public domain." During the Olympic fortnight, the massive police presence was hardly visible. It was easy to travel by metro to the Plaça de Espanya, walk through the towers, imitations of the campanile in Venice's St. Mark's Square, and ride on the brand-new escalators up the side of Montjuïc while watching the city unfold below. Escalators in the open air always seem extra-luxurious. The trees brush past your fingers, you rise slowly above the grandiose pomposity of the Royal Palace, and you turn to see the city open out behind like a child's model.

The Barcelona Games employed the richness of contemporary Catalan culture. Victoria de los Ángeles, daughter of a porter at the University of Barcelona, sang *El cant dels ocells,* The song of the birds. She was the local girl who had conquered the world's opera houses, back in her home town. And singing before the world's cameras the song most closely associated with one of the twentieth-century's greatest musicians, the cellist Pau Casals, who had dedicated the last decades of his 97-year life to the peace movement and to keeping alive Catalan nationalism in exile, messages he took to the tribune of the United Nations. In October 1971, aged 95, cello gripped in one hand, Casals stood and addressed the General Assembly in Catalan:

"I am Catalan. Today Catalonia has been reduced to a few provinces of Spain. But what was Catalonia? Catalonia was the greatest nation in the world... I will tell you why."

And he explained that Catalonia had had a Parliament before England and that in the eleventh century it had discussed peace among nations, in a sort of precursor to the United Nations. He said too that, after many years of not performing in public, he was going to play a Catalan folk tune:

"...El cant dels ocells. The birds in the sky sing 'Peace, peace, peace' and it is a song... that is born from the spirit of my people, Catalonia."

Thus Casals in the culminating performance of his life united his three life-long passions: music, the fight against war and Catalonia. As Victoria de los Ángeles sang *El cant dels ocells*, there wasn't a dry Catalan eye in the stadium.

Bridging high and mass culture, Montserrat Caballé sang the electrifying anthem, *Barcelo-o-o-ona*, that she had recorded with the late Freddy Mercury. Josep Carreras, recovered from leukemia, sang the theme-tune of the Games, the sugary *Amics per sempre*, Friends for Ever, a slight advance perhaps on the 1988 Seoul Games' *Harmony and Progress*. At the closing ceremony the organisers let loose La Fura dels Baus, avant-garde multimedia theatre group, reminders that Catalans are capable not just of *seny*, good sense, manifested here in the form of excellent organisation, but of *rauxa* too. Of wild spectacle.

The Games could not just evoke Catalan identity, but had to be finely balanced so that the Spanish State, which was after all the main financial backer of the event, and the King, who was Head of that State, were not neglected. This was publicly shown in the theatrical terms in which events such as the Olympics are composed by the tall handsome heir to the throne, Prince Felipe, carrying Spain's banner at the opening ceremony. The tears shed by those listening to that Angelic voice singing *El cant dels ocells* were matched by the apparently spontaneous and widely televised tears of Princess Elena applauding her brother.

Fears of the monarch being booed in his own country were well founded. In September 1989, it had occurred when King Juan Carlos had opened the Montjuïc stadium. Demonstrators, among them President Pujol's youngest son Oleguer, had hissed the Spanish national anthem (as *Barça* fans had in 1925) and unfurled banners demanding, in English, *Freedom for Catalonia*. Independence fervour, not high anyway in Catalonia, as opposed to regional autonomy, was skilfully neutralised by Pujol through a high-cost international advertising campaign that reminded readers of *Time*, *Corriere della Sera* or *Le Monde* that the Games were being held in Catalonia, a nation within the Spanish state. Pujol was Janus, always facing two ways with more skill than principle. Thus, in turn, to balance the adverts, in 1991 Pujol's party had assuaged Spanish centralist sensibilities by promoting a statement in the *Parlament*, the Catalan Parliament in the Ciutadella Park, that Catalonia did not aspire to independence.

The Barcelona Games produced no great sporting star, a Mark Spitz, Jesse Owens or Olga Korbut. This allowed politicians of various stripes to proclaim *The people of Barcelona are the stars*. Yet, not only in the opening and closing ceremonies, but on the track and field, the Games gave moments of high emotion: Fermín Cacho romping home clear in the blue riband, the 1500 metres, to win Spain's first-ever Olympic track medal; Linford Christie emerging at last from the shadows of Carl Lewis and Ben Johnson and proving he was a Number One in the other great track event, the 100 metres. And the other side of the coin, Gail Devers tripping as she led over the last hurdle and falling only inches from the 110 meters hurdles tape; and Derek Redmond, muscular Londoner who had overcome injury to be in with a chance of a 400-metre medal, breaking down with a snapped ligament on the back straight in the semi-final. Redmond's father evaded the security to jump onto the track and comfort the runner weeping in pain, frustration and pride as he hopped round the rest of the course. The photos of this security lapse humanised the games, as much as the Princess's tears and the beautiful singing voices.

When the two-week Games reached their conclusion, sighs of relief were heaved by the organisers. The three nightmare scenarios had been avoided: the threatened attack by the Basque terrorist group ETA had not occurred, no high-profile doping had come to light, and no-one had insulted the Spanish Royal Family. Pasqual Maragall, Mayor of Barcelona and the person most associated with the '92 Games, had done it. When he closed the Games, the IOC (International Olympic Committee) President Juan Antonio Samaranch could say: "We have brought it off... the best Games in all Olympic history."

It might be said that competition was weak. Despite its self-proclaimed role as a promoter of peace among the peoples of the world, in 1992 you had to be middle-aged to recall a peaceful Olympics. In Seoul in 1988, thousands of opponents of the military dictatorship had been arrested and beaten in the weeks preceding the Games. In the '88 Games itself, Ben Johnson had been disgraced for taking steroids to help him win the 100-metre final; and the boxing results were so scandalously rigged that, to their great credit, 50,000 Koreans rang in to protest the victory of the Korean boxer Park Si Hun in the light-middleweight final.

Before that, the 1984 Los Angeles Games had been boycotted by the Russians; 1980 Moscow, by the Americans; 1976 Montreal had lost a billion dollars; 1972 Munich saw the death of eleven Israeli athletes at the hands of Black September; in Mexico in 1968 hundreds of demonstrators were slaughtered by police in Tlatelolco Square a few days before the Games opened. It was not too difficult for Samaranch to pronounce the Barcelona Games "the best in history."

The Chameleon

Samaranch had deeper and more personal reasons for satisfaction. The most extraordinary moment of the Barcelona Games was when Samaranch and Maragall shook hands on the stadium field. This was a public meeting of two worlds: the ex-Falangist and the ex-radical socialist. For Samaranch had been a member of Franco's National Movement, and Maragall a 1960s activist in the opposition FLP, *Popular Liberation Front*. Maragall's sister had been imprisoned under Franco. As IOC President, Samaranch received state acceptance; as President (non-executive) of Catalonia's most powerful bank *La Caixa*, he had the acceptance of big business. But Samaranch had been an outcast in democratic opinion: the handshake and the success of the Games sealed his long and tortuous path back to public recognition in Spain. It was a handshake that illuminated the strengths and weaknesses of post-Franco Spain.

Fifteen years before, on April 23 1977, *Sant Jordi* and a really political book day that year, Samaranch had ordered the barricading of the doors of the *Diputación*, the Barcelona Regional Council, of which he was President. The *Diputación* was then lodged in the Palace of the Generalitat described in Chapter Six, its home since Franco abolished the Generalitat and Catalan autonomy in 1939. Outside, in the Plaça Sant Jaume, 100,000 people were chanting: "Samaranch, fot el camp!" which can be more or less translated: "Fuck off, Samaranch!" It was the climax of Juan Antonio Samaranch's long political career as a faithful servant of the dictatorship.

Born in 1920 into a family of textile manufacturers, the young Samaranch was a well-known playboy in impoverished post-war Barcelona. His ambition ran further than girls, night-clubs and fast cars, though. From as early as 1943 he was involved in sports organisation. To start with, he chose a minority sport in which Spain was prominent and financed out of his own pocket the Spanish roller hockey team. This investment paid off when the world roller hockey championships were held in Barcelona in 1951. Such an event — and the Spanish team won — was one of the first cracks in the wall of an international boycott. Sport, as already seen in the Kubala story, played a part in ending the political ostracism of Hitler's and Mussolini's ally.

The playboy's first major contact with the Olympic world was in 1955, when eight IOC members attended the Mediterranean games held in Barcelona. Samaranch had been Vice-president of the organising committee and was rewarded for the Games' success by a post on Barcelona City Council. Doubts were expressed, though, about his inappropriate life-style. He had to meet two requisites if he was going to be a serious politician: formally join Franco's *Movimiento nacional*, the Falange, the blue-shirted equivalent of Mussolini's black-shirts, and get married. These two formalities dealt with, he then rose rapidly to take charge of sport in Catalonia. In the 1950s and '60s Samaranch made his own fortune to add to the family money. He was a founder member of the Banco de Madrid, whose direct contacts with the Franco family smoothed any obstacles to its projects. His construction companies built both resort complexes on the Costa Brava to meet the tourist boom and cheap, high-rise blocks on the outskirts of Barcelona to house migrants from other parts of Spain.

In 1965 Samaranch was present when Franco himself opened the IOC annual meeting in Madrid; and in 1966 he was nominated to a vacant post on the IOC. In the same year he became Spain's equivalent of Minister for Sport. In none of these promotions was Samaranch exposed to anything so vulgar as an election. His advances were achieved through the standard practices under a dictatorship: contacts and favours.

In recent years, Samaranch has succeeded in retiring from his twenty-year Presidency of the IOC without being spattered by the bribes and gifts scandals, associated most blatantly with the awarding, or *rewarding*, of the 2002 Winter Olympics to Salt Lake City. When this scandal washed over the IOC in the late 1990s, the dignified elder statesman Samaranch stood apart in Olympian disdain for the corrupt IOC members. Six scapegoats were forced to resign in 1999 for accepting gifts, a polite word for bribes. These *gifts* were not just the standard petty graft of free lunches, plane tickets and hotel accommodation. They also consisted of gold watches, clothes, furniture, travel, holidays, presents for family members...

After the death of his patron Franco and the democratisation of the Barcelona Regional Council, Samaranch had to *fotre el camp* all the way to Moscow. He managed to get the job of Spanish Ambassador to the Soviet Union, where he was in place in the lead-up to the Moscow Games to win the glittering prize, the Presidency of the IOC, on July 16 1980.

The IOC had been a thoroughly amateur organisation, run on a shoestring. It was infused with the British public school ethos of amateurism, service and paternalism under the American Avery Brundage (President 1952-1972, see below) then Lord Killanin. It was wide open for professional politicians like Samaranch, who knew how to build the international alliances to win power. It jumped from an operation with eleven members of staff run out of three rooms in Lausanne in the 1960s to an organisation with over sixty employees, its own buildings in delightful grounds and a multi-million dollar turnover today.

Mexico in 1968 had been the first games to be satellite-broadcast round the world. The world then was amazed that TV companies paid a fabulous ten million dollars for rights. By the 1984 Los Angeles Games (profitable, unlike the Montreal disaster) this had reached 225 million dollars. By Barcelona 1992 the total sum paid to the IOC by the world's TV companies for coverage of the Games was calculated at 633 million dollars. With blanket TV coverage, a second source of income opened. Corporate sponsorship took off after Los Angeles, such that at

Barcelona there was a *Top 12*, consisting of companies who paid a fortune for exclusive sponsorship in their fields of the Games. Olympic accounts are not transparent, but the 'contributions' of the *Top 12* are estimated at about 30 million dollars each. The Barcelona *Top 12* consisted of Coca-Cola, Kodak, Brother, Panasonic, Philips, *Time Magazine*, Mars, Bausch & Lomb (Rayban sun-glasses), EMS parcels, 3M, Ricoh and Visa. Any doubts about spending such sums were doused by the deal's exclusivity: this meant competitors, whether Pepsi, Fuji, *Newsweek* or American Express, were excluded.

The President of Coca-Cola had been decorated by Samaranch with the Olympic Order in 1988 for his company's "profound sense of a positive concept of life." Coca-Cola and the rest of the *Top 12* believe that companies associated with the Olympics brand become associated with Olympic qualities: fair competition, healthy youth and, most of all, gold medals. Undoubtedly the spending companies are right, but how could the Olympic movement justify such prostitution of its values?

It was President Samaranch who oversaw this process of commercialisation. It is the moment to step back and consider the beliefs of this man who spent almost his entire working life in the service of a fascist state, then his later years, when most people have retired, apparently furthering the aims of the Olympic movement, whose Charter explicitly commits its members to resisting "all pressures... including those of a political or economic nature."

Samaranch has argued that: "It is right to practise politics in order to improve sport, but wrong to use sport in the service of politics." This truism is designed to play down his career as a militant supporter of Franco. It is the shrug: what else could someone living in Spain at that time do? It is the implicit suggestion that he had no choice but live in Franco's Spain, yet followed the most honest path possible by dedicating himself to neutral activities such as the furthering of sport. Samaranch's selective telling of the past ignores the importance of sport in breaking down Spain's isolation. It also whitewashes his membership of the Falange, whose blue shirt and military white jacket he still donned after he became an IOC member. He was President of the Barcelona Regional Council from before Franco's death to 1977, a period when in the Barcelona area members of the urban guerrilla movements, ETA and GRAPO, were executed by firing squad in 1975 and the anarchist Salvador Puig Antich garrotted in 1974. Samaranch was not just the kindly old gentleman of his recent photographs, dedicating himself to sport during the dictatorship. He is responsible for things that the dictatorship did. It is not anything he has ever publicly apologised for. Indeed in his recent memoirs (*Olympic memoirs*, 2002) his defence is the alarmingly false one that a lot of other people did the same as he.

If I have devoted space to the remarkable rise, fall and resurgence of Samaranch, it is because his story illustrates a key aspect of the Spanish transition discussed earlier: a pact of silence about past crimes. The handshake with Maragall on the grass of the Montjuïc stadium represented an uneasy victory for Maragall. At the moment of his triumph as Olympic Mayor, he was granting democratic credentials to the old Falangist.

In being excused his responsibility for the dictatorship, Samaranch was allowed to carry on in the same old way. The IOC, this club of mainly rich, mainly old, mainly men on a gravy train until the age of 75 (extended in Samaranch's case), resembles nothing so much as the Franco dictatorship. President Samaranch played the role of the old dictator, famous for his inscrutability, never committing himself, balancing different factions. When Samaranch announced in the early '80s that he would be completely neutral in the contest to host the Games involving Barcelona, he was playing this game. Of course everyone knew what the old fox, the granter of favours, the maker or breaker of careers, really wanted. Samaranch changed his colours, but not his nature. The chameleon merely extended the practice of the first part of his political career into the second. As Simson and Jennings, in their exposé of the modern Olympics, the wittily titled *The Lords of the Rings*, summarised:

> *"Like a monarch – or a dictator – he [Samaranch] occasionally descends for photocalls with selected athletes and other supplicants. But like the astute politician he was for twenty-five years, Samaranch has not only re-invented himself, he has refashioned the Olympic movement in his own style of politics: the leader grants and accepts audiences with heads of state; the leader issues orders; the leader selects new IOC members and imposes them on the movement; the leader knows best; the leader's will is carried out; the leader appears at press conferences flanked by the banners of the movement."*

The People's Olympiad

This chapter has tried to express two contradictory features of the 1992 Olympics: its genuine popularity among tourists and residents alike as a relaxed festival of sport, and its profoundly undemocratic nature as a jamboree for multinationals and a source of power, privilege and money for the Olympic family. The next chapter examines the Barcelona model of development that reached its moment of apotheosis in the Olympics, but first I want to look back to Barcelona's previous Olympic Games, for which the Montjuïc stadium was originally built. Games that in the end never took place, yet indicated a different path the Olympic Movement could once have taken. Instead, it opted for Hitler's monumental, flag-waving, patriotic route.

The tourist bus up to the Olympic Stadium drops you before a brown 1930s building with towers, the outer cladding within which the modern stadium is fitted. Just recently renamed the Lluís Companys Stadium, in honour of the President of Catalonia shot in the fortress just a stone's throw up the hill, the stadium is a reminder of Barcelona's noble alternative Olympic tradition, forgotten in the self-blown fanfares of 1992. In 1928 the first stone of the Montjuïc Stadium was laid in the presence of the then IOC President, a man with the improbable name of Comte Henri de Ballet-Latour. Barcelona was a front-runner for the 1936 Olympics. The stadium was also seen as part of the urbanisation of Montjuïc for the 1929 International Exhibition.

The IOC was due to meet in Barcelona in late April 1931 to decide on the venue for the 1936 Games. On 12 April, 1931, the municipal elections forced Alfonso XIII and his family into exile and the Spanish Second Republic was declared. Most of the IOC, many of them aristocrats like their President, were understandably chary of going to Barcelona in the circumstances and only seven turned up for their meeting at the Ritz on April 24. These seven decided to organise a postal vote to decide on the venue, and it was announced on May 13 that Berlin had been chosen to host the 1936 Games. The fall of the Monarchy had scared the IOC off Barcelona.

In January 1933 Hitler became Chancellor of Germany. This led to an international movement to boycott the Berlin Games, which was at its strongest in the United States. Avery Brundage, then President of the US Olympic Committee, at first expressed doubts about Hitler: "The very foundation of the modern Olympic revival will be undermined if individual countries are allowed to restrict participation by reason of class, creed or race."

In 1934, however, Brundage convinced himself on an IOC inspection visit to Berlin that Jewish and black athletes would be treated fairly. He opposed the *Committee for Fair Play in Sport* movement with the age-old plaint that politics had no place in sport: "The Olympics belong to the athletes not the politicians." By 1935, under greater pressure, the democratic mask slipped and Brundage was denouncing a "Jewish-Communist conspiracy" to keep the USA out of the Games.

Barcelona organised the 1936 People's Olympics as an alternative to the Berlin Games: the only time a credible counter-initiative has got off the ground. After the Popular Front came to power in Spain in February 1936,

259

the Barcelona Games were supported by the Spanish government. Construction of the Montjuïc Stadium, a brazen challenge to the brooding fortress of the Spanish Army on top of the hill, was completed. Spain and the Soviet Union were the only major European countries to boycott Berlin. The Barcelona Games, a focus for anti-nazis from round the world, were due to open on 18 July. Some 1,500 athletes from sixteen countries arrived in Barcelona in the preceding days, paid for by the large protest movements and labour organisations. In the United States, half a million signatures in favour of boycotting Berlin were collected and the contributions of this movement financed the small US contingent that arrived on Friday 17 July. On the Saturday the Americans trained in the Montjuïc stadium, but they never got to compete, for on the Sunday the revolution described in Chapter Three erupted and the People's Olympics was cancelled. Some athletes joined in the fighting: a French runner was killed. The British Workers' Sports Federation athletes and the Americans demonstrated in support of the militia. A few days later they were shipped out to Sête in France.

Hitler's Games may seem, in retrospect, a victory for the anti-fascists. It was there that the black American athlete Jesse Owens entered history as the person who disproved Hitler's racial theories on the track by winning four gold medals. At the time, however, the Berlin Olympics gave Hitler international publicity and support. *The New York Times* reported that the Games put Germany "back in the fold of nations." Leni Riefenstahl's famous propaganda film *Olympia* persuaded millions that Germany was not so bad after all. *Olympia* shows Hitler's skilful use of mass propaganda, the great hanging banners and blocks of marching athletes. In its use of spectacle in the service of patriotism, Berlin set the tone for Olympic Games since. The fact that German Jewish champions were excluded from the German team was not internationally publicised. The Berlin Games of August 1936 were a defeat for the opponents of fascism. The attendance of the USA and the rest of Europe signalled to Hitler that he would not be opposed in his support for Franco and march towards war.

Chapter 15
The Jewel in the Crown?

"Barcelona today is a model of urban planning that may prove sustainable... a model 21st century city, combining historic buildings with modern architecture in a fusion that has helped to make it one of the most popular tourist destinations in Europe."
THE BARCELONA BLUEPRINT.

Not Bulldozing

There are several lessons in the Barcelona Olympic experience for how London should build for the 2012 Games. It is disturbing that Richard Rogers, an influential figure close to Ken Livingstone, leapt in the day after the July 2005 winning of the Olympic bid with uncritical praise of Barcelona '92. He concluded in his *Guardian* article: "The Barcelona standard is what we have to achieve." Despite the excellences of the Barcelona water-front, there are several negative lessons from Barcelona: its expensive private housing, its love of roads, and air and noise pollution. It is becoming increasingly uninhabitable.

Do Londoners want the Olympic cash to be spent on prestige stadiums, new roads and private housing? The stakes are high. If they don't, if they want leisure and sports facilities for all, a pedestrianised city with better public transport and cheap, public housing, they have a fight on their hands. They can learn from Barcelona's success and failure.

These two final chapters examine the view expressed in the quote that opens the chapter, praise originating in the Council itself and repeated by its many admirers. Narcís Serra of the Socialist Party, who became in 1979 the first elected Mayor of Barcelona since the 1930s, claimed: "In no other place has an Olympic Games been so transcendental for a host city." In 1979, after decades of neglect on the one hand and *porciolista* speculation on the other, Barcelona was in urgent need of attention. Serra and his successor as Mayor from 1982, Pasqual Maragall, opted for hanging the whole development of the post-Franco city on the Olympics. Serra explained:

> *"The Olympic candidature was decided in the summer of 1980, when the city was suffering a cultural crisis, a lack of projects, the misery of a fierce economic crisis, and it was made public in May 1981, just after the attempted coup on 23 February, so we were very aware of the need to generate enthusiasm, to set out some tangible goals that people could see."*

Serra's words are revealing. 'The need to generate enthusiasm' expresses paternalism — the Council was dubbed by Vázquez Montalbán *enlightened despots*, term that brings to mind not socialist democracy but Medici Florence. Even the architect Richard Rogers, a great supporter of both Council and city, told me: "In Barcelona there is no question that everything is very top-downwards."

Serra's suggestion of the need for 'tangible goals' is evasive, given the extremely detailed proposals for parks, housing and urban reform that the Residents' Associations drew up during the transition. The Residents' Associations' agenda of wholesale reform was not Serra's, however. "The Socialist Party, not the Residents' Associations, won the elections," he made brutally clear. At the same time as the victorious Socialists rapidly distanced themselves from the more organised, left-wing section of Barcelona's voters, Serra appointed as Chief Planner the radical architect Oriol Bohigas, of the MBM (Martorell, Bohigas & Mackay) partnership. As well as a working architect, Bohigas was a writer, theoretician and Director of Barcelona's College of Architects from 1977 to 1980. Between 1980 and 1984 Bohigas left his mark on the first stage of Barcelona's post-Franco development.

Bohigas believed in "stitching together not bull-dozing." Long before, in his 1962 broadside *Towards realist architecture*, he had stated his credo:

> *"We are in favour of the given environment, against personalised exhibitionism and for the fragment of living city around a new building. Greater attention to detail and to the people who have to live in the house, and against the all-absorbent concentration on structure or abstract composition problems."*

This approach held good when Bohigas became city Planning Supremo. "We didn't want to demoralise ourselves, like other inexperienced democratic councils, in revisions of general plans," he explained. Thus the Council developed numerous small-scale reforms in outlying neighbourhoods to provide a park or square here, a children's play-ground there. Bohigas favoured de-centralisation of economic activity: he was aware of the 'doughnut' dangers of a city with its business and shops all in the centre. David Mackay told me, and his view here can be taken as little different from his partner Bohigas':

> *"...Cities have suffered from planning laws, which have been restrictive to zones: this is where you live, this is where you work, this is where you shop. Society's still under this sort of zonification. The real city is that city where everything goes on and there's an opportunity for new things to appear. If it's too regulated, the city can go dead, it can become like Venice, which is a museum-city for tourists."*

The use of sculptures to embellish bleak squares and blocks of flats also started under Bohigas. This public art programme boasted 550 pieces by 1995. Many of these were acquired brilliantly cheap, by the Council offering a 20,000-dollar flat fee plus costs of manufacture and installation. Thus Barcelona got the *Matches* in Horta from Claes Oldenbourg, Chillida's 80-ton spider in the Creueta del Coll, Botero's three-ton cat now in its fourth location on the Rambla del Raval, Rebecca Horn's *The wounded shooting star* (Ch. 16), to name a few of the best. Unlike Francoist architecture or most state monuments, and despite the large size of many of these sculptures, they were anti-monumental: in the sense that they did not glorify a historical triumph or famous personality. The down-side is that their abstraction lays them open to the accusation of lack of ideology, of becoming accomplices in the post-transition amnesia. In 1996 Maragall explained his view:

> *"Open-air sculpture becomes part of the urban system, and thus enriches it. Today, Barcelona is a city that invites one to stroll... The sculptures, standing proud day and night, defying inclement weather and merciless graffiti, have earned their respectable place in the city. They beckon us to start walking."*

One of many walks the visitor to Barcelona could undertake is a sculpture tour. It would lead to the most inhospitable outlying areas, their asphalt and tower-blocks sweetened by an internationally famous sculpture. The sculptures aroused controversy: populist politicians threatened to bull-doze some. Yet most have become a happy and popular facet of the city-scape. Maragall is right: works of art improve public space.

In the *Ciutat vella*, Bohigas developed the policy of *esponjament*, such as in the Plaça Orwell. As sculpture was small-scale embellishment, so *esponjament* was small-scale demolition to open up a small space, giving air to a *barri* like the holes in a sponge. Richard Rogers had a nice phrase to illustrate how Bohigas saw planning and architecture as one single combined activity: "...influence on the quality of space between buildings, as well as the high quality of the buildings themselves."

Serra asserted Council independence of the Residents' Associations proposals of large-scale reform. Nevertheless, many Council projects in the early years did indeed respond to the Associations' pressures: both because their demands often fitted into Serra's priorities and because it was politically expedient to cede to local demands and thus reap the electoral harvest. The *Plaça de l'Espanya industrial*, the huge *Parc de l'Escorxador* (slaughter-house), now renamed less vividly the *Parc de Joan Miró* and dominated by a remarkable palm forest and Miró's towering *trencadís 'Woman and Bird,'* and the *Plaça de Sant Martí* are all examples of victories for strong Residents' Associations demanding open space.

Space in cities is contested. Most people want parks, sports centres, decent housing, good local shops and markets. Private interests, always dominant historically, have different priorities. Once they had got over the brief fright of Socialists coming to power for the first time ever in Barcelona, real-estate owners and developers saw business could be done. The Council did not have the kind of cash it needed to make up for forty years of neglect. Nor, it was quickly clear, did it have the political will to use its popularity to challenge entrenched power. It is significant that Serra, though he had the legal power to do so, took no land into public ownership.

Under Serra and Maragall, the now-common practice began of reclassifying green areas to allow blocks of flats to be built, on condition that the property developers landscaped a small public park, square or gardens. The Council could get its park free and the private developer was happy: the park or garden increased the price for which the flats could be sold. Thus the Socialists, despite their anti-Franco credentials, were happy to work with private capital to inflate the price of housing. As in *Alice*, names in post-transition Spain have not meant what they were meant to mean: Socialists have not been socialists, Communists have not been revolutionaries and Nationalists haven't wanted Independence. Serra and Maragall were anti-ideological pragmatists, managing the system with a radical gloss.

The Socialists' room for manoeuvre was limited by the economic crisis of the early '80s, which contributed to the general disenchantment with the mundane reality of post-Franco Spain (Ch. 9). Spain's structural unemployment was extremely high. It still is: the reduction under the conservative *Partido Popular* (governing Spain from 1996 to 2004) had little to do with the creation of real, permanent jobs. The economy, with a narrow industrial base, depends disproportionately on tourism and construction. In the early '80s, the threatened closure of SEAT, the Zona Franca car plant, then its sale to Volkswagen and a moratorium on building projects exerted additional pressures on the Council. The Council built its way out of the early '80s crisis. Their extensive construction programme is still going on today. If the State and Generalitat paid for large parts of it, as occurred under the Olympics and Forum projects, so much the better. However, the main financier — and beneficiary — was the private sector.

In 1984 Bohigas resigned to return to his practice (MBM took on overall responsibility for the Poble Nou Olympic village) and was replaced by Josep Acebillo, still today the city's Chief Planner. Acebillo is identified with the big projects that turned Barcelona into a building boom town, soaking up early '80s unemployment: the ring-roads and the Olympic building programme. This latter focused on three main areas: the Vall d'Hebron, in the upper part of the city, where a mini-village for journalists was built; Montjuïc, where the main stadiums were located; and, most famously, the Olympic Village. David Mackay told me:

> *"The Olympic village was very complex, in the centre of the old Poble Nou industrial area. It would have been much simpler to follow what every other Olympic city had done and set up in a suburb. We had two years to get all the design through, negotiate with the railways, the sanitation of the city, the flooding, the metro, the archaeological problems, the whole problem of containing the sea, the new shores. There were an enormous amount of problems and people involved. Of course, if we hadn't won the Olympic nomination, it would have taken thirty years to build."*

Olympic Housing

On the 17th November 1986 in Lausanne, IOC President Samaranch announced that Barcelona had won the right to hold the twenty-fifth Olympiad. Serra's and Maragall's gamble on Olympic-led development had paid off. Barcelona's intensive lobbying had won them the 1992 nomination against Amsterdam, Belgrade, Birmingham, Brisbane and Jacques Chirac's Paris, their main rival. The 1985 Hayward Gallery exhibition had pitched out Barcelona's tent on the 'cultural front.' And a whole separate folder of Barcelona's exhaustive Olympic dossier evoked the twentieth-century artists associated with the city: Casals, Gaudí and its Holy Trinity of painters, Picasso, Miró and Dalí. The problem, though, was Paris. Any famous figure or cultural image that Barcelona could lay on the table, Paris could trump. It was the City of Light, the City of Art. Therefore, the Catalan application also hammered away at a major weakness of Los Angeles 1984, perceived to be a difficulty too for a conurbation so big as Paris: the difficulty of getting from one place to another. All Barcelona's main facilities were to be close to each other. They reckoned Carl Lewis could be driven from village to stadium in ten minutes, as fast as he could run. This was the pay-off for the bold measure of building the village on an inner-city brown-field (ex-industrial) site rather than on green fields outside the city. Special road lanes, continuously circulating buses for the 10,000 journalists, staggering of the city's commercial hours, were all planned in detail and aimed at putting first the needs of the 'Olympic family' itself. Despite Samaranch's implicit support for their bid, the city leaders had not been complacent. Chirac complained about undue influence, complaint which, as winners and as producers of an excellent dossier, Barcelona could shrug off.

For the next six years, the Games dominated every facet of Barcelona life. The Olympics was seen as a re-run of the 1888 and 1929 Exhibitions: a major event as the excuse to reconstruct large chunks of the city. It coincided with the get-rich-quick culture of late-80s Spain (much the same as in Thatcher's and Lawson's Britain). As Sagarra wrote of the 1929 Exhibition in *Vida privada*, "someone who failed to steal in the most bare-faced manner was someone missing fingers."

Eduardo Mendoza's *City of Marvels* shows how the 1888 and 1929 Exhibitions served to enrich entrepreneurs and make grand the city, but did little to address the underlying problems of health, housing and poverty of most *barcelonins*. Not for nothing did Mendoza later call this, his most famous book, published in that same 1986, "so anti-Olympic and so premonitory."

In one of his flares of iconoclasm, doubtless feeling the strain of so many small-scale interventions, Bohigas once said that everything done in the Franco years should be bull-dozed: precisely what he had refused to do when Planning Supremo. One assumes he meant, too, that the architectural jewels bulldozed in the Franco years should be un-bulldozed. With the Olympic Village, however, Bohigas and his partners also got the chance to bull-doze and design big: a whole new neighbourhood. Mackay said in 1998:

> "The Olympic village is an incredible place. I live there myself... I find I've gone back to a Barcelona that I found in 1958, where children can play in the street again... You meet a lot more people. There are about 2,000 families, which means a population of about 8,000, and another 8,000 who come to work there..."

Not all is as rosy as Mackay claimed. The village has not been wholly successful: well over a decade later there is still a lot of shop space untaken, leaving the bottom floors of classy blocks bricked up. In addition, part of the Olympic village was originally announced as cheap housing. The Council boasted: we will build this new neighbourhood, and it will be for everyone, even the housing. This did not happen. After its two-week occupancy by the world's top athletes, prices soared on the open market, with no control exerted by the Council. As Mackay says, it is a green neighbourhood, where children can play outside, as in the 1950s, but the comparison he makes is false. 1950s quiet was because there were few cars; in the 1990s, children could only play outside in the fenced-off protected gardens of the green middle-class enclave the Olympic Village has become. When Robert Hughes, in his 1991 BBC film *Barcelona*, with characteristic chutzpah asked Oriol Bohigas, by then City Arts Supremo: "This development was never intended for workers' housing, was it?", Bohigas side-stepped the question.

Names are cheap, however, and the main street of the Olympic Village was dubbed the Avinguda d'Icària after the *Icària* commune founded by utopian socialists, including some from Barcelona, in Louisiana in the 1840s. With Olympic village flats at 500 dollars a square metre even in 1992, Hughes spluttered in radical indignation, "you might as well call a luxury condo on Manhattan Karl Marx Towers." Maybe the Council in this naming was celebrating the failure of the Louisiana venture, which sank into the Mississippi swamps. They're probably not so cynical, though. Like Genet or Orwell, Icària was just a name associated with the city.

The central claim for Barcelona's urban renewal was stated some years ago by Richard Rogers as follows:

> *"Barcelona is the ideal for most planners and architects in that it's the jewel in the crown which we are trying to achieve in other cities... They've got nearer to dealing with the industrial past which is a very difficult period because we're seeing the end of heavy industry."*

When you go to Sants and look at the *Parc de l'Espanya industrial* on an old industrial site or the former Güell factory converted to a public library, few would disagree that this is good use of abandoned nineteenth-century factories. Yet it is not just the visible, visited results that should be assessed. What happened to all the other factories and slum housing demolished? In Sants and Poble Nou most indus-

270

trial sites have been or are being transformed into housing. This sounds praiseworthy, just what the Residents' Associations wanted in 1979. However, these are all private flats, with most of their owners fully mortgaged. In 2005, an average first flat cost over 100% of an average income. It is only affordable if both partners in a childless couple work.

New expensive flats do not alleviate Barcelona's horrendous housing problems. The young, bar the 10% of rich and high-flying graduates, cannot buy a flat without family help. And you need a permanent employment contract to rent a flat on the minuscule rental market, yet 80% of under-30 year olds in work are on short-term contracts. At the bottom end of the scale, this leaves many people without housing: forced to live in distant suburbs, live with their parents, squat or sleep in the parks.

Barcelona has created beautiful parks, full of sculpture, public spaces and facilities; of clear benefit to its residents as well as tourists. But if the city has no programme of public housing and cannot house its citizens, how can one talk of sustainable development as Barcelona's champions do? It cannot be sustainable to have a city for tourists and the wealthy, with those around them in slums.

It was Franco who persuaded Spaniards of the importance of becoming home-owners. Before, people in Spain rented, as most French still do. Often soaring property prices are attributed to Barcelona being squashed onto its narrow plain between Collserola and the sea. The argument is contradicted by Madrid prices, which are as high despite the availability of space for expansion. Not geography, but policy is the explanation: whether or not the Council has the political will to control land by taking it into municipal ownership, stopping speculative building, providing cheap municipal housing or by limiting prices.

Like Mackay, Carles Prieto (see Ch. 9) believed that, though many individual decisions of the Council can be criticised, there was no alternative to the Olympic model of development. He told me: "Go to Poble Nou on a Sunday and you will see how people use the village and

271

beaches, now only a metro ride away." However, the popularity of the beaches does not close the argument. The marine park created right along the front is clearly popular; but few do not desire cheaper housing.

The *Pla de la Ribera*, the Shore Plan, was an attempt, in the bad old 1960s, by the owners of factory land in Poble Nou to multiply their fortunes by getting the land reclassified for building. The *Pla de la Ribera* was strongly opposed then by the very opposition professionals who were to govern the city in the 1980s. Yet in the '80s the Council implemented this *Pla de la Ribera* as the Olympic plan, instead of compulsorily purchasing the unused ex-factory land in Poble Nou in the early '80s and then controlling its development. The Council's evident lack of money for compulsory purchase did not inhibit them from becoming heavily indebted in the Olympics.

A similar example of the Council's obeisance to private interests can be traced in the career of Romà Sanahuja. In the 1950s this builder was responsible for tiny flats in the Turó de la Peira in the district of Nou barris, a vertical shanty-town for immigrants. In 1991 two of these blocks collapsed, causing the death of one resident, due to the high-aluminium, cheaper concrete originally used. The rebuilding of all twenty blocks is still going on, at public expense not at Sanahuja's. In the 1980s, Sanahuja had been named a "social benefactor" by the City Council and his firm co-built *L'illa*, the up-market shopping mall on the Diagonal in Les Corts. The Council allowed *L'illa* to exceed municipal building limits by 77,000 square metres, so increasing Sanahuja's profits. Sanahuja is just one example of several constructors who made their fortunes under Franco and then continued to expand those fortunes whilst working closely with the democratic Council.

Olympic Motoring

If housing prices are making it hard to find a place to live in Barcelona, traffic is making the city uninhabitable.

Something it shares, of course, with most cities, but nevertheless which invalidates its claims to be a city for the twenty-first century.

In a recent newspaper article on well-known people's fondest memories of the city, it was shocking to read that ex-Mayor Maragall recalled his pleasure on riding his bike on a car-free day (this occurs once a year) along the Passeig de Gràcia. Shocking because Council policy has been completely pro-car, despite its 2005 creation of pedestrian-only streets: notably in parts of Gràcia and the *Ciutat vella*. Such pedestrian streets are part of the conservation of some of the old hearts of city *barris*, but do not reflect a general, integrated transport policy.

In Barcelona, cars jump lights, park on pavements, double-park, ignore zebra crossings, stop in the middle of crossings so you have to thread your way across, and break the speed limit as a matter of course. These are just symptoms of the reverence in which cars are held. Most importantly, they are welcomed into the centre of the city – right to the edges of the pedestrianised areas. The prestigious new developments of the *Palau nou* (Ch. 1), Santa Caterina and the Illa Robadors, all in the *Ciutat vella*, are amply provided with underground car parks.

In the 1980s increasing prosperity brought a sharp rise in the number of cars on the road. The Council responded by a massive road-construction programme, especially the ring-roads, *rondes*. Most of the *rondes* were uncovered ravines enclosing the city — and dividing neighbourhoods, as in the Vall d'Hebron or Badal. The best-organised Residents' Associations fought to have the *rondes* covered over and turned into tunnels with parks on top. Ironically, this has meant that more militant working-class areas such as Nou barris have their part of the *ronda* covered, whereas some wealthier *barris* do not.

I asked Richard Rogers how he could defend Barcelona as a sustainable city when it was so traffic-ridden[1]. His view was that private cars were little questioned in Spain, and that with the late growth of the consumer society they are still seen as a democratic right. He is probably right, but the reply begs the question. Whatever Maragall's private dreams of pedalling down the Passeig de Gràcia, the Socialists have not had the courage to take a step they perceive as unpopular and to challenge car worship.

No serious policy to take cars off the road has been attempted. The Council, as it tends to do when it feels pressured to do something it does not really want to do, mounts advertising campaigns. These praise the public transport system, or urge people to walk. No practical measures, such as reduced public transport fares or car-parks on the outskirts with rapid transport in, have been adopted. Rather, the Council has encouraged the car and construction industries by building more roads. Not just the *rondes*, ring-roads, but a tunnel through Collserola under Vallvidrera, and another planned by Horta – though this has been stopped for the time being by the swing to the left in the 2003 municipal elections.

Despite the decline in Barcelona's industries, pollution is rampant. Car love, of course, is a major cause. A popular, sarcastic novel, Pablo Tusset's *The Best Thing That Can Happen to a Croissant*, summed up the city of the first decade of the twenty-first century:

"... she just takes my hand and drags me through a series of anonymous streets, although I can tell we're in Barcelona – the smell and the traffic noise are unmistakeable..."

Later, the loutish anti-hero of Tusset's novel decides to welcome the spring:

"For the first time since the previous autumn I opened the living room window, and a mixture of air, carbon monoxide, and heavy industrialised metal fumes wafted into the room. After a few seconds the entire room smelled like bus exhaust fumes... I love the smell of Barcelona – I don't know how people can survive in the country, with all that raw air drilling away at your lungs."

Alternatives?

Is the above not just radical carping? After all, nothing's perfect. Was there any real alternative to the Council's model of regeneration? Maragall and his successor as Mayor, Joan Clos, argue there wasn't. The central state was not going to provide the money and Barcelona had too narrow a tax-base to raise enough. In the twenty years from 1968 to 1988, the city lost half its manufacturing jobs. By the Olympics, 70% of jobs were in the service sector.

Was there an alternative model of development? I put this question to university economics professor and Residents' Association activist in Nou barris, Albert Recio:

> *"There were definitely other possibilities when the Socialists came to municipal power in 1979. The Olympics were not essential. In fact, they distorted development in favour of big business. Remember it was an exceptional situation: the Socialists had enormous support and good-will. There was mass rejection of Porcioles-style speculation. They could have mobilised their electorate in favour of radical policies. They could have conducted systematic education in favour of taxes. If constructors had entered into conflict with the Council, it had the popular backing to insist. At the start of the '80s it had a golden opportunity to oppose the domination of the motor-car, but the SEAT and Nissan crises pushed them into the enormous road-building programme."*

Vázquez Montalbán and Eduard Moreno, in their book *Where are You Going, Barcelona?*, developed a less radical but just as telling line of criticism. Whereas Recio rejected the Olympics as unnecessary, these two were more pragmatic and argued that the Socialists could have exerted greater control over land even within the grandiose Olympic programme. A Socialist Council could have experimented with "the formula of a *market economy with a social brain*" (Montalbán). The influx of Olympic money from the State and Generalitat gave it a one-off opportunity to radically improve the situation of the city's poor. The Council blew it.

In his *Olympic Death*, Vázquez Montalbán criticised the Olympics fictionally. He expressed his own and his detective's *desencanto* (disenchantment) fourteen years on from *The Angst-ridden Executive* (Chapter 9). His Carvalho books, his social chronicle, had tackled a number of themes, with particular success in *Southern Seas*, *Murder in the Central Committee* (the crisis in the Communist Party) and *Off-side*, which satirised football and denounced property speculation. *Olympic Death* (1991) was to have closed the series: and pity perhaps that it didn't, for the several novels that followed it declined. In *Olympic Death*, Montalbán sees the insertion of a new middle-class in a rebuilt once-proletarian Poble Nou as symbolic of the social settlement that emerged from the transition. Montalbán places great emphasis on the importance of feeling familiar in your surroundings. He scrupulously tries to separate this from nostalgia for a lost past. Thus, he welcomes the destruction and rebuilding of uninhabitable slums, but he is opposed to the "brutal cleansing plans" that "occur at the expense of the weakest residents."

In *Olympic Death* Carvalho is in a bad way. He is no longer able with his fists and weapons; he is overweight and weary. He is also worried about his old age, for private eyes lack pension schemes. This mid-life crisis is reflected in an urban landscape so scarred by Olympic redevelopment that the detective loses his way. He makes mistakes. Carvalho can no longer interpret a Barcelona that has become "broken images... It was hard to tell where the destruction ended and where the construction began."

The physical destruction of the old landscape leaves Carvalho unable to read his city. Thus memory, in Montalbán's terms, can no longer give meaning to *barcelonins*' life. The final erasure of memory is the final victory of the ruling class. Samaranch's smile as he shakes Maragall's hand is the lizard smile of he whose version of history has triumphed. All that is left is an effort, where memory has gone, to commemorate the past, as Rebecca Horn's sculpture portrayed in the next chapter does. But merely to commemorate, instead of still fighting to win, is an admission of defeat.

Vázquez Montalbán wrote in melancholy in 2002:

> *"The real cities that exist are in the end built by the powerful. We read them almost always without posing what they would have been like if their citizens really had built them."*

---

[1] *Telephone interview with Richard Rogers, November 2002.*

THE FRONT

CIUTADELLA PARK

POBLE NOU

OLYMPIC VILLAGE

BARCELONETA

AVINGUDA DEL GRA

RONDA DEL LITORAL

PASSEIG MARITIM DEL PORT OLIMPIC

PORT OLIMPIC

LA MARINA

UNIVERSITAT POMPEU FABRA

HOSPITAL DEL MAR

PASSEIG DE FRANCA

CARRER DE R

PLATJA DE LA BARCELONETA

PLATJA DE BOGATELL

PLATJA DE LA MAR BELLA NUDIST BEACH

SITE OF FORUM 2004

MEDITERRANEAN SEA

HOTEL ARTS

TORRE MAPFRE

GEHRY'S FISH

"HOMAGE TO BARCELONETA"

Chapter 16
The Shore

"The most successful coastal development I can think of, anywhere. It's a stunning regeneration, five or six kilometres along the front, live, work, leisure, park, shops, restaurants, there's no real comparison anywhere."
RICHARD ROGERS, ARCHITECT.

The Harbour

This chapter takes a walk along the four miles of Barcelona's water-front, much of it only opened to the public since the Olympic Games. It is a modern, new walk for the last chapter to match the centuries-old stroll down the Rambles of the first chapter.

The Rambles proper end at the harbour, by the French-style Port Authority and Columbus' Column. From there you can go two ways into the sea. The passenger-boats known as *golondrinas* — swallows, literally — cross the port to and from a point near the end of the outer break-water. On this trip the fresh sea-breeze and occasional whiff of engine oil bang against you as the swallow lurches through the waves. If you peer into the oily water near the quays, black fish, fat on waste from the boats and drains, loiter. "Not to be eaten," the boat-man states severely. The *golondrina* passes the container-ships with cranes probing about in their entrails like surgeons, the white multi-storey ferry to Mallorca, the squat 1990s World Trade Centre building, and often a cruise ship spilling its passengers down the Rambles for an afternoon, just as in Genet's time. Whereas then the cruise-ship tourists paraded "their inherent right to find these archipelagoes of poverty picturesque," now they are persuaded to admire

Barcelona's transformation into a "model for the twenty-first century."

The *golondrina* trip to the sea-wall is a journey thirty years back in time. Stalls sell over-fried potato crisps and *churros* (sticks of deep-fried dough) wrapped in grey paper cones. The smell of re-heated vegetable oil mingles with the tang of weed and fish entrails. The passengers climb stained and crumbling steps to the top of the sea-wall. On the open-sea side, old men fish off the big concrete blocks dumped in a jumble, like a Cubist painting, to break the waves slapping the harbour wall. A hundred years ago there were squatters' shacks along here, photos show, but they were washed away. Family groups take the air, young women sun-bathe, the old men not fishing stare at them. This is a Barcelona without time and money to head up or down the coast.

At the bottom of the Rambles, there is a modern alternative to the *golondrinas*: the 1990s Rambla del Mar, wooden causeway with slats like a pier leading out over the water to the Maremagnum, the shop/club/cinema/restaurant complex reclaimed from the old harbour. The Maremagnum has a plaza with a giant distorting mirror and a fountain throwing fine spray across the benches. In the aquarium, "the biggest in Europe" (Valencia's new one is, too), you can walk through transparent underwater corridors and stare at sharks face to face. The Maremagnum could have been more public, assuaging the lack of open space in the Old City. However, its owners *Crédit Suisse* developed it as a shopping mall with 88 outlets: new, smart, post-92 Barcelona, the future projected over the sea.

The Maremagnum has not worked. Peaceful by day, at night it became club-land, and grew a vicious edge. Numerous racist incidents climaxed in January 2002, when Wilson Pacheco, a young immigrant from Ecuador, was beaten up by a group of disco door-men and tossed into the water. Wilson Pacheco drowned after several minutes. One of the three later convicted of murder had said:

*"I'm not jumping in and wetting my mobile for a fucking South-American (*sudaca de mierda*)."*

All three discos in the Maremagnum have been found guilty of excluding Gypsies and black people. Like the Camp Nou when Roberto Carlos steps out, the Maremagnum reveals the racism fermenting beneath the liberal veneer of Spanish and Catalan society. Barcelona Socialist politicians tend to say all the right things, but do little. Too much fuss, a real educational campaign against racism, could seriously damage Barcelona's international reputation for civic behaviour and good living.

The Maremagnum in 2003 and 2004 lost custom. Shops closed, disco attendance dropped off: a salutary reminder that Barcelona's upward tourist curve is not eternal. It was relaunched in 2005, with a quieter image of a place to stroll, a *rambla* over the sea, rather than a disco complex.

The Meadow

The sea-front walk of this last chapter can start here, or a few kilometres South of Barcelona, in El Prat, *The Meadow* in Catalan, where the AVE (TGV-style high-speed train) to Paris and Madrid will run into the airport, which is being expanded with a third run-way[1].

Carles Prieto, Residents' Association activist throughout the transition, whom I quoted in Chapter Nine, also talked to me about El Prat. He is Head of the Delta Programme, the project to conserve and redevelop the River Llobregat delta.

> *"Aren't redevelopment and conservation contradictory?" I asked.*
> *"Not at all," he grins. "We have to juggle conservation of the delta, the expansion of Barcelona's airport, and considerable social problems and housing shortages here in the town of El Prat." The Sant Cosme area, rather crudely concealed by advertising hoardings from the tourist taxis speeding out of the airport, is an area of burnt-out cars, drug dealing and badly constructed 1960s flats. "We're*

doing it up," Prieto says. He points enthusiastically to the map on the wall. "All this will be housing. This is the third run-way, here the line of the AVE running into the airport, here the new underground line, and here the new mouth of the river."

"You're moving the river!"

"Yes, if we move the river mouth south, it gives us the space we need."

"But what about the famous artichokes and blue-foot chicken?" For the loamy Llobregat delta is also a rich agricultural area, known for these two products. The train from the airport to Sants takes you past fields of lettuce and artichokes among the abandoned factories.

"— There will be space for them. By making a general plan, we're re-designing the whole area. Obviously there will be less agricultural land, but without a plan everything would have been swallowed by unplanned development. The Delta Programme will take housing up to here but no further, protect the River with its nature-conservation areas, and create space for the railway and underground without eating up unnecessary land."

"— I can see that. But there's nothing to guarantee that the next generation won't change the rules."

"— No. But we never know what the next generation will do, do we? All we can do is plan in a logical and rational way. Because what's the alternative? Savage capitalism. Uncontrolled development run by land speculators. Here we do a deal: housing here, park there, agricultural land there. Less agricultural land, yes. But the alternative was to have none left in a generation."

Carles Prieto is characteristic of a generation of anti-Franco activists who have become politicians or, in Prieto's case, administrators in the post-Franco town councils. Having fought against the wild speculation under Porcioles in the 1960s, this generation set themselves to govern Barcelona and its surrounding area, Greater Barcelona, in a pragmatic way.

Because of the harbour mouths, the industrial plants of the Zona Franca and the river, it's not possible to walk along the coast from El Prat. But one can walk down to the shore at El Prat, and a very strange shore it is. An enormous pile of containers, big as a block of flats, is stacked behind the beach. To my ignorant eyes, these containers never change. They seem the dock-yard equivalent of the lost suit-cases piled beside the airport carousels. Did no lorry ever turn up to collect them? Behind the containers, a flock of sheep crop the reedy grass that grows out of the dunes.

El Prat used to be a beach-comber's dream: wood carried down the river by the mountain storms, plastic bottles, rusted cans and all the other non-degradable débris from the ships moving in and out of the port of Barcelona, and from the Barcelona sewage plants: used ear-wax removers, condoms and plastic parts of sanitary pads, all washed completely clean. Yet just beside this sea-side tip, ducks and migratory birds quack in the reeds and land on the lagoons of the Nature Reserve. Part of the beach is roped off to protect birds laying their eggs. Farmhouses are scattered across the plain. You see them from a window-seat as you come in to land. Right on the sea-shore, a house is abandoned: the delta is receding.

Ignasi Riera, in his eccentric book *Off Barcelona* about the remoter corners of the city, proclaims rhapsodically:

> *"The Llobregat Delta, colourful contrast of birds and planes, of crops and technology, of rural and urban worlds, of wretchedness and triumph in the mud, becomes symbol and example of the diversity of Catalonia."*

Riera is right. The anarchic mix of nature and hi-tech is just what Carles Prieto is trying to plan. This is either conservation or the final nail in its coffin. The beach has changed. For the first time in two decades, it is 'clean.' *De rigueur,* the portly town councillors took a dip to prove so.

Barceloneta
Or the coastal walk can start up on Montjuïc, from where you can look down on the industrial harbour with its lines of spider-claw cranes, the quays stacked with brightly-

coloured containers, and the queues of lorries pulling onto the ring-road. If you don't mind being hung from vibrating wires over water from a great height, you can take the *teleféric* from Montjuïc across the harbour to the tip of Barceloneta.

Barceloneta (Little Barcelona) is a promontory of land within whose embrace the old fishing port huddles. There is still a fishing-fleet, though it shares the inner harbour with the yachts of the marina. The clock tower on the quay is where the catch used to be auctioned, though now this is sold through Mercabarna, the Central Market in the Zona Franca. You can sit at the end of the Maremagnum in the late afternoon and watch the fishing-boats chug in. Almost an anachronism: fish and diesel smelling of an older pre-tourism Mediterranean.

Barceloneta was built in the eighteenth century, on a straight-line grid basis, but much more humbly than the later Eixample. The original inhabitants were those evicted when their quarter was razed for the Citadel's construction after 1714. The houses were kept low and the streets at right angles to the Citadel, so that the cannon could look and shoot over and through the neighbourhood. A wall from the citadel down to the beach enclosed Barceloneta within the city. Verdaguer wrote:

> *"The unlucky hated Citadel,*
> *born in Barcelona like a poisonous rash*
> *in the middle of a beautiful face."*

Today, Barceloneta is a lively, attractive area, full of very narrow streets and flats so small they are hard to gentrify. Hans Andersen saw it in 1862:

> *"The low houses look like the poor-house. There are clothes stalls, stands selling food, junk and trinkets everywhere; overloaded carts and mule wagons criss-cross; half-naked children smoke fag-ends; workers, sailors, peasants and city-dwellers lie about in the sun and dust."*

284

"But if you want," Andersen continues, in more upbeat vein, "you can take a refreshing swim." Barceloneta has always been a working-class beach: the city's only beach before the Olympic reforms. Today, from the wooden board-walk that separates beach and promenade, you can plunge into the water and look back to see the tiny flats of Barceloneta with the washing hanging — flags of poverty — from their windows.

Along here, as mentioned earlier, used to be rows of fish restaurants. A Sunday lunch of black rice at Barceloneta on a crystal-clear winter's day, with a walk along the sand and harbour wall afterwards, was the highlight of a working week in 1980s Barcelona. Gaudí liked this Sunday walk too, but after high mass not black rice. There were, too, numerous private swimming-pools and bathing clubs — some, refuges of gays in the difficult Franco years, others of young Falangists fanatical on bodily fitness, another (the Oriental baths) for women only where men hung like apes on the wire fence gaping at the sun-bathers. These baths have disappeared in the modernisation of the front.

Right on the sand now is Rebecca Horn's 1992 sculpture *The wounded shooting star*, commonly known as *Homage to Barceloneta*. This rusted-iron four-storey tower, with each storey stacked higgledy-piggledy on the previous one, its windows filled with jumbled light, was one of Maragall's best sculpture bargains. It's particularly beautiful silhouetted against the sea at dusk. In the '80s and early '90s, this German artist created a number of sculptures evoking the history and memory of place, of which *The wounded shooting star* is one. It is designed to commemorate the lost, rusted beach restaurants, the landscape that had developed over generations before the sudden shock of demolition and their replacement by new white sand and new palms (non-native, but *expected* by visitors). It is both a light-house in the night and a shooting star plunged to earth.

The Front

The walk along the promenade from Barceloneta towards the two towers of the Olympic village is broad and traffic-free. Cyclists, runners and roller-skaters are the only people not strolling or lounging. Views of Barcelona are not just those from the hills behind walked in Chapter Four. From the front you can look across the city to the back, to the Collserola range and its landmarks: the 1600-foot hill of Tibidabo, with its ugly 1920s utilitarian church transformed into a glistening star in the sunlight, and the 1992 telecommunications tower, known after its architect as the *Torre Foster*. Bound by cables to the Vallvidrera hill-side, Norman Foster's tower is a slender spear thrusting up towards the aeroplanes, which alarmingly often fly right over the city. If the weather changes, clouds swirl rapidly over Collserola and these skyline buildings turn into fairy castles in the mist.

Approaching the water-front twin towers, you pass the *modernista* water tower, all polished and shiny now it is just a memento of the industrial age. It is a reminder too that *Aïgues de Barcelona* was a major owner of the water-front. The gas company was, too, and its 20-storey crystal sky-scraper has also risen here. Barcelona never had high-rise before: its promotion now is part of the city's adoption of the international style. Surprising, when Planning boss Acebillo is on record as being "very worried" about the Americanisation of Barcelona and consequent loss of local identity.

Port Olímpic

One of the twin towers at the Olympic village is the luxury Hotel Arts, not actually finished on time for the Olympics. Ross Montgomery, who laboured on the project in 1991/2, told me:

> *"It was chaos. No safety regulations were enforced. Building workers were flown in from London, housed in Blanes and coached down every day to the site. They had no*

contact with Spanish unions, no legal recourse. Any com-
plaint and you were out. Flown straight back to London."

A reminder that Barcelona's monuments were not built by
the famous architects named throughout this book, but by
the unknown thousands. Some of whom died. Spain's construction industry has had, for decades, the highest
accident rate of any industry in Western Europe.

When the Olympic village was built, no-one foresaw its
port's spectacular take-off as a site of all-night discos,
restaurants and bars, prospering where the Maremagnum
stumbled. Whilst the gaudy front and port area buzz with
youth at play, the village proper has settled into its more
sophisticated identity, separated from the port by steadily
thickening vegetation along the line of the buried ring-road.

In the morning, the Port Olímpic is quiet. The dancers
are sleeping. Pigeons waddle among the *Pan's* and *Pizza
Hut* tables, pecking at the left-overs. In front of the towers,
Frank Gehry's giant latticed fish, made of criss-crossing
strips of what looks like golden aluminium, floats in the
air. The dazzling fish presides over the shopping walk-ways
and ponds above the marina. When it catches the sun, it
imposes itself on the entire front. A complete contrast to
Rebecca Horn's rusty sculpture in Barceloneta, which
attempts to set itself into its environs and history. Gehry,
the guru of Los Angeles architecture and famous in Spain
for Bilbao's Guggenheim Museum, describes many of his
works as 'stage sets,' thus cleverly accepting what others
use as criticism. Perhaps Ocaña would have approved: the
architect as performance artist. Here architecture is no
longer William Morris' dream of beauty lying in function,
an ideal seen in Gaudí's houses, but buildings as show, as
spectacle. If art and architecture create a stage-set, the
people walking on the front are in a play. It is, though, real
life: those picturesque locals on the scattered benches are
not acting. They actually are unemployed and have nothing
to do. Yet a common response to Barcelona is that it is *a
simulacrum* (Vázquez Montalbán) or a *stage-set*.

Mike Davis describes Gehry as "the 'human face' of the corporate architecture that is transforming Los Angeles — uprooting neighborhoods and privatizing public space..." It is a comment that may appear inapplicable to Barcelona's Olympic village which, built on brown-field sites, made private land more public. Yet, more subtly, this freed-up Barcelona front is controlled by its enclaves of private space, *viz.* the private gardens of the village, patrolled at times and in places by uniformed security guards, the privately-run Diagonal Mar public park, the Hotel Arts, the mall, the yachts.

Nevertheless, Gehry's headless, tail-less fish is light, happy and fun. It does humanise the complex it fronts. It even bears a relation to place: after all, it's a *fish*, and there's the *sea*. It is also, for the Barcelona authorities, a trophy sculpture, a big catch: *Yes, we have a giant Gehry, too.*

The Port Olímpic area is the most Americanised chunk of Barcelona. This is L.A. on the Med. Gehry, the shopping mall, the fountains and luxuriant plants (they're not really growing, they're just replaced frequently). The *Baja Beach Club*, right by the sand, looks like a parody of a Beach Boys album cover, with its tacky bright-yellow and green entrance and flashing neon strips. The lamp-posts are elegant, elongated, vandal-proof cylindrical lights in metal sheaves. The restaurants and bars huddle shoulder to shoulder round the marina, white canopies extended over the terrace tables in successive bulges like the segments of a bleached centipede. The familiar noise of wealth — yacht lanyards tapping masts in the sea breeze — accompanies a waterside coffee.

The people on the walk along the front on a week-day are similar to those on the hill path from the Park Güell. Elderly women paddle in the waves; male pensioners watch the sea as if there was an event expected. The only sights ever visible out there are wind-surfers, private yachts and the container ships waiting to enter the harbour. The unemployed poke about on the beaches or annoy the fishermen on the piers by asking if they've caught anything. In addition to these people with enforced leisure, well-off young people with well-combed dogs read the papers at the cafés. Dogs are a problem on Med beaches: there is no tide to cleanse their droppings and no enforcement of bye-laws to keep them off the sand. It's not the only problem. The artificial beaches are quite regularly washed away in storms: no-one's quite worked out how to shape them to withstand nature's currents.

Who can doubt that the people of Barcelona have gained in public space? These are some of the contradictions of the city: the Council's model of development has favoured a consumerist American-style fast-food culture; its housing policy forces masses of people to live in private flats that are too expensive and often too small. The State has not guaranteed stable employment; pensions are low. Yet the city's open space means people can walk, run, cycle, sit or swim along several kilometres of sea-front. Richard Rogers says this is the best bit of sea-front regeneration in Europe, and I will take his word for it, as he claims to have visited a hundred. Yet, as the last chapter argued, public space was gained without the housing problems of the people of Barcelona being solved. Indeed, the model of reform of Barcelona contributed to these housing problems, by forcing prices up and up as the city gained in glamour. Glamour doesn't let people eat, though they can watch glamorous people eating on the best marine front in Europe.

The most imaginative part of the front is not the rather bland California tack of Gehry and the two towers, which will date rapidly as places without history do, but beyond the towers towards the Forum site. Here the roads have been pushed back and the old pre-tourist Costa Brava has been re-created. A mini pine forest has been planted; grassy dunes introduced. And a great piece of sculpture: a steamship sunk into the dunes, only its prow and its funnel 100 yards away protruding. Thick reeds shadow a rough track down to the nudist beach, called the *Mar Bella*.

Intelligent City

Behind this part of the front, inland from the *Mar bella* beach, is Poble Nou, still a lively working-class quarter. Its Rambla is full of life, its shops and cafés packed. Poble Nou, at the time of writing in late 2005, is a mass of contradictions. The old factories have come down or are scheduled to fall. There is bitter conflict between various Residents' Associations and the Council over the building of multi-storey blocks of flats and of the new computer-industry area, the *city of knowledge* known as the *22@* (*22 arroba* — the *at* sign is known as *arroba* in Spain). The Council proclaims this as the "transformation of industrial land into land for the new economy." Clos argued more lyrically in late 2002:

> *"The city of knowledge is the city we have, but better, richer, more connected to the world. It is the city that replaces old industrial chimneys with the bits and neurones of the revolution in knowledge. It is an intelligent city, with ideas and the ability to carry them out, which are translated into better quality of life for its residents."*

It is not just that former industrial land is becoming intelligent land, but perfectly good housing is being demolished too. Up to 40% of Poble Nou is due to disappear. As in Clot, Sant Andreu, Horta or Sants, Council strategy is to give *carte blanche* to builders whilst conserving the old low-rise heart of a *barri* to provide 'village' atmosphere. In Poble Nou, for example, the Plaça Prim, among streets of low housing being done up, conserves the classy restaurant *Els Pescadors* and bulging, twisted-rooted ombu trees pushing up the pavement.

The construction-led economy thrives, with owners of the land and builders making fortunes with high-rise blocks, thousands of workers taking home a wage, and thousands of middle-class workers (though they may not perceive themselves as workers) mortgaging themselves to buy flats they can't afford. This is a cameo of how people live in Barcelona. Not surprising that residents threatened with eviction for these new blocks are fighting hard to stay put. One lamented to me:

> *"We just want to go on living where we've always lived. We're not revolutionaries. The compensation they're offering won't let us get anywhere else, housing prices being what they are."*

The Universal Forum of Cultures

Beyond the *Mar bella* beach, the front approaches what was the desolate site of the mouth of the polluted River Besòs, with a water purification plant, the Besòs power station whose three chimneys parody the Sagrada Família's, and the grim memory of the *Camp de la bota*, the beach site of many of Franco's post-39 executions. With characteristic public-relations panache, the Council opened at the *Mercè* Festival in 2002 the huge Diagonal Mar park on the site of the old Macosa engineering plant: factory turned into public park gives the right message, even if this is then managed privately. Beyond the park, the development of the front has been rounded off with the 100-acre site of the First Universal Forum of Cultures.

The Olympics had been so successful that in 1996 Mayor Maragall announced that the city would organise an Expo, a World Fair like Sevilla's in 1992. However, the international organisations that control such events clarified that an Expo fair could not be held in Spain so soon after Sevilla's. Embarrassed at Maragall's *faux pas*, though outwardly undaunted, the Council invented the UNESCO-backed First Universal Forum of Cultures. This took place in 2004.

Maragall's eagerness to have an Expo, or a Forum, or *something big*, reflected not just Olympic success but considerable post-Olympic anxiety. The City Council was in deep debt as a result of the Games. The Olympics transformed the city and tourists came in unimagined numbers. But what next? The fear was that from the Olympic peak, only decline could follow. But no. Whilst '80s Barcelona had been the city of design, of frantic building, everything subsumed to those two summer weeks in 1992; the 1990s saw it become the city of culture and good living, of an ever-rising graph of tourists. The success of the Olympics was not just the culmination of its change, but launched Barcelona towards a yet higher peak. To the triumph, unimaginable ten years before, of replacing Paris in 2000 as the Number One destination for UK week-end breaks, no less!

Even before it opened, the Forum 2004 took a lot of flak because of the vagueness of its aims. Critics maintained it would just be a five-month jamboree of congresses, concerts, exhibitions and other cultural events, with nothing clear pulling it together. The fuzzy verbiage of the constant, glossy publicity heightened the feeling of improvisation, *viz.* the City Council's monthly magazine in April 2001:

> *"The Forum is a project that Barcelona wants to offer the world... The Forum is being worked out, day after day, as a project based on real values: cultural diversity, sustainability and conditions for peace."*

The Forum flopped. 2.4 million people attended the 141 days of events, leaving 28.5 million euros in entrance money. Beforehand, the organisers had been rash enough to set a target of 5 million visitors and 61 million in gate money. There was a considerable short-fall in covering the budget of 324 million euros, though lack of transparency in the accounts makes it hard to know exact figures. Extra contributions from industrial sponsors were asked for and all sorts of extras (such as the exhibition in Madrid after the Forum of the famous Chinese Xiang terracotta warriors) were scrambled into the profit-and-loss account, allowing the organisers to make the generally derided claim, "we've broken even."

But what was it all for? The Forum's three vague values or "axes," of cultural diversity, sustainability and conditions for peace, gave a feel of progressive well-being, whilst concealing three other implicit aims. These real aims were

much less abstract: promotion of cultural tourism, speculative building and the ideological promotion of social
democracy or, as things are today, neoliberalism with a
social democratic face. These unstated aims sum up most
of what this book has argued is negative in the development of modern Barcelona.

The first aim, to promote *cultural tourism* to Barcelona,
benefits above all hoteliers, restaurateurs and shop-keepers. It is hard to argue that the 100,000 or so people
employed in the tourist industry benefit, as most of them
are on short-term, seasonal contracts and rock-bottom
wages. As such, the Forum 2004 flowed on from Gaudí
Year in 2002 and dovetailed with Dalí year 2004. The formula was spectacular exhibitions and big-name events to
bring in the tourists and enhance Barcelona's image as a
progressive city of culture. Yet there is a danger. If
Gehry's fish presides over a stage-set, the Forum was a
theme park, a cultural *Port Aventura*[2]. Barcelona as a specific place with its own history producing its own culture
is drowned under this international splurge of culture
events. In the end, such events are self-defeating. Why
come to Barcelona for the bland, international culture that
can be as easily consumed in London or Paris? The Forum
failed dramatically in this aim of attracting cultural
tourism, as the event achieved no international resonance.

The second aim of the Forum was economic: to bring the
Diagonal down to the sea, so completing Cerdà's 1859 proposal, and re-develop the area between Poble Nou and the
River Besòs. This is Barcelona's real "Golden Triangle,"
with its hypotenuse along the front traversed in this
Chapter. Golden in the sense of bringing gold for the owners of the land. The Forum site itself, with its huge plaza
and conference halls, is only a part of this development. In
addition, some 30,000 new flats have been constructed,
along with hotels, offices and a shopping mall, *Diagonal-
Mar*: yet another 'cathedral to consumerism.' That makes
eight in Greater Barcelona, and a ninth is on the way in
Richard Rogers' re-development of the *Las Arenas* bull-

293

ring by the Plaça d'Espanya. Rogers strongly defends these large spaces: for him, in a post-industrial age, in which people are atomised and alienated in big cities, these shopping-leisure complexes enable people to meet. They meet whilst consuming food, art and leisure. The Rogers argument is that this improves city life. This may be so, in some respects: no open plaza or arts centre should be spurned. The main argument against is that the money could be better spent: on local libraries, municipal housing, youth centres, sports centres, public transport and the regeneration of the outlying quarters unvisited by tourists. The second argument is that public space is being constructed, not for itself and under control of the inhabitants, but as an antechamber to palaces of consumption, under control of the big companies.

One symbol of the building round the Forum site is Jean Nouvel's 142-metre Torre Agbar, the suppository as it is known, politely, due to its rocket shape. It is similar to Norman Foster's 180-metre 'gherkin' in London. The Torre Agbar, consisting of two superimposed cylinders of glass, is designed as an ecological building, and yet fills the night sky with spectacular lights of many colours. In addition, a dozen high-rise blocks have changed the shore sky-line. This Forum-stimulated construction is much more clearly speculative than the pre-Olympic building spree. In 2004 there was no pretence that cheap housing was on offer; and there are fewer installations that are going to be of general benefit. Building on the brown-field Forum site regenerates dead land and raises property values around it. Culture adds economic value to land and property, just as Richard Meier's MACBA has in the inland part of the Raval.

One of the great questions is what will happen to La Mina, Barcelona's worst slum, an area beside the Forum site of ten thousand inhabitants where few outsiders venture. Andrés Naya, President of the Barcelona Federation of Residents' Associations (FAVB), affirmed: "The remodelling of La Mina is the litmus test of the Forum." Indeed, the FAVB withdrew support for the Forum because of disagreement on the La Mina remodelling. The Council has affirmed it gave priority to employing people from La Mina at the Forum, but short-term jobs do not solve the social problems, chronic unemployment and bad housing of a marginal area. It is grotesque that the Forum site and its surrounding flats were put up in a couple of years, whereas La Mina beside it has been rotting away for decades.

Culture and Politics

The third aim of the Forum was more ideological and evolved as the world's political situation so rapidly changed. The Egyptian socialist and feminist writer Nawal El Saadawi averred in Barcelona on receiving the 2003 Premi (*prize*) Catalunya: "Now there are two world powers: imperialism and the peoples standing up." She meant by this a US-driven international war against terrorism, on the one hand; and a rising anti-capitalist movement, with one of its centres in Barcelona, on the other.

The Forum was presented by the City Council as an alternative to both the mass anti-capitalist movement on the streets and George Bush's foreign policy. The Socialists were in power in both Catalonia and the Spanish state as a whole. Along with the Barcelona Socialist Council, the force on the ground, they sought to involve in the Forum sufficient sectors of the anti-globalisation movement to weaken the more radical sectors of the movement. Measures such as debates on the Iraq war, contracting Intermon-Oxfam to provide fair-trade coffee at the Forum or enticing speakers such as Susan George of Attac France were designed to achieve this. Despite their consistent efforts to talk up their radicalism, hardly anyone confused this Forum with the anti-capitalist movement and the mass European Social Forums.

The Forum organisers got the shock of their lives, because what started out as a typical, minority anti-Forum protest movement suddenly found its meetings overflowing. *Barcelonins* then voted with their feet by not paying the 21-euro entry fee to tramp round the site. The Forum did not convince. How could it be 'promoting sustainability,' when it was sponsored by ENDESA, a Spanish energy giant that is Europe's fourth biggest emitter of carbon dioxide? Or 'creating conditions for peace,' when it was sponsored by the arms company, INDRA? The Council treated the Forum as if it were the Olympics, repeating corporate sponsors such as Coca-Cola. They did not grasp how good will towards them had been eroded and that the anti-war movement had changed many people's perceptions.

The Forum organisers' 'third-way' strategy was the subtext to the assertion of Joan Rigol, President of the Parliament of Catalonia until Summer 2003:

> *"The Forum is a cry going out round the world in the name of cultures... Culture creates dialogue where politics cannot."*

Fair-trade coffee is window-dressing. Or perhaps one should use in a more political sense the word *simulacrum* applied by Vázquez Montalbán and other readers of Baudrillard to architecture for show. Pretending that fairer-priced coffee or cultural events help make poverty history is a *simulacrum* of anti-capitalism.

World City or Habitable City

In June 2001 Barcelona's Joan Clos became the first city mayor to address the United Nations General Assembly, normally a forum for representatives of states. A special session had been convened to review progress on the Habitat Agenda, an action programme for city regeneration coming out of the 1996 UN City Summit held in Istanbul. Clos's moment in New York marked the increasing size of cities, and their growing influence within their states. "Globalisation," argued Gary Lawrence, ex-Planning Director for Seattle, in *The Barcelona Blueprint*, the TV film issued to coincide with Clos's intervention, "has meant a shift from national agendas to the agendas of economic regions." Such a concept, placing cities at the forefront, fits the ideas of Barcelona's rulers well: they see the city as the centre of a new high-tech area stretching from Montpellier and Toulouse to Valencia. One could say that, given that Catalonia as an independent state is not on the agenda, Barcelona city seeks to emulate such a project in the economic field.

The choice of Clos to address the United Nations reflected Barcelona's prestige, for he was then President of Metropolis, the organisation of major world cities. *The Barcelona Blueprint* film opened thus:

> *"Welcome to Barcelona, set to be one of the most successful cities in the 21st century... an old industrial city that could all too easily have become a burnt-out rust-belt town, left behind by the globalised world... Barcelona is a city of three million people, which could have had three million visions of the future — but the city listened to people's hopes and fears and produced a single, coherent vision."*

The Residents' Association of Carmel (Ch. 4) refuted this idea that the Council has "a single, coherent vision" by drawing attention to the inequalities of investment. From the Forum, among the high-rise private developments, one can visualise these inequalities by looking up at the hill on which Carmel was built, and where corner-cutting and lack of proper investment led to the collapse of the underground tunnel.

Another frequent theme of praise for Barcelona, the idea of popular participation (that "the city listened..."), was questioned in Chapter Fifteen. Few in the city, even Council supporters, make such a claim: it is very much for external consumption.

In New York, Clos presented Barcelona as the *city of opportunities*, two centuries ago in the forefront of the Industrial Revolution and now leader of the New Economy. The Valencia-to-Marseilles axis suddenly swelled, in the hot-house of the United Nations, to a grandiose idea of Barcelona as centre of an axis "from Lisbon to Naples," which would shift the motor of European development from North to South in the coming years.

I asked Marçal of the group *En Lluita* (In Struggle), activist in Barcelona's enormous, though disperse anti-capitalist movement, if they saw Barcelona as the *city of opportunities* or had taken part in the Forum 2004.

> *"The Assembly of the European Social Forum in Paris in 2003 voted to boycott this Forum. We considered it useless to debate peace with multinationals up to their necks in the arms trade. Outside Catalonia, Clos presents the anti-capitalist and anti-war movements as a sign of Barcelona's civic and progressive character. But here he strews all sorts of obstacles in our way. He defended, for example, police provocation in the demonstration against the World Bank. The half a million people who demonstrated in Barcelona against Capitalist Europe in March 2002, the million in the General Strike of June 2002, then millions in various demonstrations against the Iraq war in 2003 and 2004 weren't deceived by the Forum. As for opportunities, well, Barcelona for us is a city where the big companies sponsoring the Forum have opportunities to make money, but for young people it's almost impossible to get a decent job or find somewhere to live."*

Such is the popularity in Barcelona of the general proposals of the movement against capitalist globalisation (polls in early 2003 showed 60% in favour of anti-globalisation ideas and 91% against the invasion of Iraq) that Clos went to speak in 2003 at the World Social Forum in Porto Alegre. At the same time as Clos was in Porto Alegre, the Council, through Metropolis, was taking part in World Bank projects in the Third World.

In Chapter Two I posed the question, in reference to the Old City, of whether: *too sanitised a city may become too boring to visit.* Barcelona is popular and famous for its architecture and art, its style and ambience. Its culture, all its attractions, spring from its history. Inasmuch as the re-invention of Barcelona has followed Richard Meier's standard big-city museum, the Gehry stage-set fish, higher rise and faster food... in the short term it may appear more glittering, more attractive and "modern." In the medium term, it will become not only a city more and more uncomfortable to live in, but less interesting to visit. Quim, whose views on migration I report in Chapter Ten, commented the day I interviewed him:

> *"This morning on the radio I heard Clos say something about how Barcelona has to be the best city in the world. What a load of crap! Who cares whether it's the best city or a world city? What it has to be is a habitable city for its residents."*

---

[1] *Ten million passengers in 1992 had become 24 million by 2004.*

[2] *The Generalitat-sponsored Universal Studios theme park at Salou.*

TIBIDABO

SARRIÀ

NOU BARRIS

PARK
GÜELL

CARMEL

CAMP
NOU

GRÀCIA

SANT ANDREU

SANTS

SANTS
STATION

CASA
MILÀ

SAGRADA
FAMÍLIA

TORRE AGBAR

PLAÇA
CATALUNYA

CASTLE
OF
MONTJUÏC

RAVAL

PLAÇA
SANT
JAUME

COLÓN

OLYMPIC
VILLAGE

POBLE NOU

FORUM SITE

BESÒS RIVER

CEMETERY
OF
MONTJUÏC

TOWERS

BARCELONETA

BARCELONA

Bibliography

I've divided the bibliography into five sections: firstly, works of fiction; then the main non-fiction books used, chapter by chapter; third, other background books; fourth, articles cited; and fifth, films on Barcelona.

There is a deliberate bias towards books available in English.

In English, there are several background books to Barcelona. Robert Hughes' lively, boisterous *Barcelona* sets the standard, especially in history and architecture; Vázquez Montalbán's *Barcelonas* is sardonic and leftist; more analytic, if you want to look closely at Council policy, is Donald Mcneill's *Urban Change and the European Left: Tales from the New Barcelona*. If you can read Spanish, try José María Carandell's *Guía secreta*, full of history and spicy gossip about the *Ciutat vella*. The most detailed survey is in Catalan, Fabre and Huertas' *Tots els barris de Barcelona*.

Colm Tóibín's spare *The South* is the most beautiful modern novel written in English and set in Barcelona. Many of Vázquez Montalbán's best are available in English: start with *The Pianist* or *Southern Seas*. Don't miss Raúl Núñez's short gem *The Lonely Hearts Club*. Going back to the 1930s, the first half of Victor Serge's outstanding *Birth of our Power* is set in Barcelona. To my mind, the most impressive body of work in modern Spanish literature are Juan Marsé's novels set in the La Salut-Guinardó area. Rosa Regàs' ferocious *Luna lunera* is excellent on growing up under Franco. Try and find Mercè Rodoreda's classic *The Pigeon Girl*.

Works of Fiction

English-language editions cited whenever possible. The number in brackets refers to the chapter the book informs.

Agustí, Ignacio, *Mariona Rebull* (Planeta, Barcelona 2001) (1). 1890s high society.

Bataille, Georges, *Blue of Noon* (Penguin, London 2001) (2). Originally 1957. Low-life 1930s.

Burgen, Stephen, *Walking the Lions* (Constable, London 2002) (3). Contemporary thriller rooted in Civil War.

Cervantes, Miguel de, *Don Quixote* (Secker & Warburg, London 2004) (Intro).

García Márquez, Gabriel, *Maria dos prazeres* in *Strange Pilgrims* (Penguin, London 1994) (5). Woman organising her funeral.

Genet, Jean, *The Thief's Journal* (Penguin, London 1967) (2). 1930s poverty and lust for crime.

Goytisolo, Juan, *Marks of identity* (Serpent's Tail, London 2003) (5). 1960s rejection of Spain.

Goytisolo, Juan, *Forbidden Territory* (Verso, London 2003).

Hall, David C., *No quiero hablar de Bolivia* (Júcar, Barcelona 1988). Noir set in *Ciutat vella*.

Malraux, André, *Days of Hope* (Penguin, London 1970) (3). 1936 revolution.

Marsé, Juan, *Últimas tardes con Teresa* (Bruguera, Barcelona 1980) (4). Originally 1966.
The Fallen (Little Brown, Boston 1979) (5). In Spanish 1973.
El amante bilingüe (Planeta, Barcelona 1993) (10). Originally 1990.
El embrujo de Shanghai (Plaza & Janés, Barcelona 1993) (4).
Lizard Tails (Harvill, London 2003). In Spanish 2000 (9).

Mendoza, Eduardo, *La verdad sobre el caso Savolta* (Seix Barral, Barcelona 1975) (3). Gunmen defending bosses in 1917.

Mendoza, Eduardo, *City of Marvels* (Harvill, London 1989) (1 & 7). 1888-1929 gangster rise to riches.

Mora, Víctor, *Els plàtans de Barcelona* (Edicions 62, Barcelona 1994) (5). Originally 1966. 1940s misery.

Núñez, Raul, *The Lonely Hearts Club* (Serpent's Tail, London 1989 & 2002) (1 & 2). Bitter-sweet 1980s in a cheap *pensión*.

Oller, Narcis, *El febre d'or* (Selecta, Barcelona 1993) (7). Originally 1893. 1880s get-rich-quick fever.

Pieyre de Mandiargues, André, *La marge* (Gallimard, Paris 1967) (2). 1960s existential despair in *Ciutat vella*.

Regàs, Rosa, *Luna lunera* (Plaza & Janés, Barcelona 2000) (12).

Rodoreda, Mercè, *The Pigeon Girl (La Plaça del Diamant)* (André

Deutsch, London 1967) (6). 1930s working woman: the most famous post-war Catalan novel.

Ruiz Zafón, Carlos, *The Shadow of the Wind* (Orion, London 2004) (6).

de Sagarra, Josep Maria, *Vida privada* (Cercle de lectors, Barcelona 1991) (12). Originally 1932. Decadent 1920s high society.

Sánchez Soler, Mariano, *Para Matar* (Libros de la medianoche, Madrid 1996) (9). Fascists during transition.

Serge Victor, *Birth of our Power* (Gollancz, London 1968) (5). 1917 revolutionary movement, told from below.

Tóibín, Colm, *The South* (Picador, London 1995) (6). Melancholic, oppressed 1950s Barcelona.

Tusset, Pablo, *The Best Thing That Can Happen to a Croissant* (Canongate, Edinburgh 2005) (15).

Vázquez Montalbán, Manuel, *Tatuaje* (Planeta, Barcelona 1989) (13). Originally 1974.

The Angst-ridden Executive (1977) (9), *Southern Seas* (1979) (9), *Murder in the Central Committee* (1981), *Off-side* (1988) (11), *Olympic Death* (1991) (15), *The Man of My Life* (2005) (all published by Serpent's Tail, London). Pepe Carvalho detective novels, part of the author's social chronicle of modern Barcelona.

The Pianist (Quartet, London 1989) (2 & 9). Ex-POUM pianist with nothing left but his integrity.

Non-Fiction Chapter by Chapter

Chapter One

Carandell, Josep Maria, *La Rambla i els seus misteris* (Edicions de Nou Art Thor, Barcelona 1986).

Chapter Two

Carandell, José María, *Guía secreta de Barcelona* (Al-Borak, Madrid 1974).

King, Clifford, *Barcelona with Love* (Allen & Unwin, London 1959).

van Heeren, Stephanie, *La Remodelación de Ciutat Vella. Un análisis crítico del modelo Barcelona* (Veïns en defensa de la Barcelona vella, 2002).

White, Edmund, *Genet* (Chatto & Windus, London 1993).

Wright, Richard, *Pagan Spain* (Harper, New York 1957).

Chapter Three

Berga, Miquel, Introduction to: *Orwell en España* (Tusquets, Barcelona 2003).

Broué P. & Témime E., *The Revolution and the Civil War in Spain* (Faber, London 1972).

Carr, Raymond, *Modern Spain* (OUP, Oxford 1991).

Durgan, Andrew, *B.O.C. 1930-1936* (Laertes, Barcelona 1996).

Fraser, Ronald, *Blood of Spain* (Penguin, London 1981).

Orwell, George, *Homage to Catalonia* (Penguin, London 2001).

Solano, Wilebaldo, *El POUM en la historia* (Los libros de la catarata, Madrid 1999).

Chapter Four

Cirlot, Juan-Eduardo, *Gaudí, an Introduction* (Triangle Postals, Barcelona 2001).

Macaulay, Rose, *Fabled Shore* (Hamish Hamilton, London 1949).

Pevsner, Nikolaus, *Pioneers of Modern Design* (Penguin, London 1970).

Pla, Josep, *Gaudí* (from *Alguns homenots*) (El Observador, Barcelona 1991).

Chapter Five

Gibson, Ian, *The Shameful Life of Salvador Dalí* (Faber & Faber, London 1997).

Goytisolo, José Agustín, *Elegías a Julia Gay* (Visor, Madrid 1999).

Pernau, Josep, *Diario de la caída de Cataluña* (Ediciones B, Barcelona 1989).

Riera, Ignasi, *Los catalanes de Franco* (Plaza & Janés, Barcelona 1999).

Chapter Seven

Balcells, Albert, *Catalan Nationalism* (Macmillan, London 1996).

Martínez, Félix, *Los señores de Barcelona* (La esfera, Madrid 2002).

Mackay, David, *Modern Architecture in Barcelona* (Anglo-Catalan Society, Sheffield 1985).

Michener, James A., *Iberia* (Corgi, London 1970).

Terry, Arthur, *Catalan Literature* (Ernest Benn, London 1972).

Vicens i Vives, Jaume & Llorens, Montserrat, *Industrials i Polítics (segle XIX)* (El Observador, Barcelona 1991).

Wray Mcdonogh, Gary, *Good Families of Barcelona* (University Press, Princeton 1986).

Chapter Eight

O'Brian, Patrick, *Picasso* (Harvill, London 1994).

Sand, George, *Winter in Majorca* (Valldemosa, Mallorca 1956). Translated by Robert Graves.

Chapter Nine

Balfour, Sebastian, *Dictatorship, Workers and the City: Labour in Greater Barcelona since 1939* (OUP, Oxford 1989).

Crameri, Kathryn, *Language, the Novelist and National Identity in Post-Franco Catalonia* (Legenda, Oxford 2000).

Elordi, Carlos, ed., *Los años difíciles* (El País/Aguilar, Madrid 2002). Testimony of anonymous protagonists of the Civil War.

Gabriel, Pere & Molinero, Carme, *Comissions Obreres de Catalunya 1964-1989* (Empúries, Barcelona 1989).

Chapter Ten

Candel, Francesc, *Els altres catalans* (Edicions 62, Barcelona 1965).

Candel, Francisco, *Los otros catalanes veinte años después* (Plaza & Janés, Barcelona 1986).

López Bulla, José Luis, *Cuando hice las maletas* (Península, Barcelona 1997).

Tree, Matthew, *CAT* (Columna, Barcelona 2000).

Chapter Eleven

Burns, Jimmy, *Barça, a People's Passion* (Bloomsbury, London 2000).

Sobrequés, Jaume, *FC Barcelona, cent anys d'història* (edi-Liber, Barcelona 1998).

Chapter Twelve

Hooper, John, *The New Spaniards* (Penguin, London 1995).

Chapter Thirteen

Andrews, Colman, *Catalan Cuisine* (Headline, London 1989).

Boyd, Alastair, *The Essence of Catalonia* (Muchnik, Barcelona 1988).

Mendel, Janet, *The Best of Spanish Cooking* (Santana Books, Fuengirola 1996).

Pla, Josep, *La cuina del peix* (El Observador, Barcelona 1991).

Chapter Fourteen

Samaranch, Juan Antonio, *Memorias olímpicas* (Planeta, Barcelona 2002).

Simson, Viv & Jennings, Andrew, *The Lords of the Rings* (Simon & Schuster, London 1992).

Chapter Fifteen

Ecologistes en Acció, *Guia de la Barcelona insostenible* (Ecologistes en Acció, Barcelona 2004).

Mcneill, Donald, *Urban Change and the European Left: Tales from the New Barcelona* (Routledge, London 1999).

Moreno, Eduard & Vázquez Montalbán, Manuel, *Barcelona, ¿a dónde vas?* (Ediciones de la Tempestad, Barcelona 1991).

Chapter Sixteen
Davis, Mike, *City of Quartz* (Vintage, New York 1992).
Riera, Ignasi, *Off Barcelona* (Barcanova, Barcelona 1993).

General Books that Inform Many Chapters

Acento Editorial (ed.), *Barcelona, Letras de viaje* (Acento, Madrid 2000).

Arts Council of Great Britain (ed.), *Homage to Barcelona, catalogue to the exhibition* (Arts Council, London 1985).

Castellar-Gassol J., *Barcelona, a History* (Edicions de 1984, Barcelona 2000).

Cirici, Alexandre, *Barcelona pam a pam* (Teide, Barcelona 1990).

Foment de Ciutat Vella, SA (ed.), *Memòria 2001-2002* (Foment, Barcelona 2003)

Ford, Richard, *Handbook for Spain 1845*, Vol. II (Centaur, London 1966).

González, Antoni & Lacuesta, Raquel, *BARCELONA Architecture Guide, 1929-1994* (Gustavo Gili, Barcelona 1995).

Huertas, J.M. & Fabre, J., *Tots els barris de Barcelona* (Edicions 62, Barcelona 1980).

Hughes, Robert, *Barcelona* (Harvill, London 1992).

Jacobs, Michael, *Barcelona Blue Guide* (A & C Black, London 1991).

Langdon-Davies, John, *Gatherings from Catalonia* (Cassell, London 1953).

Mendoza, Cristina & Mendoza, Eduardo, *Barcelona modernista* (Planeta, Barcelona 1989).

Riera, Ignasi, *Viatgers de Barcelona* (Ollero & Ramos, Madrid 2000).

Soldevila, Carlos, *Barcelona* (Destino, Barcelona 1964).

Tóibín, Colm, *Homage to Barcelona* (Simon & Schuster, London 1990).

Vázquez Montalbán, Manuel, *Barcelonas* (Verso, London 1992).

General Background Books

Allison Peers, E., *Catalonia infelix* (Methuen, London 1937).
Andersen, Hans Christian, *A Visit to Spain and North Africa*

(Peter Owen, London 1975).

Aranda, Quim, *Què pensa Manuel Vázquez Montalbán?* (dèria, Barcelona 1995).

Brenan, Gerald, *The Spanish Labyrinth* (CUP, Cambridge 1943).

Burns, Jimmy, *Spain: A Literary Companion* (John Murray, London 1994).

Graham, Helen & Labanyi, Jo, *Spanish Cultural Studies, an introduction* (OUP, Oxford 1995).

Magris, Claudio, *Danube* (Harvill, London 1999).

Mitchell, David, *Here in Spain* (Lookout, Málaga 1988).

Nash, Elizabeth, *Madrid* (Signal, Oxford 2001).

Payne, John, *Catalonia, History and Culture* (Five Leaves, Nottingham 2004).

Pritchett, V.S., *Midnight Oil* (Chatto & Windus, London 1971).

Rivière, Margarita, *El problema MADRID-BARCELONA* (Plaza & Janés, Barcelona 2000).

Rogers, Richard, *Cities for a Small Planet* (Faber, London 1997).

Sánchez Soler, Mariano, *Los banqueros de Franco* (OBERON, Madrid 2005).

Trotski, *Escritos sobre España* (Ruedo Ibérico, Paris 1971).

Vilar, Pierre, *Cataluña en la España moderna* (Crítica, Barcelona 1977).

White, Edmund, *The Flaneur* (Bloomsbury, London 2002).

Articles

Bohigas, Oriol, *Conversación*, Firanews 18, April 2002 (4 & 15).

Bunn, Michael, *Interview with Paul Preston*, Catalonia Today, 28/4/2005 (9).

Carlin, John, *Barcelona, la ciudad de moda en Europa*, El País, 12/1/2002.

de Carreras, Francesc, *¿Tierra de acogida?*, El País, 24/5/2001 (10).

Ealham, Chris, *Class and the City*, Oral History, Spring 2001 (10).

Eaude, Michael, *Renewing the City*, Lookout, Málaga 1998 (15).

Galdón, Gemma, *Pensamiento único en piel de alternativa*, El viejo topo, November 2004 (16).

García Márquez, Gabriel, 'Mercè Rodoreda' in *Notas de Prensa, 1980-1984* (Mondadori, Madrid 1991) (6).

Glancey, Jonathan, *Barcelona beats world's greatest architects*, The Guardian, 18/3/99 (4).

Goytisolo, José Agustín, Introduction to *Elegías a Julia Gay* (Visor, Madrid 1999) (5).

Goytisolo, Juan, *Españolas en París, moritas en Madrid*, El País 2/9/99 (10).

Hitchens, Christopher, Introduction to *Orwell in Spain* (Penguin,

London 2001) (3).

Jacobs, Michael, *Gaudí mania*, Art Quarterly, Summer 2002 (4 & 7).

Makaroff, Sergi, *La sinagoga mayor de Barcelona*, El País, 30/9/2003 (6).

Rahola, Pilar, *Murieron a garrote vil*, El País, 2/11/2002 (9).

Riviere, Margarita, *Por qué los españoles no tienen hijos*, El País, 24/10/02 (12).

Robinson, Andy & Specht, Marina, *Olympic city...*, The European, 13/9/91 (15).

Rogers, Richard, *Bend it like Barcelona*, The Guardian, 7/7/2005 (15).

Ros, Manel & Solé, Marçal, *Resistencia e Inmigración*, En Lucha, February 2001 (10).

Sales, Joan, Introduction to: *La plaça del diamant* (HMB, Barcelona 1982) (6).

Sudjic, Deyan, *Homage to Catalonian planning*, The Guardian, 16/7/92 (15).

Vázquez Montalbán, Manuel, Introduction to: Stephanie van Heeren, *La remodelación de Barcelona* (2 & 8).

Wells, Caragh, *Investigating the City: Space, Place and Identity in the Detective Fiction of Manuel Vázquez Montalbán* (unpublished) (6 & 9).

Films

The stars search for peace, 1952 (11).

Pedro Almodóvar, *All about my mother,* 1998 (12).

Michelangelo Antonioni, *The Passenger*, 1975 (7).

Vicente Aranda, *Libertarias*, 1996 (3).

The Barcelona blueprint, 2002 (16).

Julio Cortázar — A Fondo, Editrama, 1977. Interview with Cortázar for TVE (Spanish TV) (4).

Federico Fellini, *Roma*, 1972 (12).

Dolors Genovès & Llibert Ferri, *Operació Nikolai*, TV3, November 1992 (3).

José Luis Guerín, *En Construcción*, 1999 (2).

Robert Hughes, *Barcelona*, BBC, 1991 (15).

Ken Loach, *Land and Freedom*, 1995 (3).

Ventura Pons, *Ocaña, Retrat intermitent*, 1978 (12).

Leni Riefenstahl, *Olympia*, 1938 (14).

Whit Stillman, *Barcelona*, 1994.

Glossary

(All in Catalan, except when **cast,** for Castilian Spanish, is put after the term)

Geographical

Ajuntament	City Council /City Hall
Barcelonins	Natives of Barcelona
Barri /barrio (cast)	Neighbourhood
Barri xinès /barrio chino (cast)	Chinatown
Camp Nou	New ground
Carrer	Street
Ciutat vella	Old city
El Corte inglés	(department store) 'The English Cut'
Drassanes	Shipyards
Eixample	Expansion
Ferrocarrils	Railways
Generalitat	Autonomous Government of Catalonia
Llotja	Stock exchange
La muntanya pelada	The bare mountain
Nou barris	Nine neighbourhoods (name of an area)
Palau	Palace
Pati dels tarongers	Orange-tree Court
Plaça	Square
Ronda de dalt	Outer ring-road
Ronda litoral	Coastal ring-road

General

Absenta	Absinthe
Autobombo (cast)	Self-promoting
Avi	Grandad/Old man
Azada (cast)	Mattock
Bodega	Wine-shop
Boixos nois	Wild boys
Caliqueño (cast)	Cheap cigar
Caixa	Savings bank
Casa	House
Castells	Human towers
Castellers	Participants in human towers
¡Catalán de mierda! (cast)	(racist) Filthy Catalan!
Cava	Catalan sparkling wine
Chiringuito (cast)/ xiringuito	'Hole-in-the-wall' — small bar

309

Churros (cast)	Deep-fried sticks of dough
Colgado (cast)	Drop-out
Corral	Sheep-pen
El català, cosa de tots	Catalan is everyone's business
Desencanto	Disappointment, disenchantment
Destape (cast)	Sudden explosion of freedom in the transition.
Entrepà / bocadillo (cast)	Filled bread roll
Esponjament	Sponging (the creation of small open spaces in densely populated areas by selective demolition)
Estraperlistas (cast)	Spivs (black-marketeers)
La feina ben feta	Doing the job well
Fer país	Construct the country
Fot el camp!	Fuck off!
El galliner	The 'gods' at the Opera
Garrote vil (cast)	Vile garrotte (method of execution)
Granja	Dairy/ farm
Guiri	Foreigner
Indiano (cast)	Rich returnee from the Indies
Locutorio (cast)	Phone-call shop (place for making cheap phone calls round the world)
Masia (masies pl.)	Farm-house
Me cago en Díos (cast)	Lit. I shit on God! (common exclamation)
Menú del dia	Fixed-price menu
Modernisme	Catalan Art Nouveau
Nou	Nine/ new
Pastisseria	Cake-shop
Pou mort	Cess-pit
Ramblejar	To stroll
Rauxa	Emotional outburst
Seny	Good sense
Senyera	The Catalan flag
Tallat	Strong coffee with a dash of milk
Terra d'acolliment	Land of welcome
Terra de pas	Thoroughfare
Tertulia (cast)	Regular conversation group
Trencadís	Mosaic of broken tiles
Turró	Nougat
'Una casa i un hortet'	'A house and vegetable garden', Macià's desire for all Catalans.
Vapor	Steam/Steam-powered factory
Venta ambulante (cast)	Street hawkers
Xoriço	Pork sausage/thief. If someone shouts 'xoriço' in the street, they are probably not selling sausages.

310

Political

Associació de veïns	Residents' Association
'Cheka'	The Russian word means the secret police of the USSR. By association, it jumped in the Civil War to mean a Stalinist secret prison.
CGT (Confederació General de Treball)	General Federation of Labour (anarchist-inspired trade union: break-off from CNT in 1980s)
CNT (Confederació Nacional de Treball)	National Federation of Labour (anarchist-led union)
Comisiones obreras (cast)/ Comissions obreres	Workers' Committees (Spain's and Catalonia's main union federation today)
Consell de Cent	Committee of a Hundred (mediaeval city council)
Convergència	Convergence (Catalan Nationalist party)
Converso (cast)	In mediaeval times, a Jew obliged to convert to Christianity.
Diputación (cast)	Regional Council (unelected)
ERC Esquerra Republicana de Catalunya	Republican Left of Catalonia (pro-independence party)
ETA	"Basque Land and Freedom" urban guerrilla group fighting for Basque independence.
FLP	Popular Liberation Front. Socialist anti-Franco group.
FAI	Iberian Anarchist Federation
Iniciativa per Catalunya	Initiative for Catalonia (left social-democratic party)
Lliga Catalana	Catalan League (pre-war big-business Catalan Nationalist party)
POUM Partit obrer d'unificació marxista	Workers' party of Marxist unification (anti-Stalinist revolutionary party)
PSC Partit dels Socialistes de Catalunya	Catalan Socialist Party
PSUC Partit Socialista Unificat de Catalunya	United Socialist Party of Catalonia (Catalan Communist Party)
Setmana tràgica	Tragic week (1909 uprising)
¡Visca el POUM!	Long live the POUM!
¡Viva Franco! (cast)	Long live Franco!